FIRST 50 SONGS

YOU SHOULD PLAY ON ACCORDION

ISBN 978-1-5400-0709-4

7777 W. Bluemound Rd. P.O. Box 13819 Milwaukee, WI 53213

Visit Hal Leonard Online at
www.halleonard.com

CONTENTS

Adiós 4
All of Me 14
Beer Barrel Polka (Roll Out the Barrel) 8
Bésame Mucho (Kiss Me Much) 20
Blue Tango 17
Bubbles in the Wine 24
Carnival of Venice 27
Cherokee (Indian Love Song) 30
Ciribiribin 36
Come Back to Sorrento 33
Edelweiss 42
The Godfather Waltz 44
Hava Nagila (Let's Be Happy) 46
Hello, Dolly! 49
Hernando's Hideaway 52
Jambalaya (On the Bayou) 55
Just Because 58
La Cumparsita (The Masked One) 60
La Marseillaise 64
La Paloma Blanca 66
La Vie en Rose (Take Me to Your Heart Again) 72
Lady of Spain 74
Libertango 69
Milord 76
Moon River 80
More (Ti guarderò nel cuore) 82
Never on Sunday 85
'O Sole Mio 88
Oh Marie 94
The Phoenix Love Theme (Senza fine) 98
Pigalle 91
Poinciana (Song of the Tree) 102
Return to Me 106
Santa Lucia 112
Sentimental Journey 114
Slow Poke 109
Somewhere, My Love 116
Spanish Eyes 119
Speak Softly, Love (Love Theme) 122
Sway (Quien será) 124
Sweet Georgia Brown 127
Tango of Roses 130
Tarantella 136
That's Amoré (That's Love) 133
The Third Man Theme 140
True Love 150
Under Paris Skies 145
Where Is Your Heart (The Song from Moulin Rouge) 152
Wonderful Copenhagen 154
Zip-A-Dee-Doo-Dah 156

ADIÓS

English Words by EDDIE WOODS
Spanish Translation and Music by ENRIC MADRIGUERA

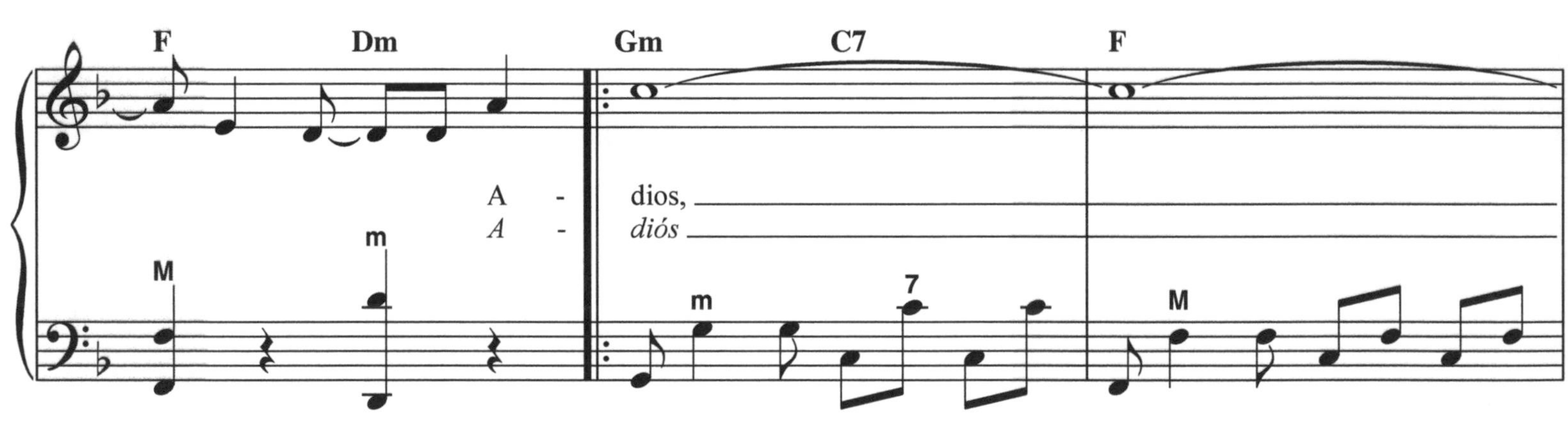

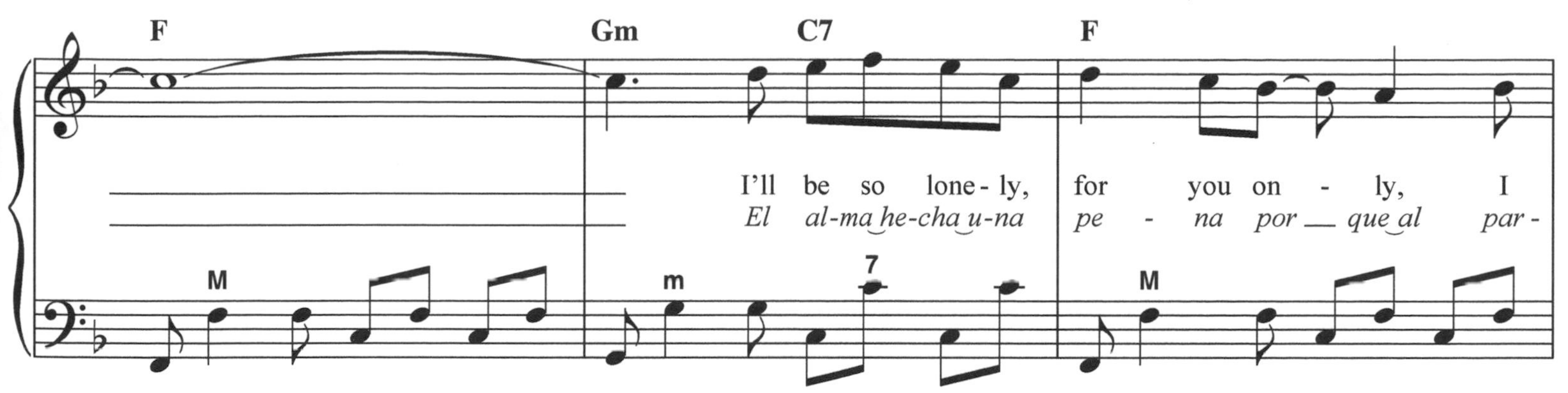
F
Gm
C7
F
I'll be so lone - ly, for you on - ly, I
El al-ma he-cha u-na pe - na por que al par -
M
m
7
M

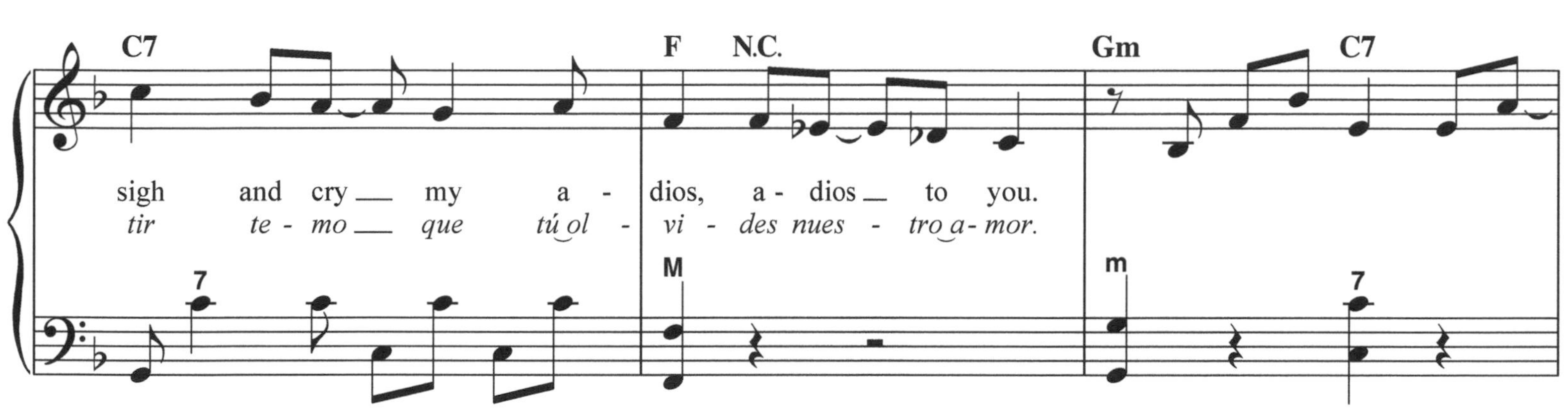
C7
F
N.C.
Gm
C7
sigh and cry my a - dios, a - dios to you.
tir te - mo que tú ol - vi - des nues - tro a - mor.
7
M
m
7

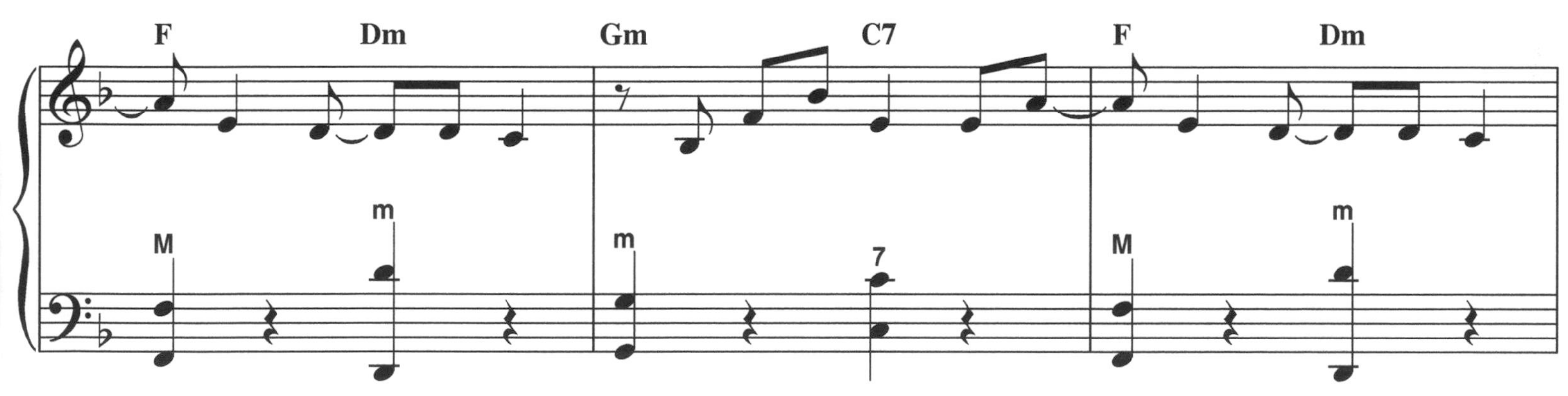
F
Dm
Gm
C7
F
Dm
M
m
m
7
M
m

Gm
C7
3
F
Gm
C7
And in this heart is mem-'ry of what
Her - mo - sa flor mi al - ma cau - ti -
m
7
M
m
7

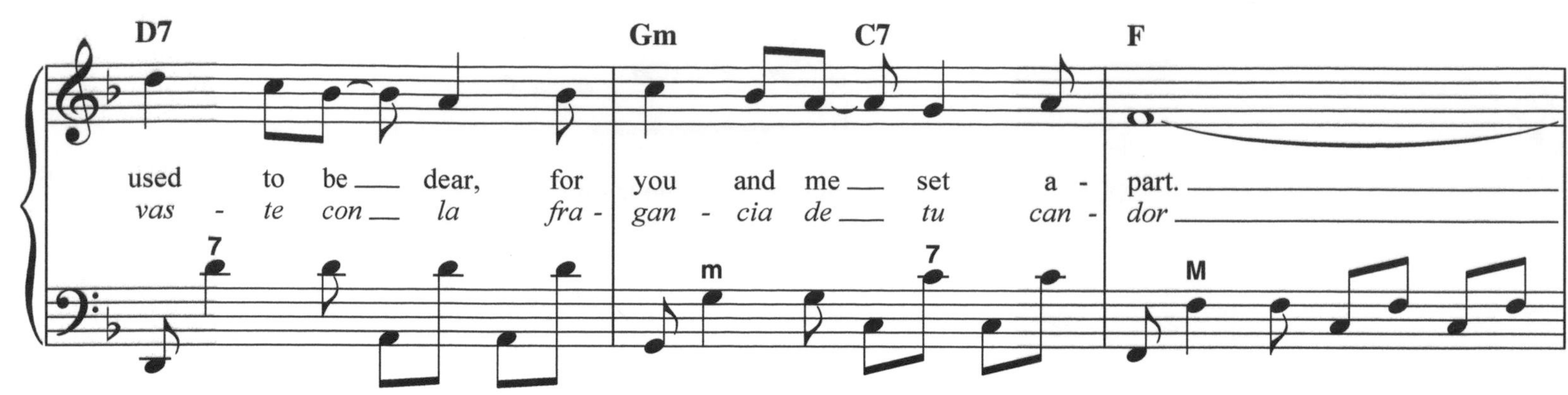
D7
Gm
C7
F
used to be dear, for you and me set a - part.
vas - te con la fra - gan - cia de tu can - dor
7
m
7
M

E7
Am
Dm
Moon
Tú
watch-ing and wait - ing a -
e - res to - da mi i - lu -
7
m
m

E7
Am
bove,
sión
soon
Tú
7
m

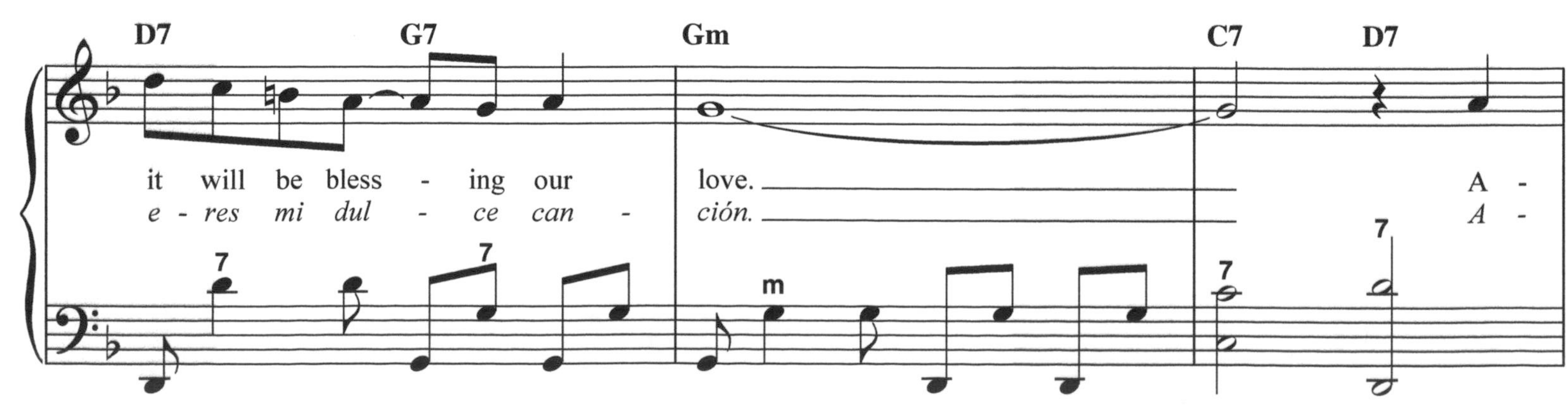
D7
G7
Gm
C7
D7
it will be bless - ing our love. A -
e - res mi dul - ce can - ción. A -
7
7
m
7
7

Gm C7 F Gm C7
dios for hap - py end - ings
diós me voy lin - da mo -
m 7 M m 7

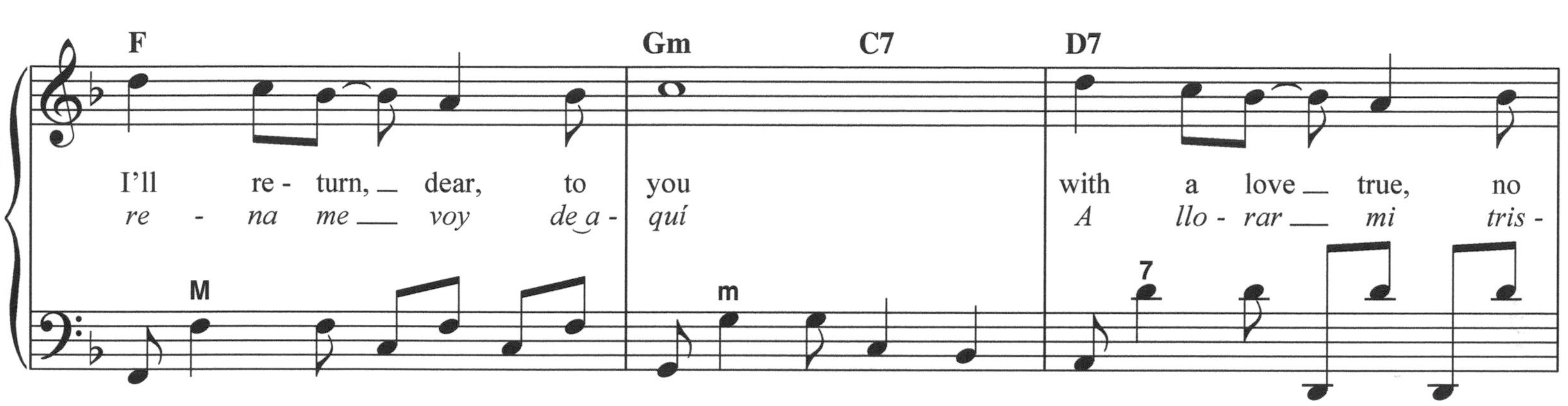
F Gm C7 D7
I'll re - turn, dear, to you with a love true, no
re - na me voy de a - quí A llo - rar mi tris -
M m 7

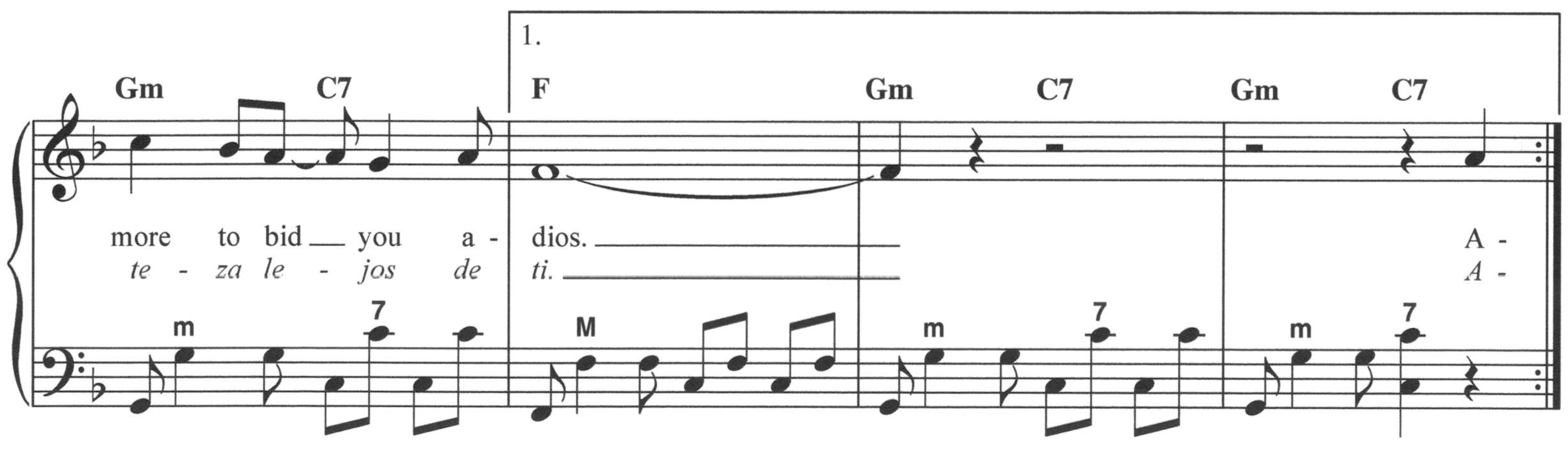
1.
Gm C7 F Gm C7 Gm C7
more to bid you a - dios. A -
te - za le - jos de ti. A -
m 7 M m 7 m 7

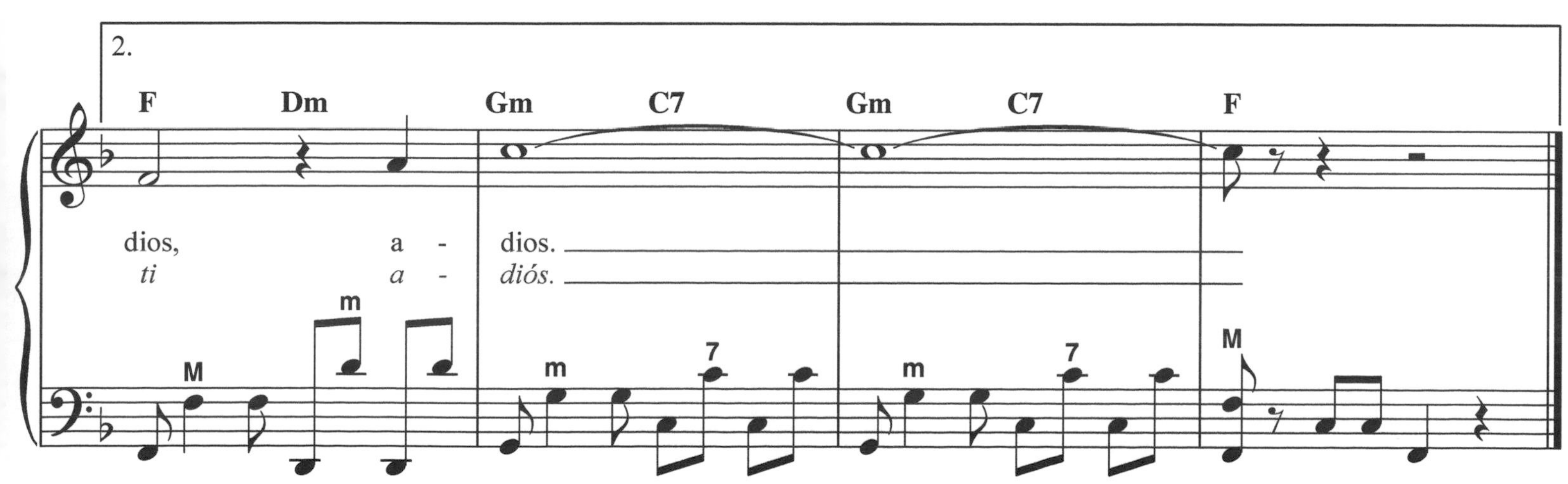
2.
F Dm Gm C7 Gm C7 F
dios, a - dios.
ti a - diós.
M m m 7 m 7 M

BEER BARREL POLKA
(Roll Out the Barrel)

Based on the European success "Skoda Lasky"*
By LEW BROWN, WLADIMIR A. TIMM,
JAROMIR VEJVODA and VASEK ZEMAN

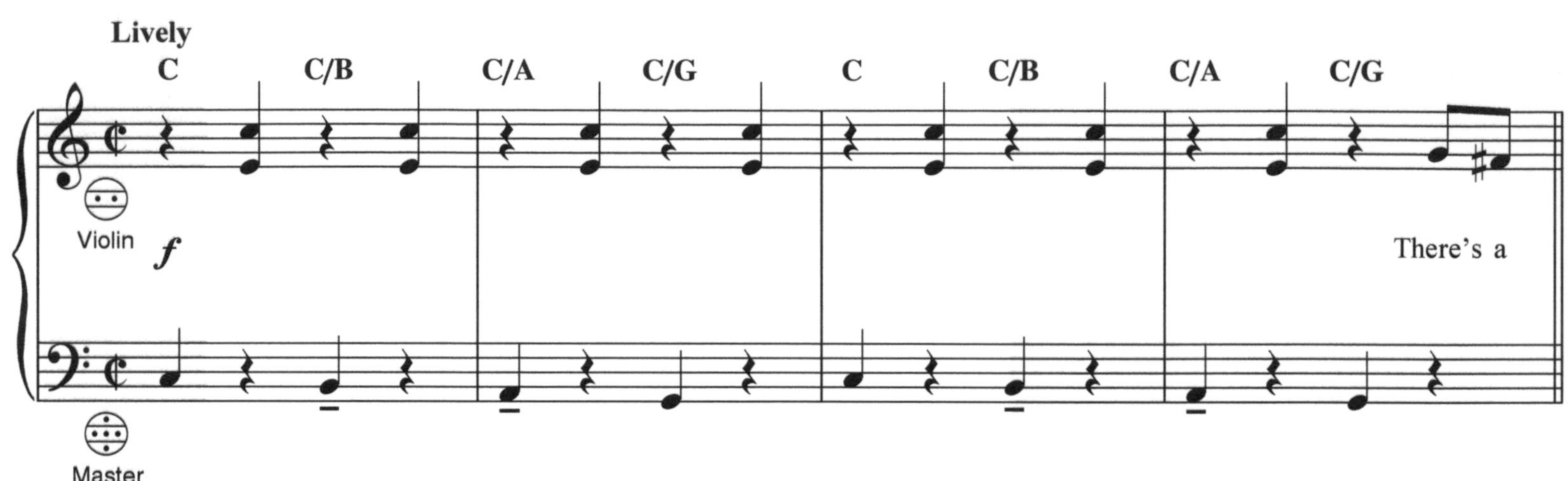

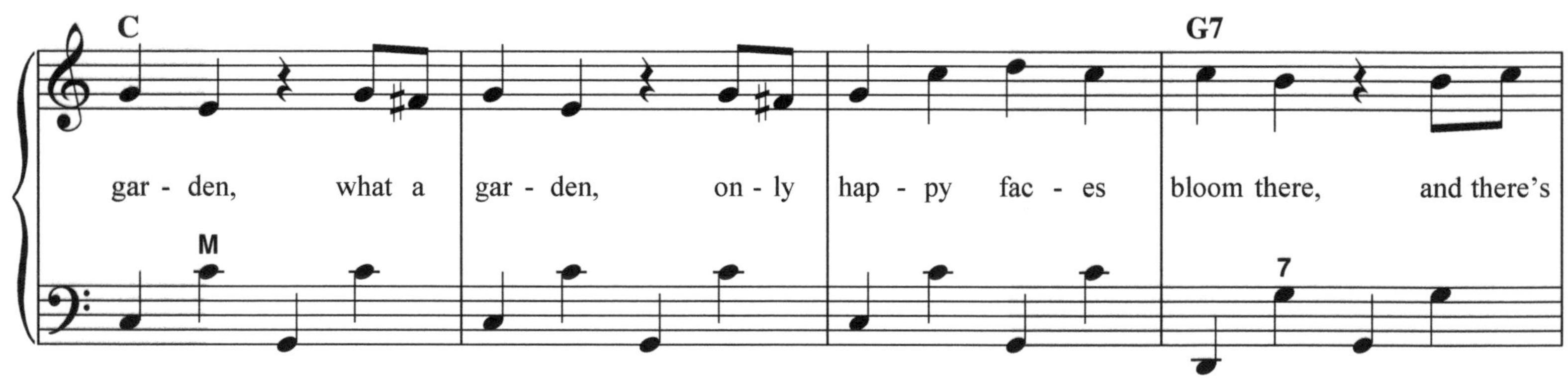

G7
mu - sic and there's danc - ing and a lot of sweet ro - manc - ing.
7

C
When they play a pol - ka, they all get in the swing. Ev - 'ry
M

G7
time they hear that oom - pa - pa, ev - 'ry -
hear a rum - ble on the floor, it's the
7

C
bod - y feels so tra - la - la. They want to
big sur - prise they're wait - ing for. And all the
M

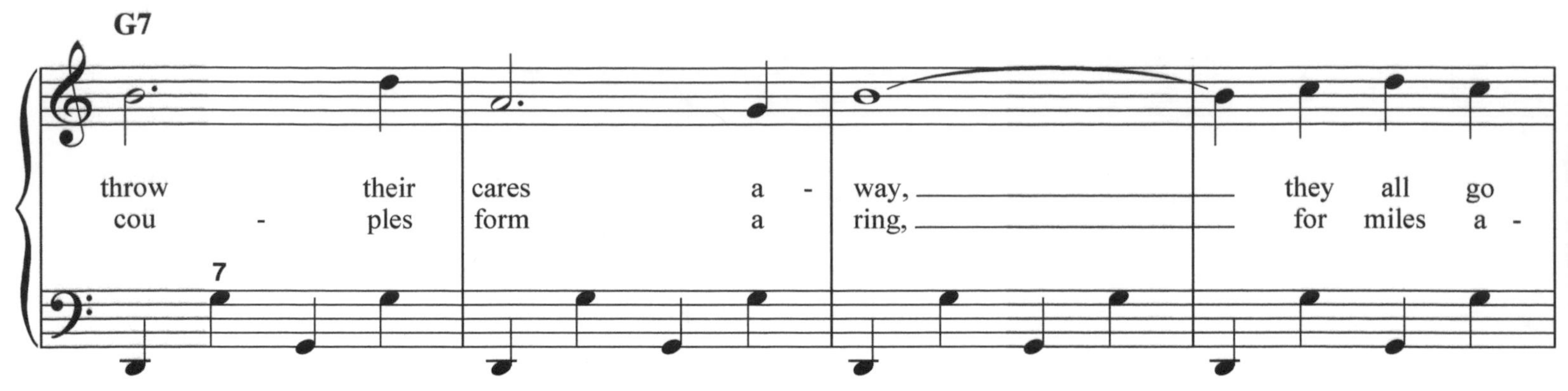
G7
7
throw their cares a - way, they all go
cou - ples form a ring, for miles a -

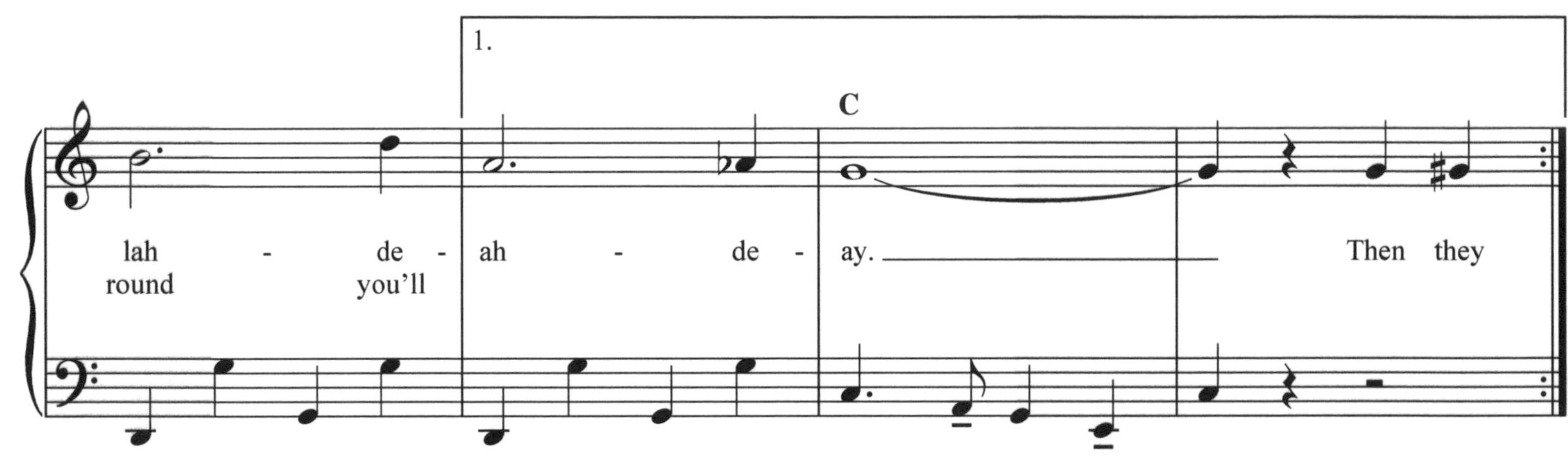
1.
C
lah - de - ah - de - ay. Then they
round you'll

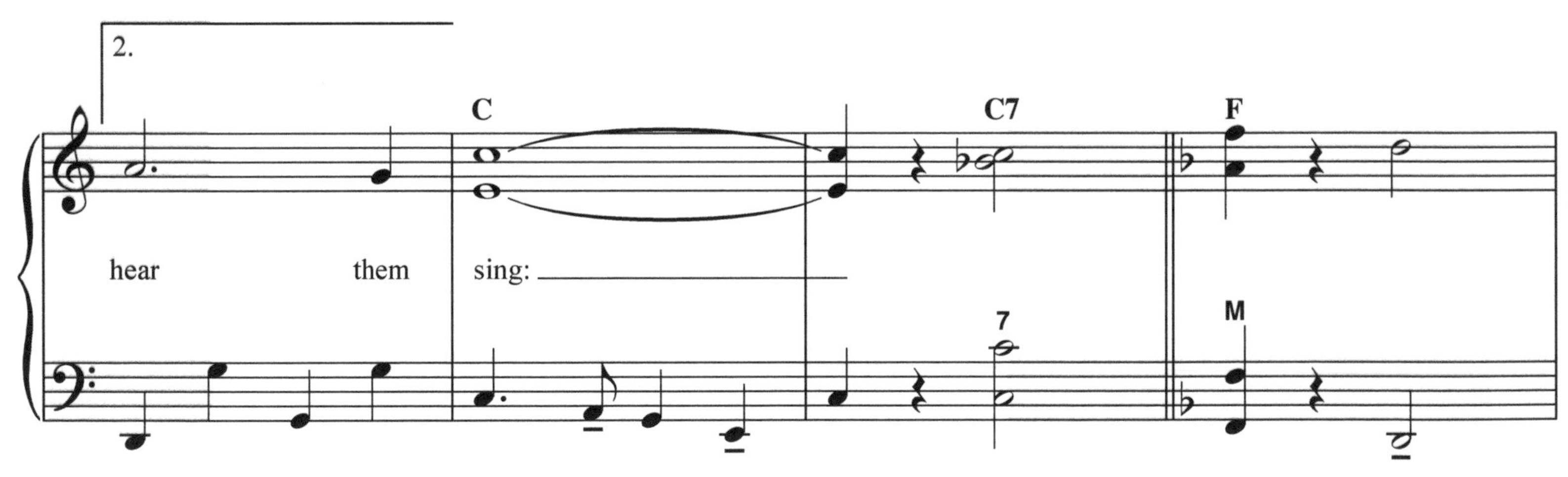
2.
C
C7
F
hear them sing:
7
M

F
Roll
M

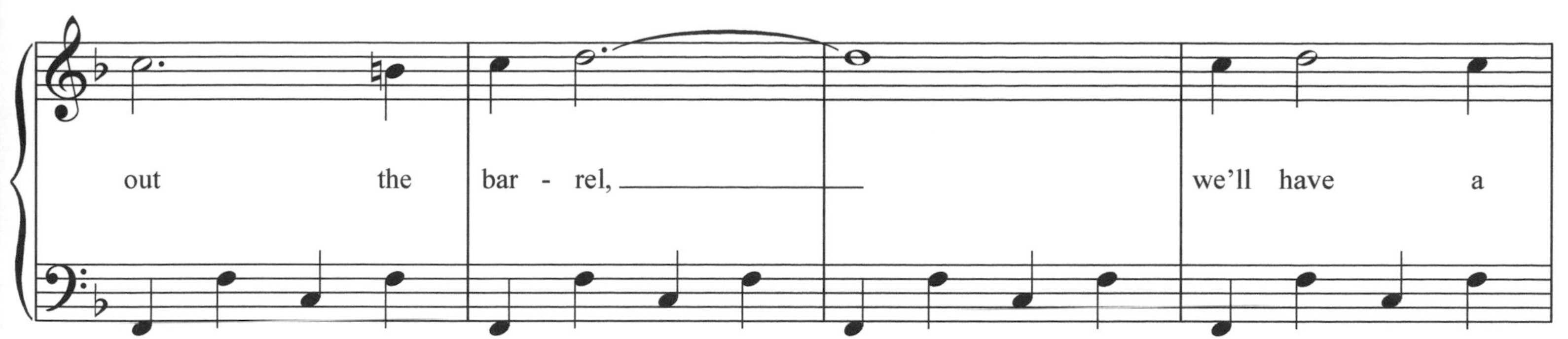
out the bar - rel,
we'll have a

C7
bar - rel of fun.
Roll
7

out thc bar - rel,
we've got the

F
C7
F
blues on the run.
Zing!
M
M

Boom! Ta - rar - rel!
Ring out a

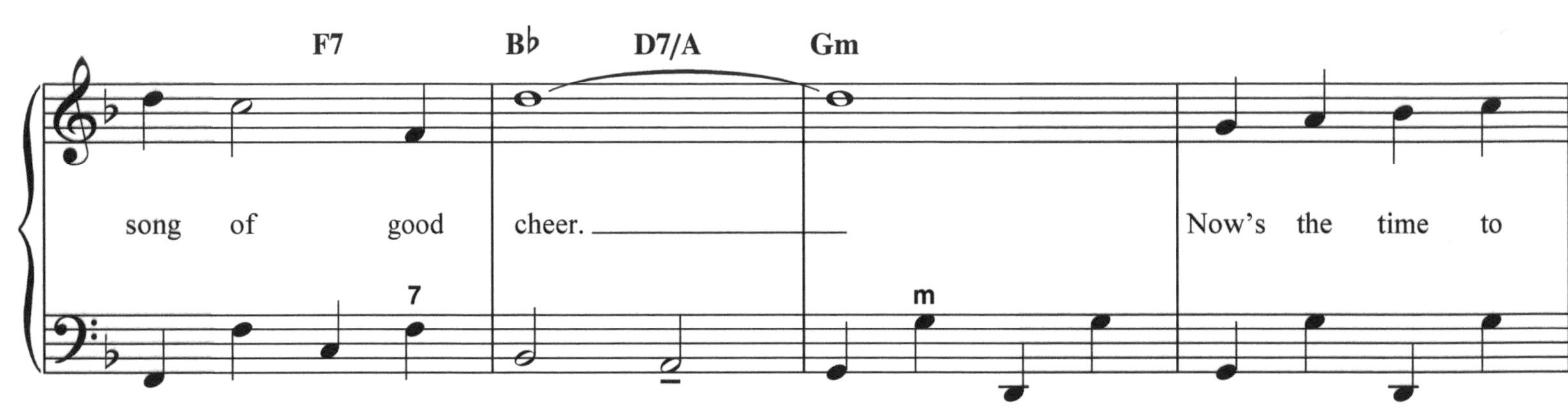
F7
B♭
D7/A
Gm
song of good cheer.
Now's the time to
7
m

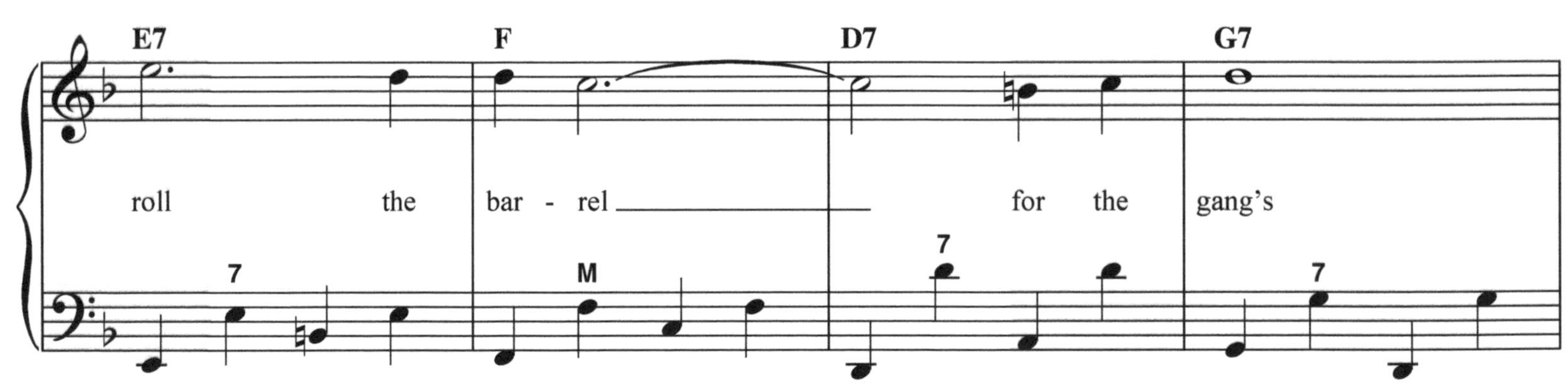
E7
F
D7
G7
roll the bar - rel for the gang's
7
M
7
7

To Coda
C7
F
Dm
all here.
7
m

A7
Dm
m
7
C
G7
M
7
C
M
D.S. al Coda
CODA
F
here.
M

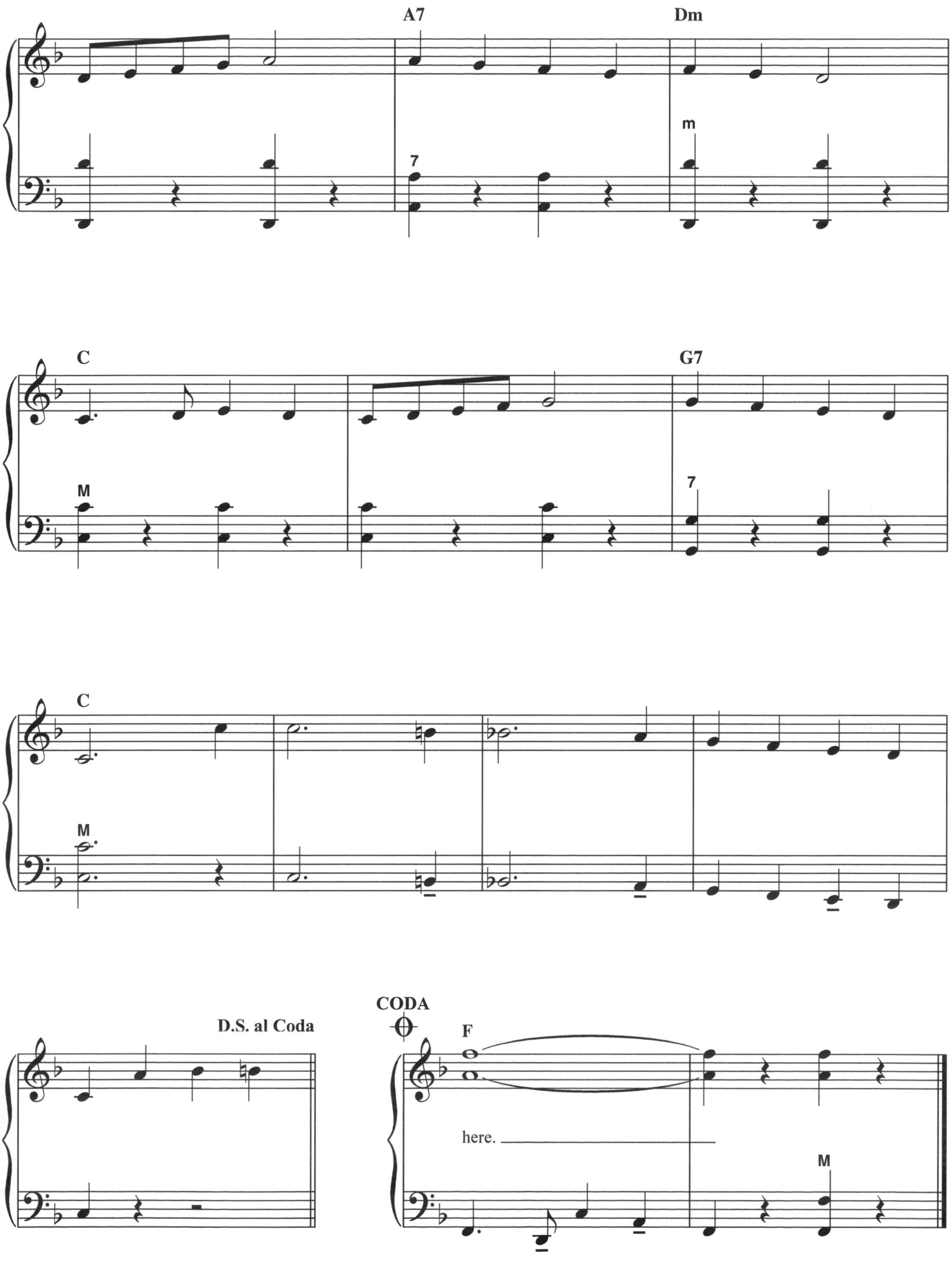

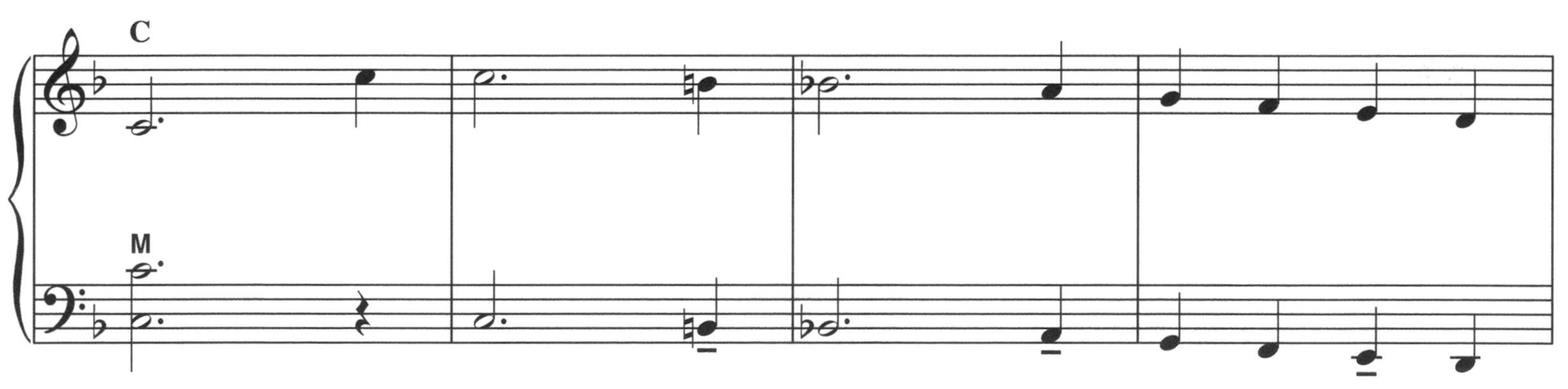

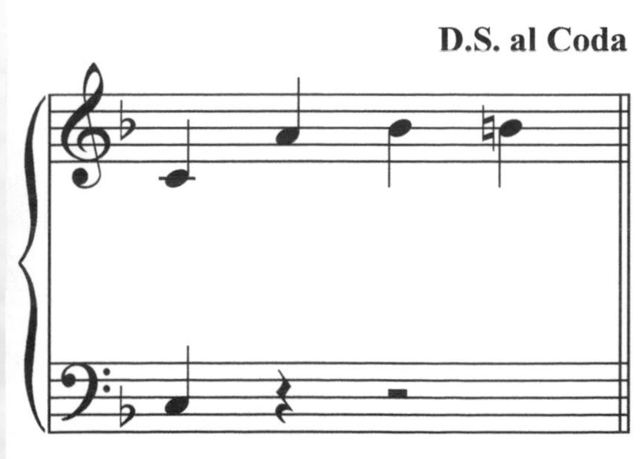

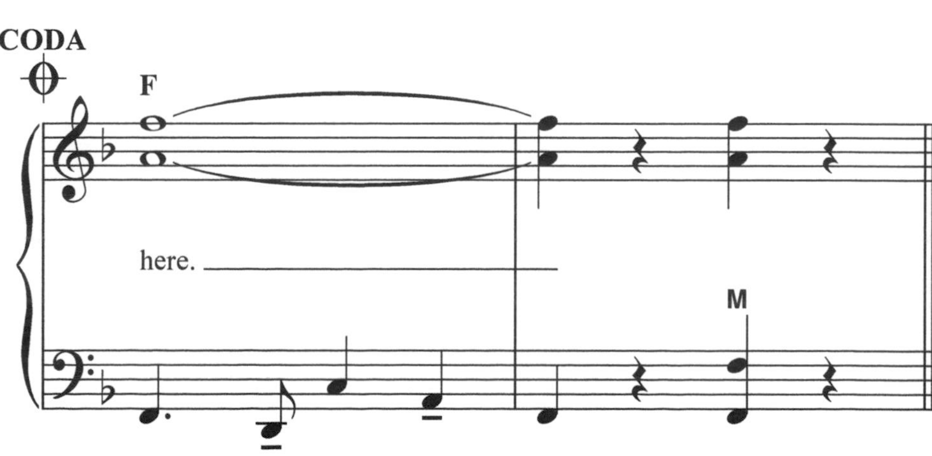

ALL OF ME

Words and Music by SEYMOUR SIMONS
and GERALD MARKS

Am
I want to lose them.
m

D7
G7
Take my arms, I'll nev - er use
7
7

C
them. Your good - bye left me with
M

E7
A7
eyes that cry, how can I
7
7

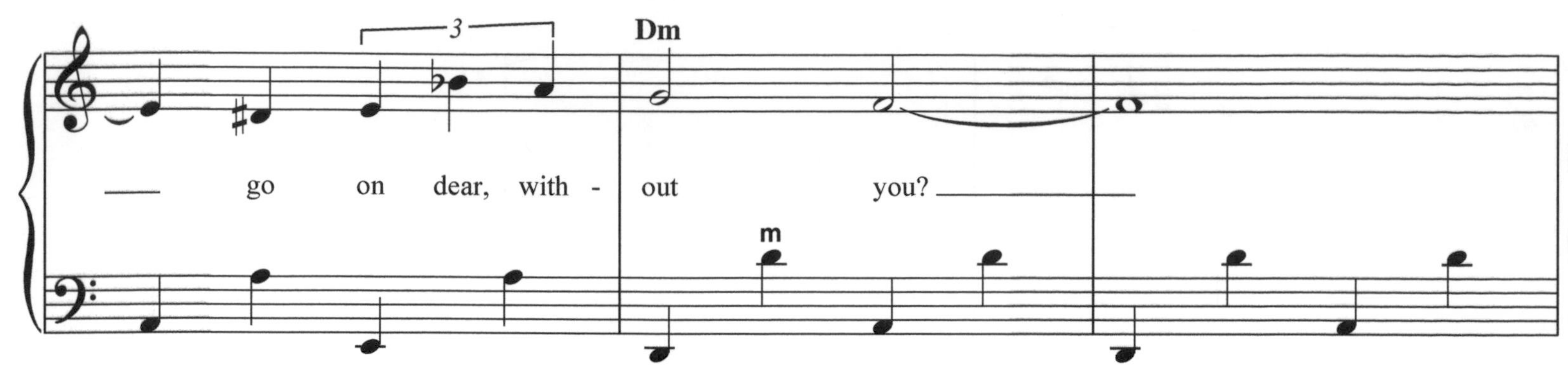
Dm
go on dear, with - out you?
m

F
Fm
C
You took the part that once was my
M
m
M

A7
Fm
G7
heart, so why not take all of
7
m
7

1.
2.
C
E♭dim
Dm
G7
C
Fm
C
me?
me?
M
m
7
M
m
M

BLUE TANGO

By LEROY ANDERSON

A7
D
we first met; _
while the
mu - sic plays,
M
7
A7
we re - call the days
when our
D
A7
D
D7
love was a tune that we could - n't soon for - get. _
As I
G
D
kiss your cheek,
we don't have to speak,
the vi - o -

A7 Em Adim/D♯ A7 D
lins, like a choir, ex - press the de - sire we used to know not long a -
dim 7 M 7 m
D7 G D
go. So just hold me tight in your arms to - night
7 M M
A7 Em Adim/D♯ A7
and this Blue Tan - go will be our thrill - ing mem - o - ry of
7 m dim 7
1. 2.
D Bm Em A7 D A7 D A7 D
love. Here am love.
M m m 7 M 7 M 7 M

BÉSAME MUCHO
(Kiss Me Much)

Music and Spanish Words by CONSUELO VELAZQUEZ
English Words by SUNNY SKYLAR

A7
Dm
Bé - sa - me mu - cho,
bé - sa - me mu - cho,
7
m
Am
Am/G
F7
E7
3
hold me, my dar - ling, and say that you'll al - ways be
que ten - go mie - do per - der - te, per - der - te o - tra
Am
Dm
Am
Dm
mine.
vez.
This joy is some-thing new,
Quie - ro te - ner - te muy
Am
E7
Am
my arms en - fold - ing you, nev - er knew this thrill be - fore.
cer - ca, mi - rar - me en tus o - jos, ver - te jun - to a mí,

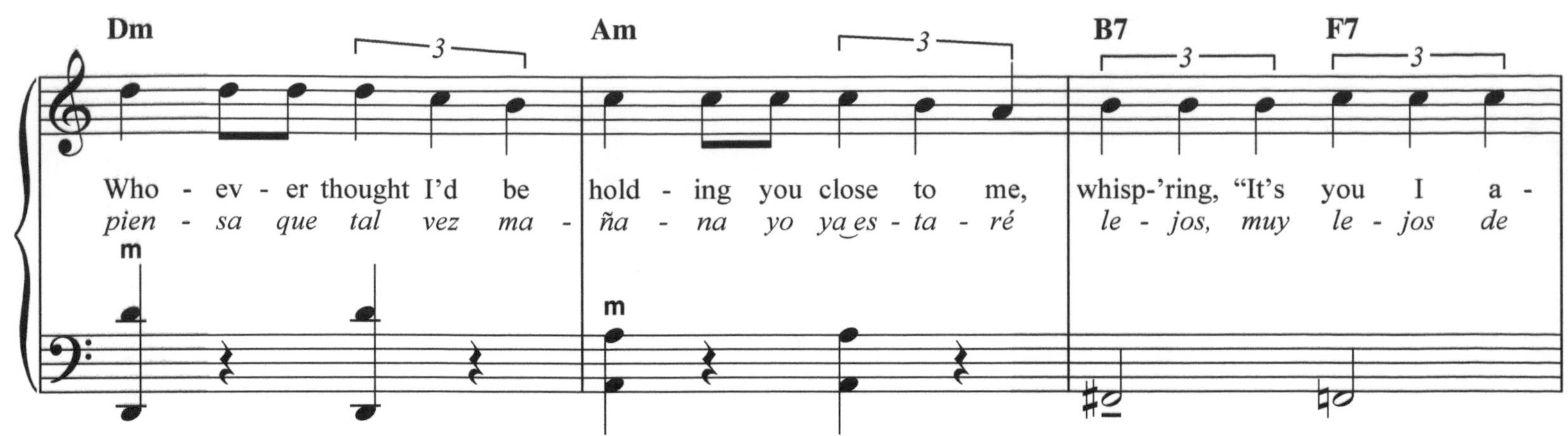
Dm
Am
B7
F7
Who - ev - er thought I'd be hold - ing you close to me, whisp-'ring, "It's you I a -
pien - sa que tal vez ma - ña - na yo ya es - ta - ré le - jos, muy le - jos de

E7
Am
dore." Dear - est one, if you should
ti. Bé - sa - me, bé - sa - me

Dm
A7
leave me, each lit - tle dream would take
mu - cho, co - mo si fue - ra es - ta

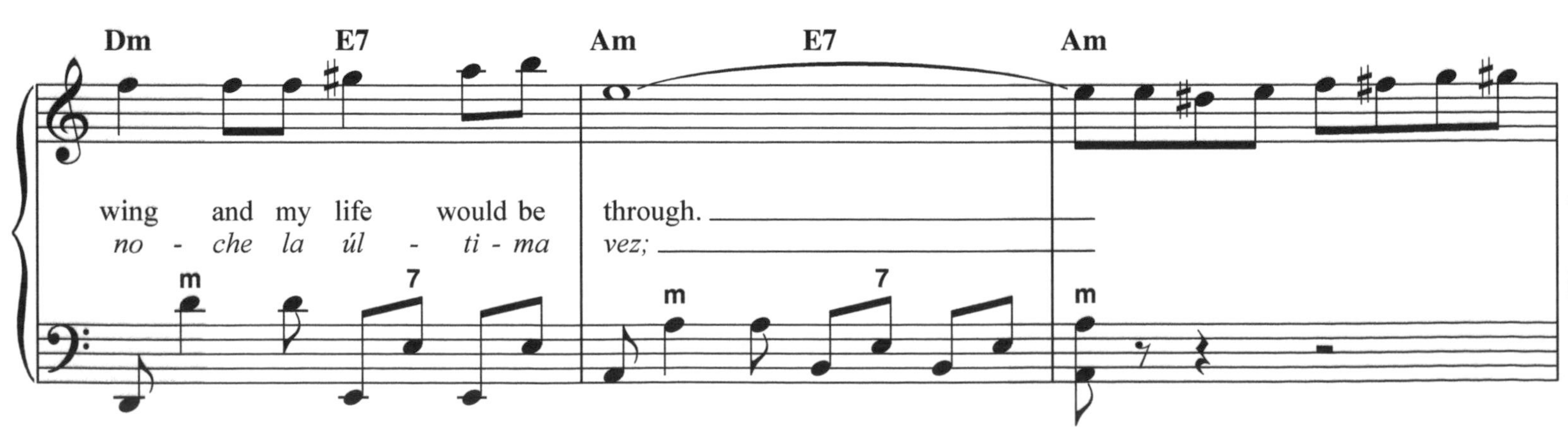
Dm
E7
Am
E7
Am
wing and my life would be through.
no - che la úl - ti - ma vez;

A7
Dm
Bé - sa - me mu - cho,
bé - sa - me mu - cho,
1.
Am Am/G F7 E7
love me for - ev - er and make all my dreams come
que ten - go mie - do per - der - te, per - der-te des -
Am F7 E7
true.
pués.
2.
Am Am/G Dm/F E7
love me for - ev - er and make all my dreams,
que ten - go mie - do per - der - te, per-der - te
Am Am/G Dm/F E7 Am E7 Am
love me for - ev - er and make all my dreams come true.
que ten - go mie - do per - der - te, per - der-te des - pués.

BUBBLES IN THE WINE

featured in the Television Series THE LAWRENCE WELK SHOW

Words and Music by FRANK LOESSER,
BOB CALAME and LAWRENCE WELK

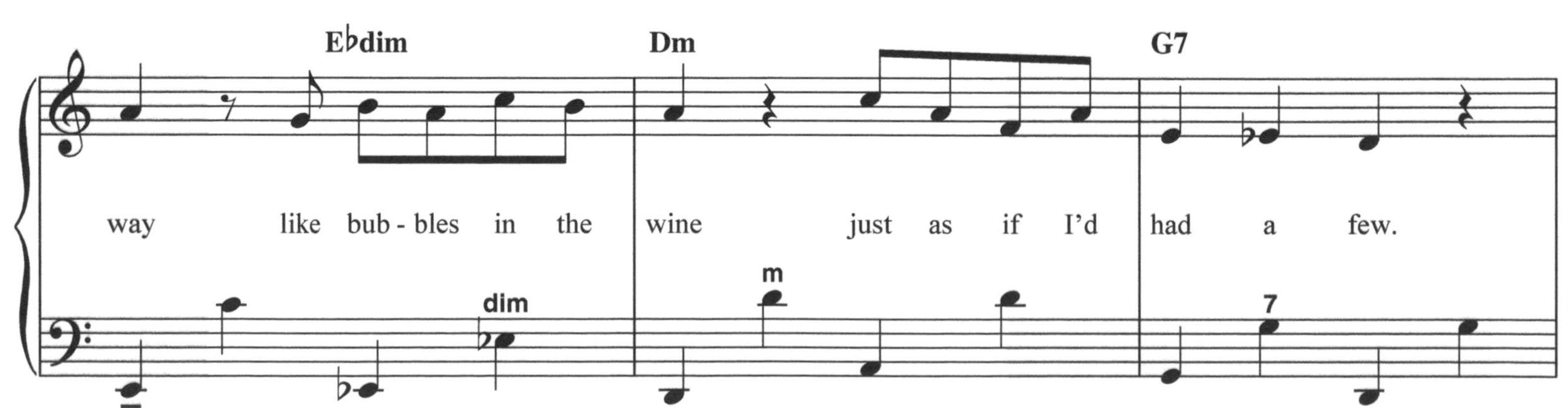

C7
F
Oh, may - be it's that moon, or may - be it's that tune, play - ing as we
7
M

D7
gen - tly sway; or may - be it's the fact that I love you.
7

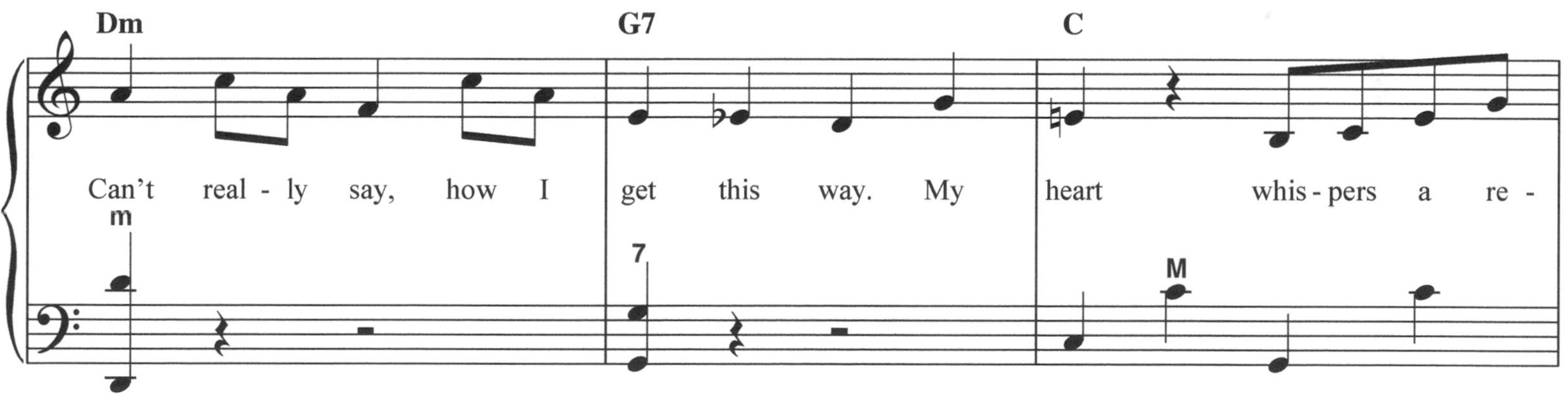
Dm
G7
C
Can't real - ly say, how I get this way. My heart whis - pers a re -
m
7
M

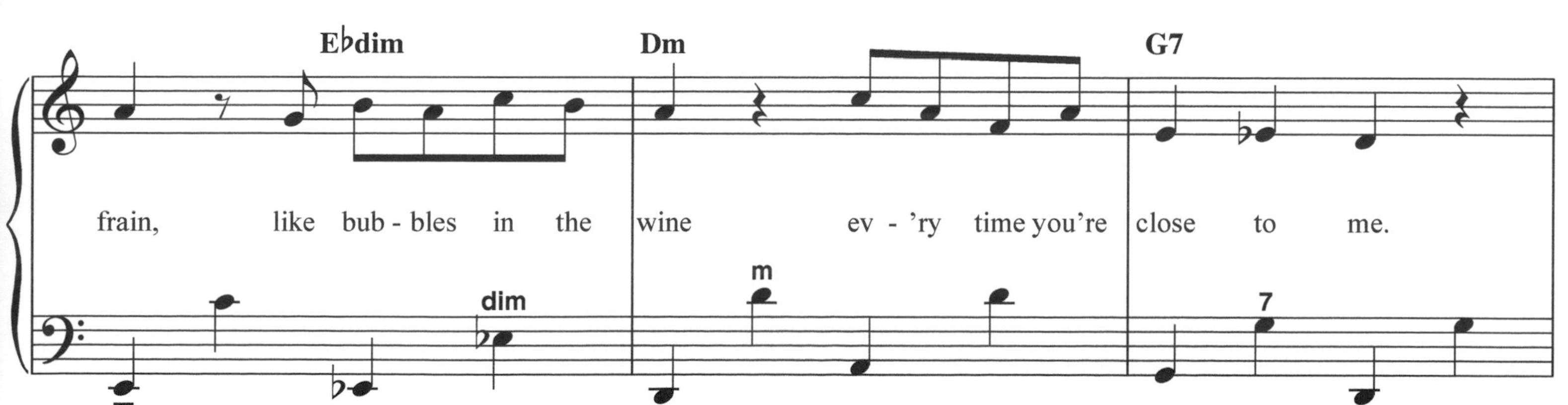
E♭dim
Dm
G7
frain, like bub - bles in the wine ev - 'ry time you're close to me.
dim
m
7

C7
F
I need - n't drink cham - pagne, a feel - ing quite in - sane lights me up and
7
M

Fm
3
sets me free. Some day I may lose you, but no mat - ter how fate may go, a -
m

C
Am
D7
G7
C
3
part or to - geth - er, when I think of to-night I know I'll hear, in this heart of
M
m
7
7
M

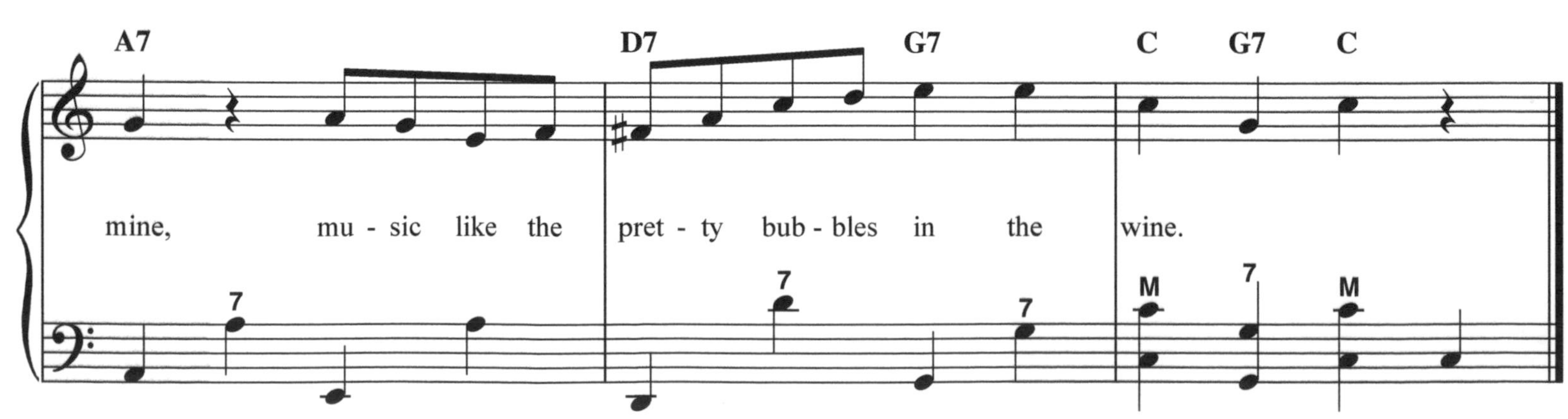
A7
D7
G7
C
G7
C
mine, mu - sic like the pret - ty bub - bles in the wine.
7
7
7
M
7
M

CARNIVAL OF VENICE

By JEAN-BAPTISTE ARBAN

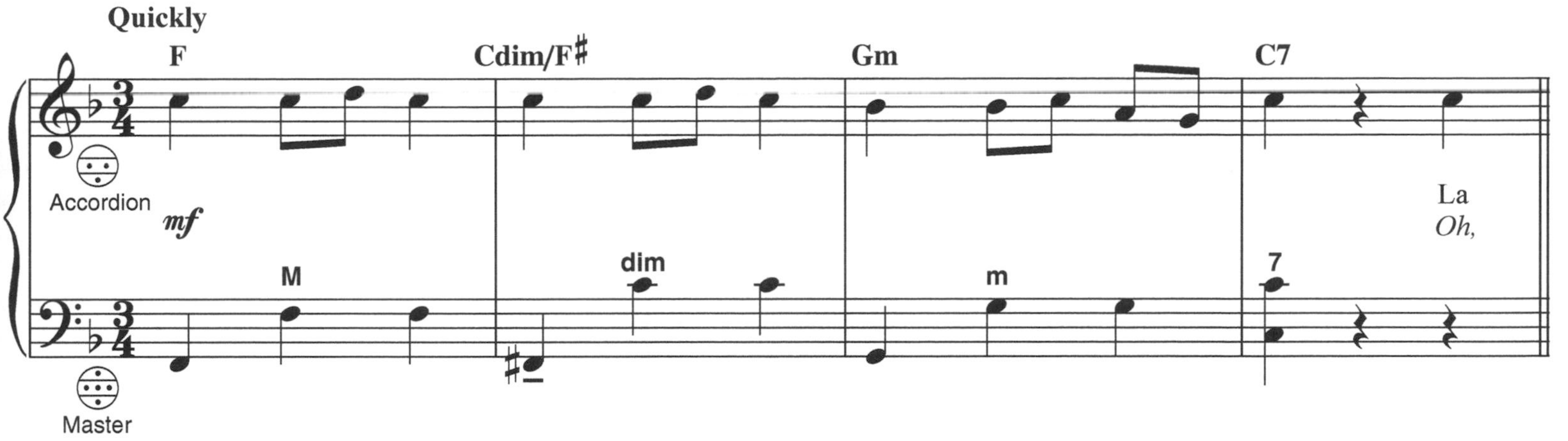

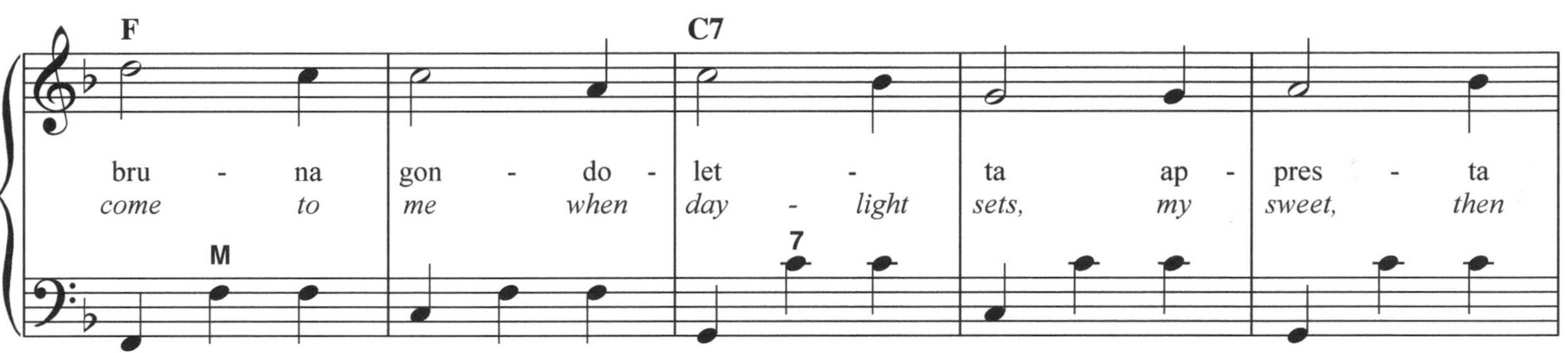

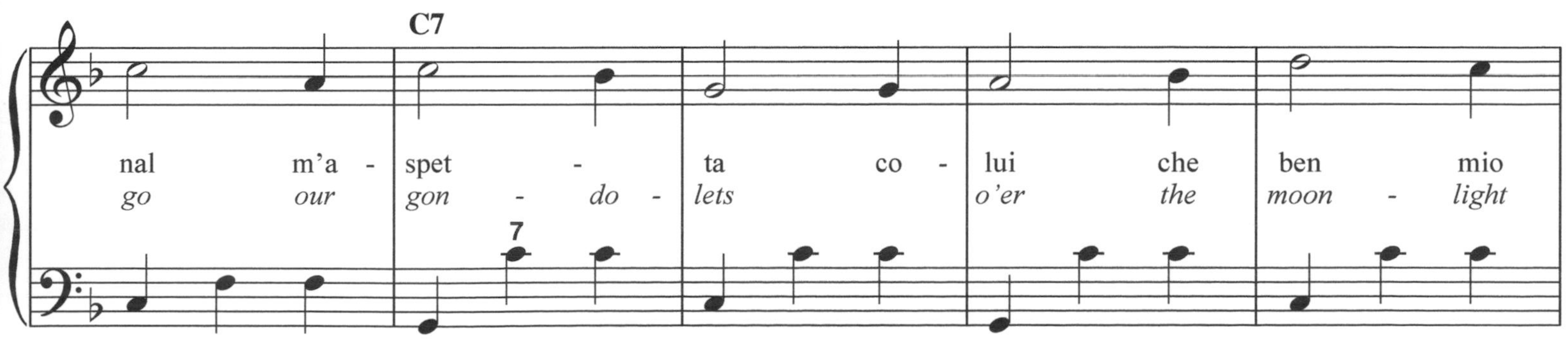

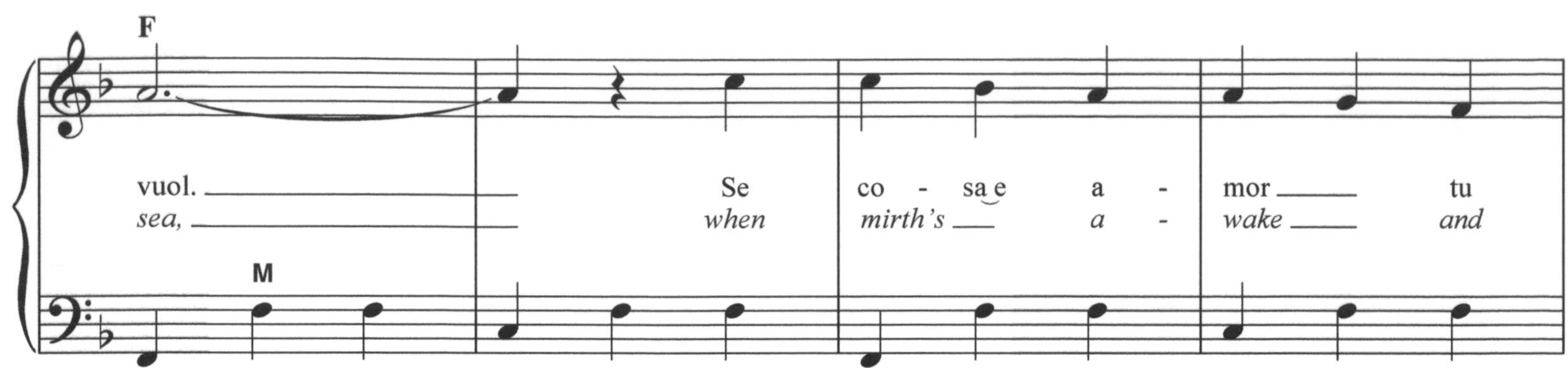
F
vuol. Se co - sa e a - mor tu
sea, when mirth's a - wake and
M

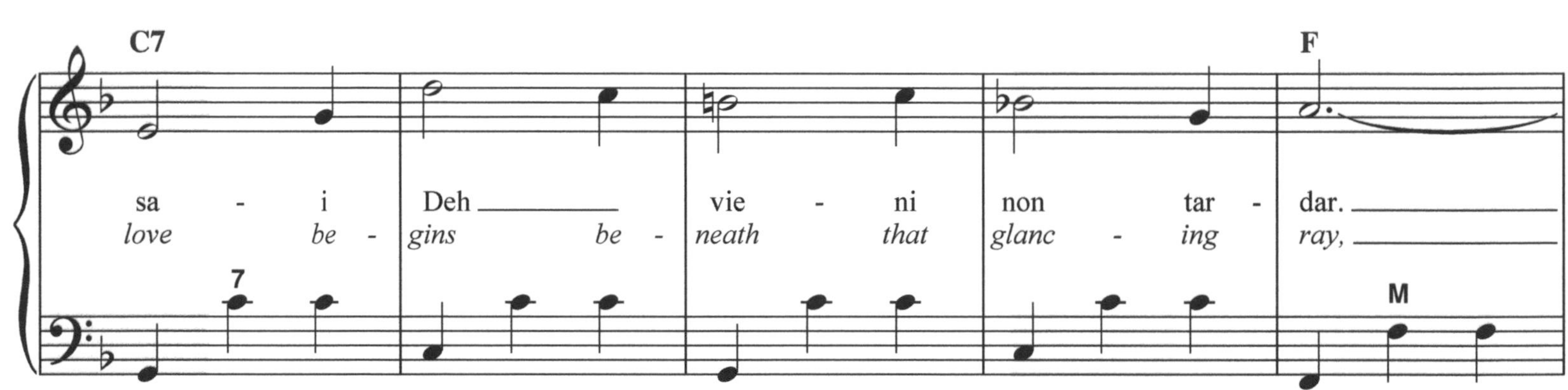
C7
F
sa - i Deh vie - ni non tar - dar.
love be - gins be - neath that glanc - ing ray,
7
M

C7
E quel che tu vor - ra - i
with sounds of flutes and man - do -
7

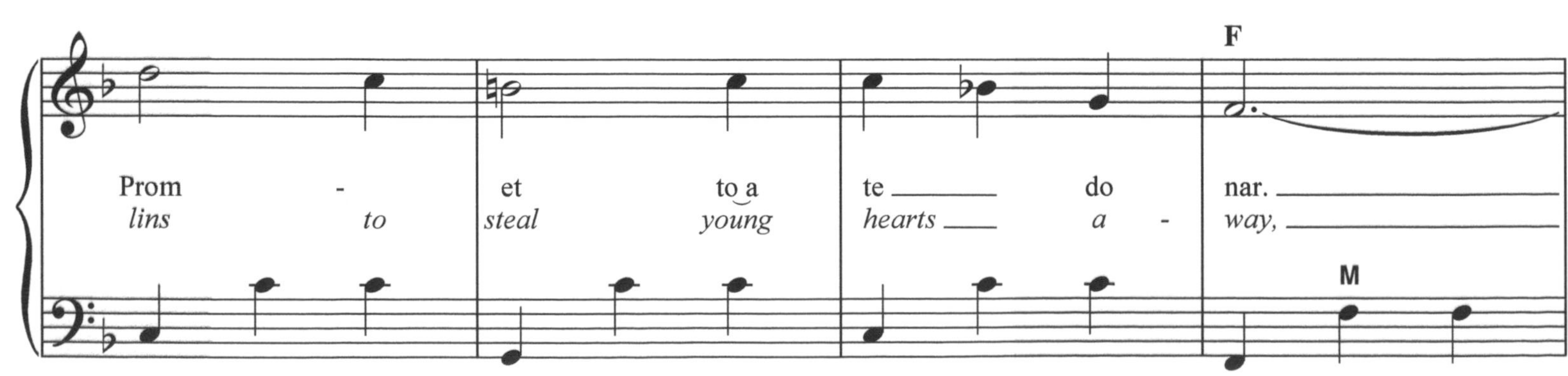
F
Prom - et to a te do nar.
lins to steal young hearts a - way,
M

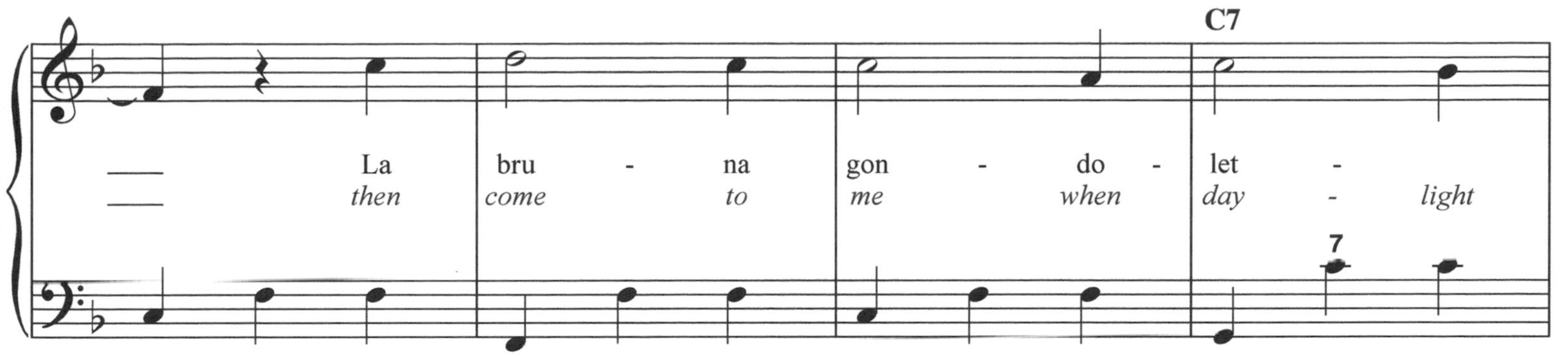
C7
La bru - na gon - do - let -
then come to me when day - light
7

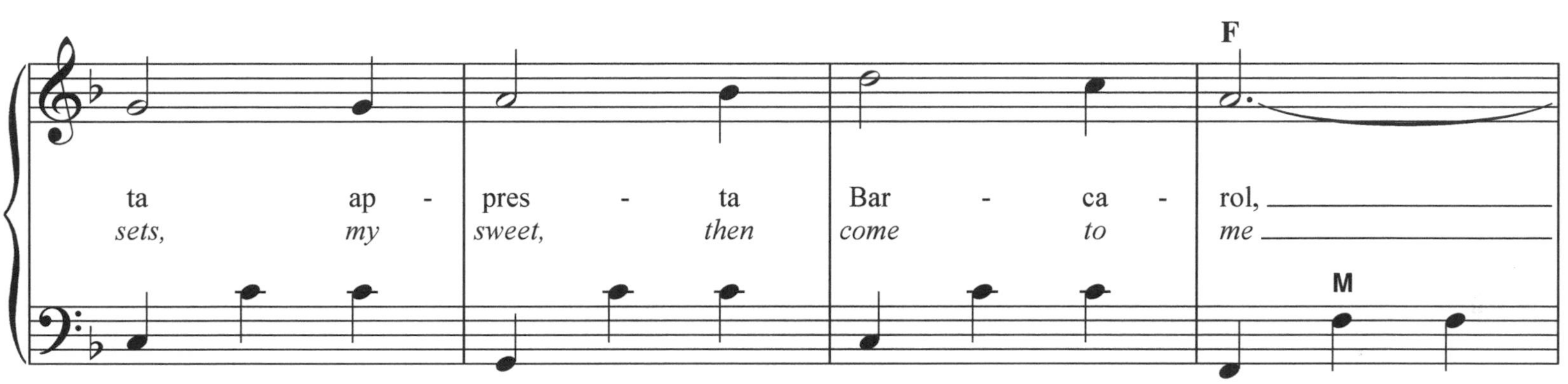
F
ta ap - pres - ta Bar - ca - rol,
sets, my sweet, then come to me
M

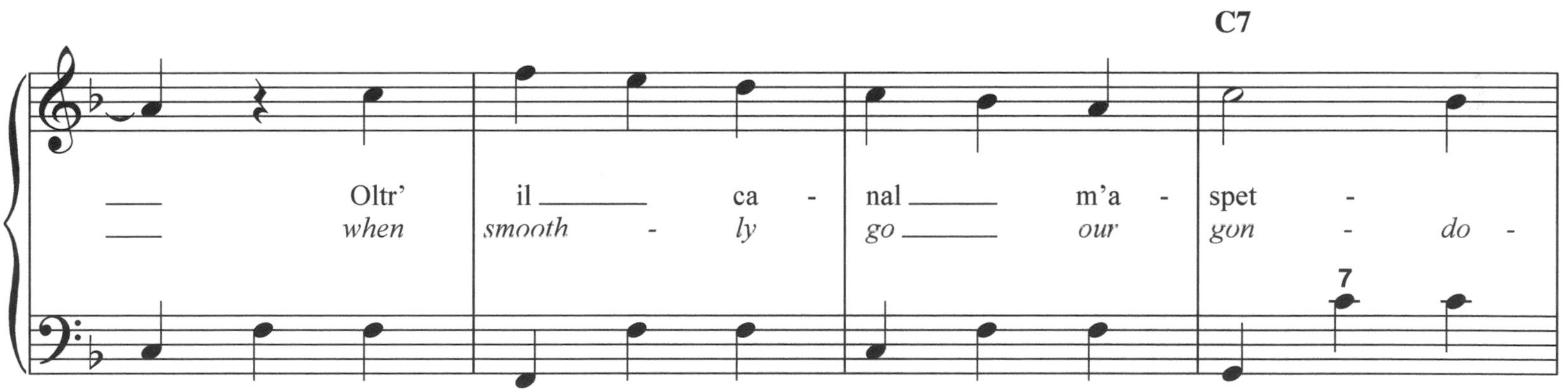
C7
Oltr' il ca - nal m'a - spet -
when smooth - ly go our gon - do -
7

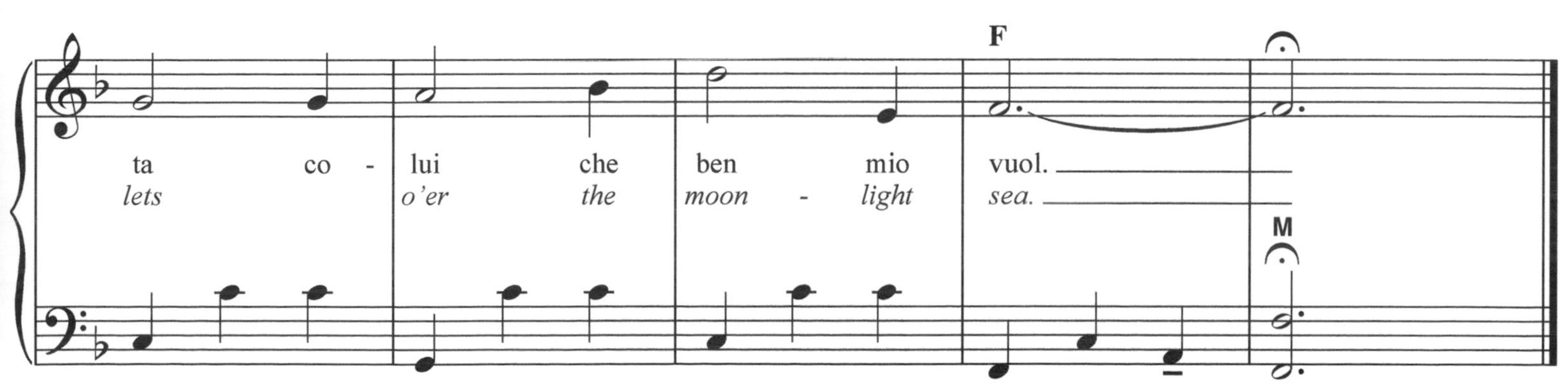
F
ta co - lui che ben mio vuol.
lets o'er the moon - light sea.
M

CHEROKEE
(Indian Love Song)

Words and Music by
RAY NOBLE

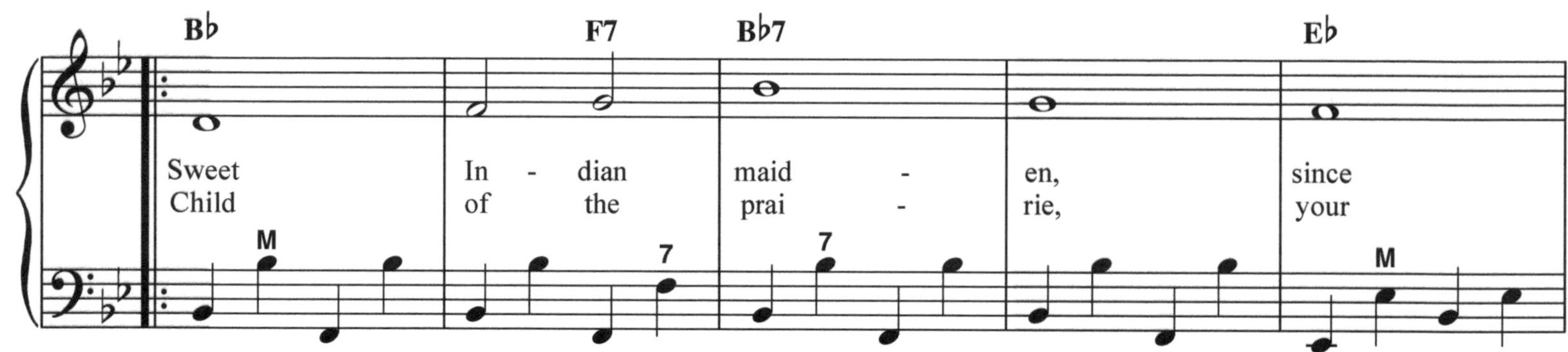

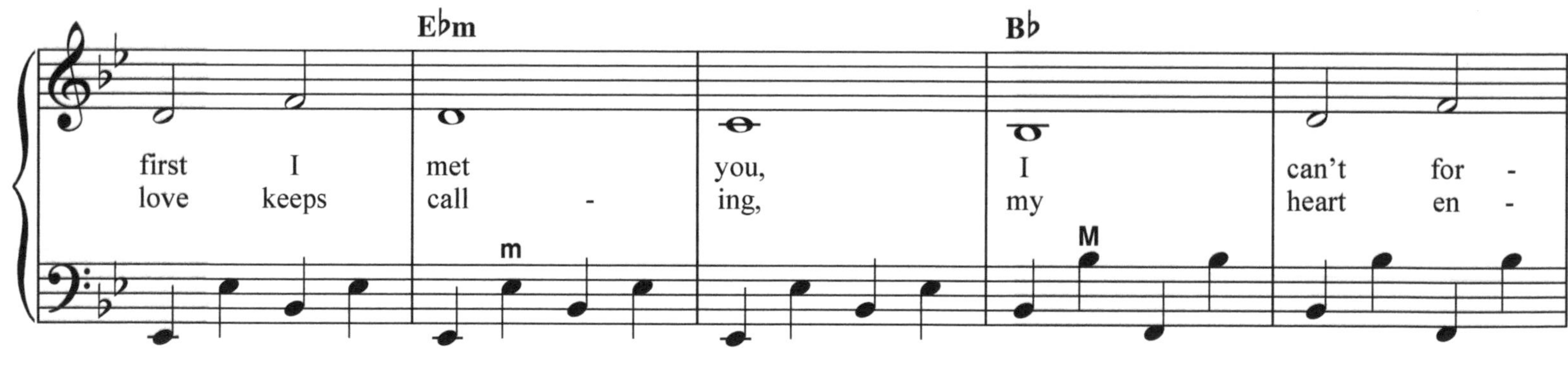

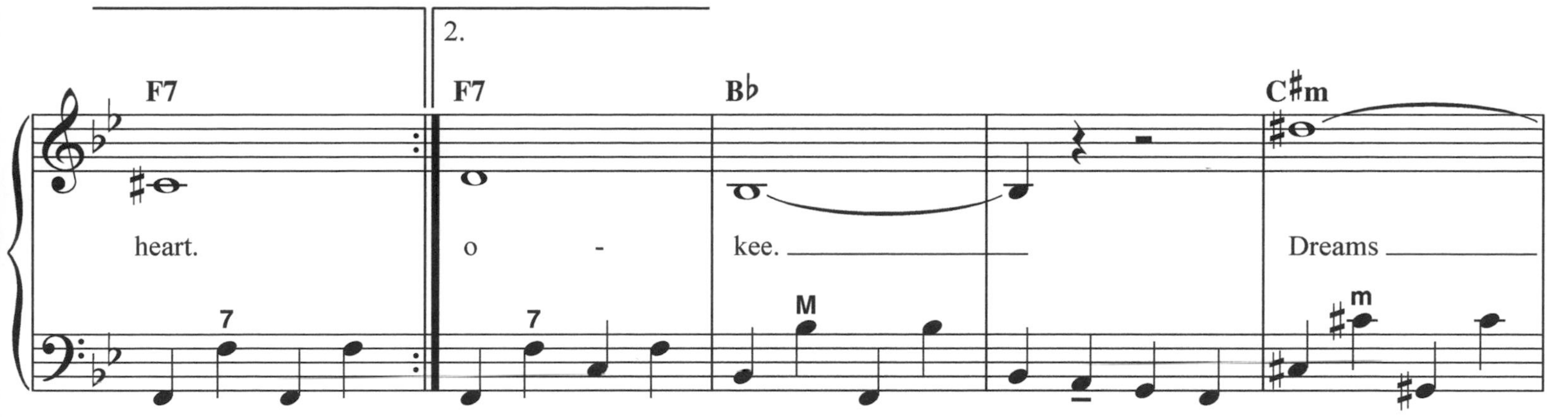
2.
F7
F7
B♭
C♯m
heart.
o - kee.
Dreams
7
7
M
m

F♯7
B
Bm
of
sum - mer - time
of
lov - er - time
7
M
m

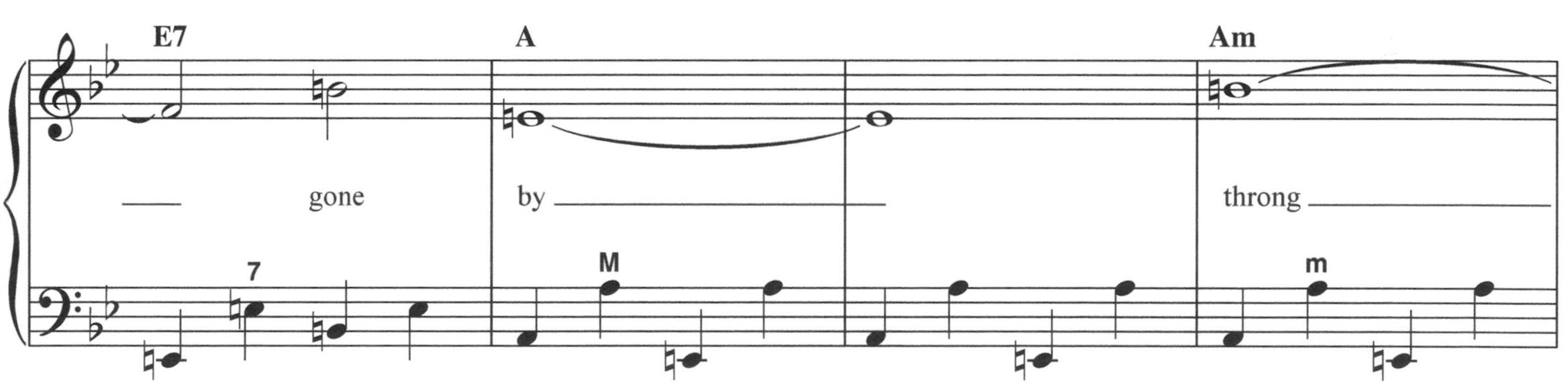
E7
A
Am
gone
by
throng
7
M
m

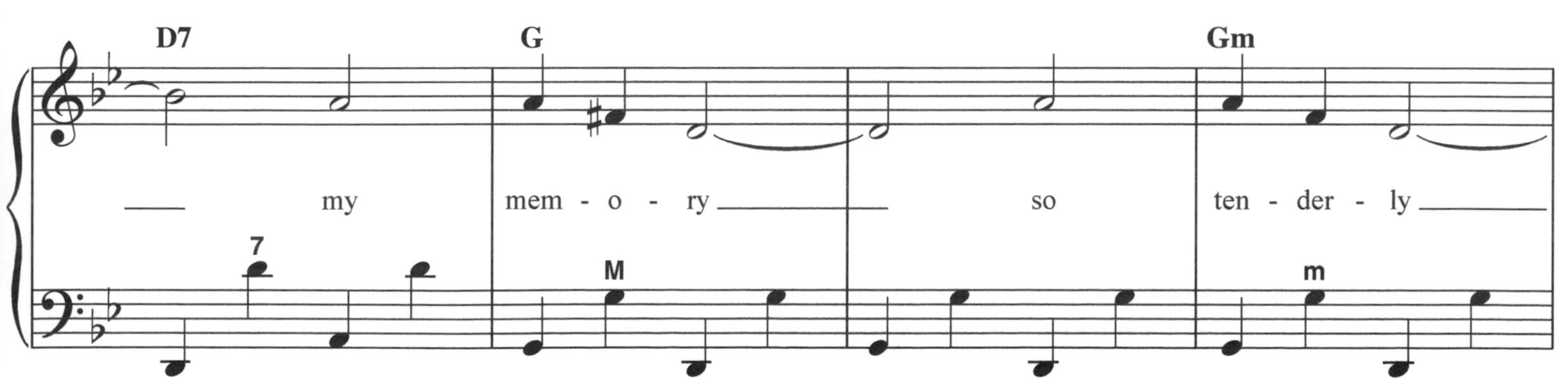
D7
G
Gm
my
mem - o - ry
so
ten - der - ly
7
M
m

C7
Cm
F7
B♭
F7
and
sigh.
My
sweet
In - dian

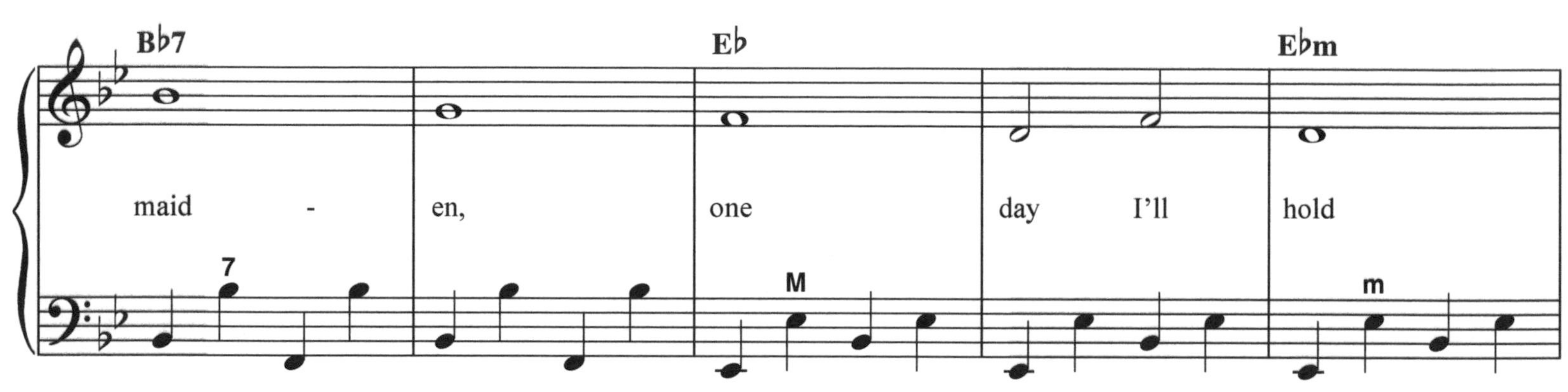
B♭7
E♭
E♭m
maid - en,
one
day I'll
hold

B♭
C7
you,
in
my arms
fold

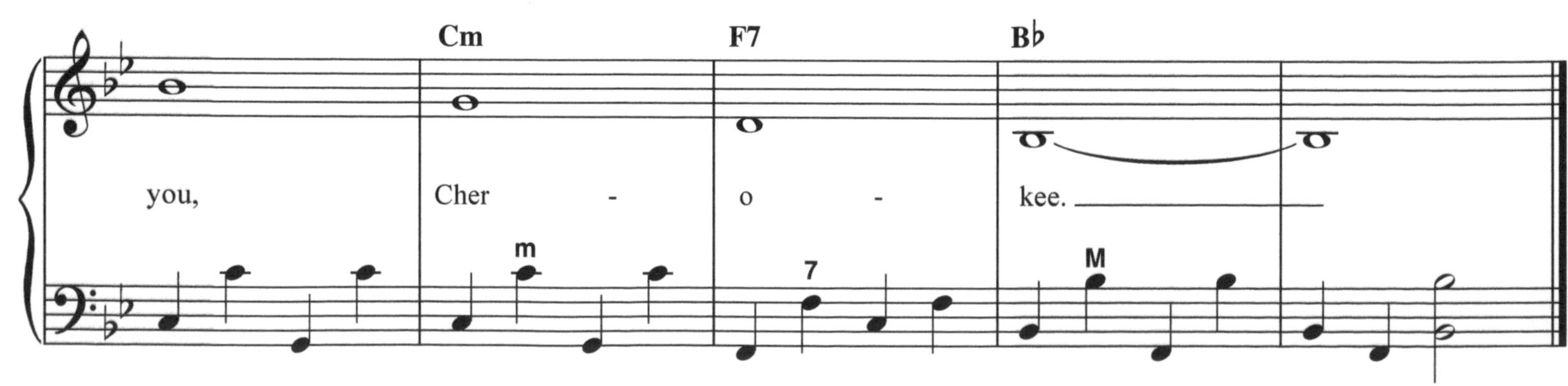
Cm
F7
B♭
you,
Cher - o - kee.

COME BACK TO SORRENTO

By ERNESTO DE CURTIS

D
Em
ran - ci: un pro - fu - mo non v'hae - gua - le
ta - te, par che vo - glia - no a te so - la
M
m

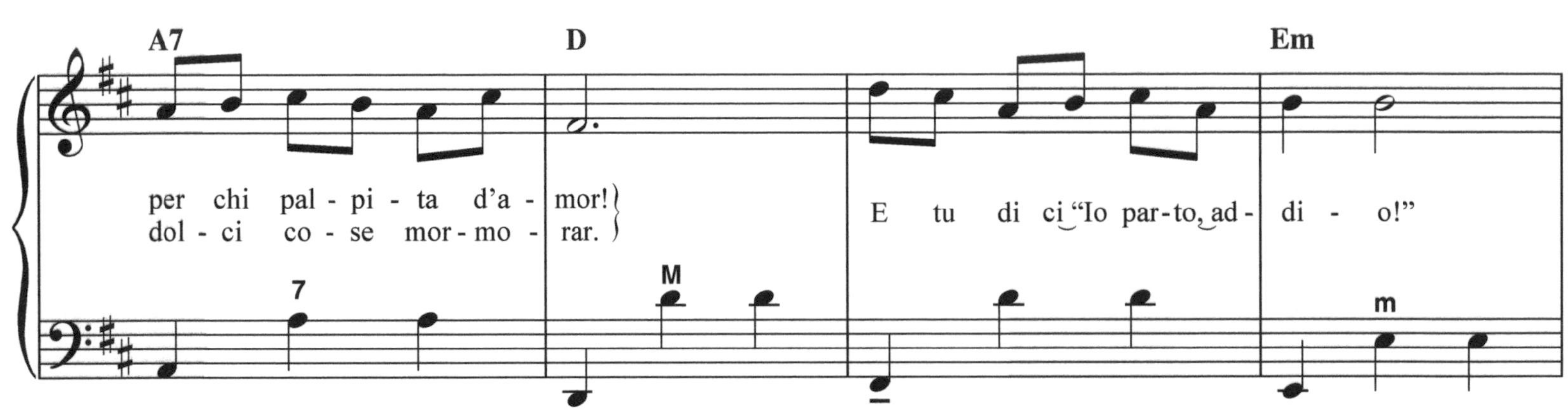
A7
D
Em
per chi pal - pi - ta d'a - mor!
dol - ci co - se mor - mo - rar.
E tu di ci "Io par - to, ad - di - o!"
7
M
m

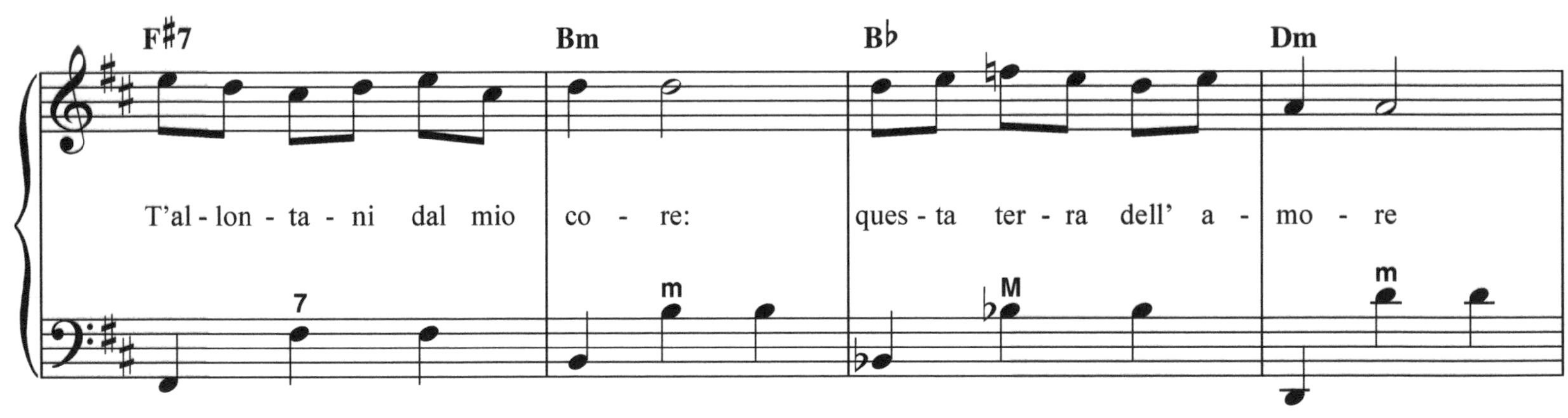
F♯7
Bm
B♭
Dm
T'al - lon - ta - ni dal mio co - re: ques - ta ter - ra dell' a - mo - re
7
m
M
m

A7
D
Em
hai la for - za di la - sciar? Ma non mi fug - gir,
7
M
m

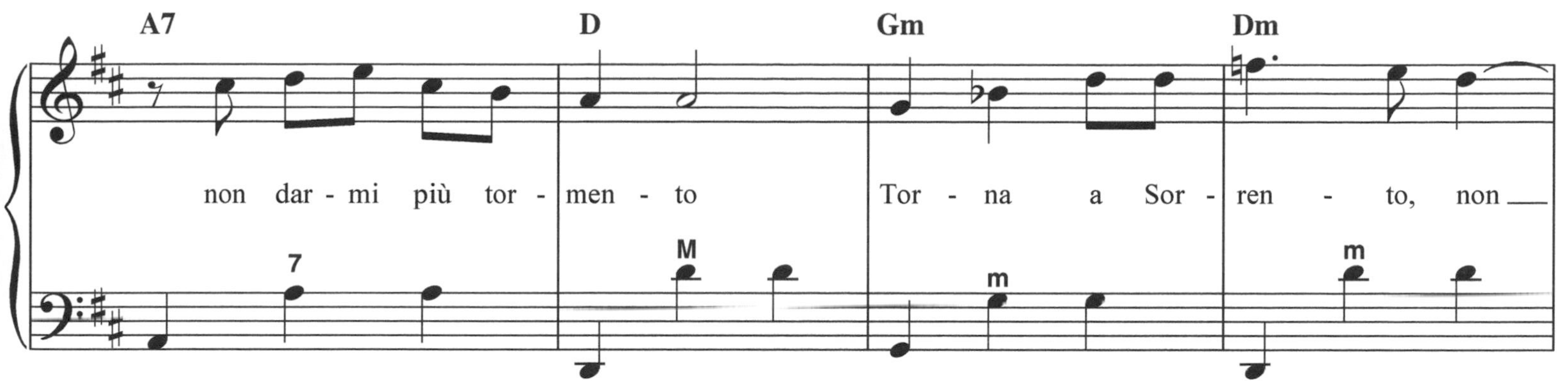

English Lyrics

1. Oh how deep is my devotion,
   Oh how sweet is my emotion,
   As in dreams I cross an ocean
   To be with a love so true.
   Once again to hold you near me,
   Once again to kiss you dearly,
   Once again to let you hear me
   Tell you of my love so true.
   As I wake, my tears are starting,
   Thinking of the hour of parting,
   Thinking of a ship departing
   From Sorrento and from you.
   I'll come back, my love,
   To meet you in Sorrento,
   I'll come to Sorrento,
   To you, my love!

2. I keep dreaming of Sorrento,
   For I met you in Sorrento,
   And you gave me a memento
   To be treasured all my days.
   Oh! the night was warm and lovely,
   Stars were in the sky above me,
   And your kiss declared you love me
   It's a memory that stays.
   Though my heart is wrapped with sadness,
   I recall that night of gladness,
   Ev'ry moment full of madness
   Will remain with me always.
   I'll come back, my love,
   To meet you in Sorrento,
   I'll come to Sorrento,
   To you, my love!

CIRIBIRIBIN

Words and Music by
ANTONIO PESTALOZZA

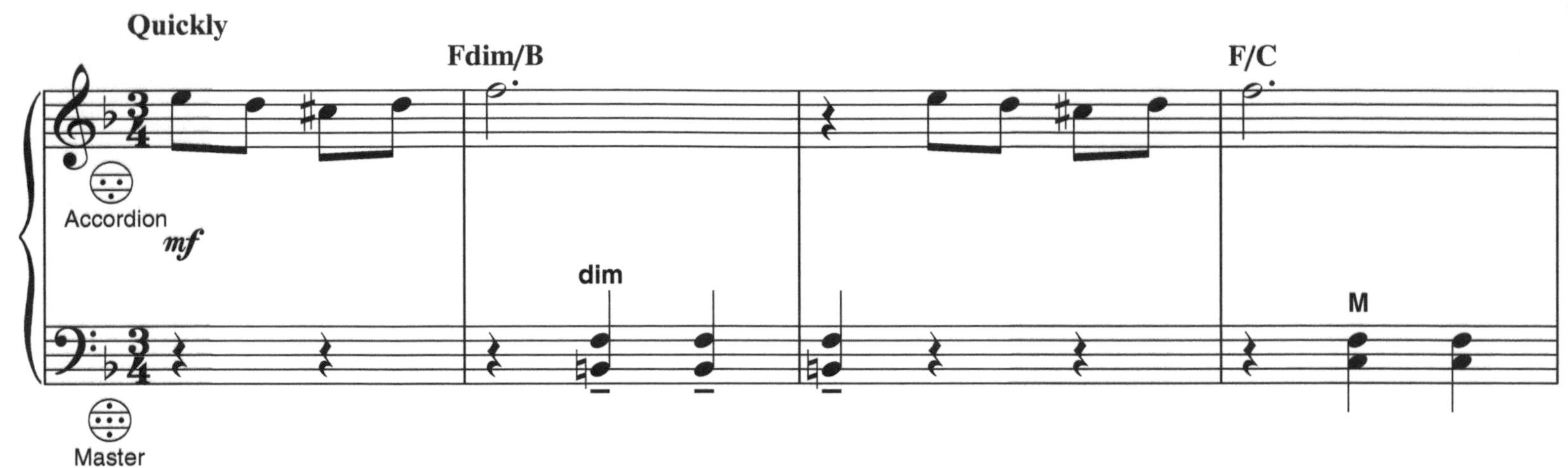

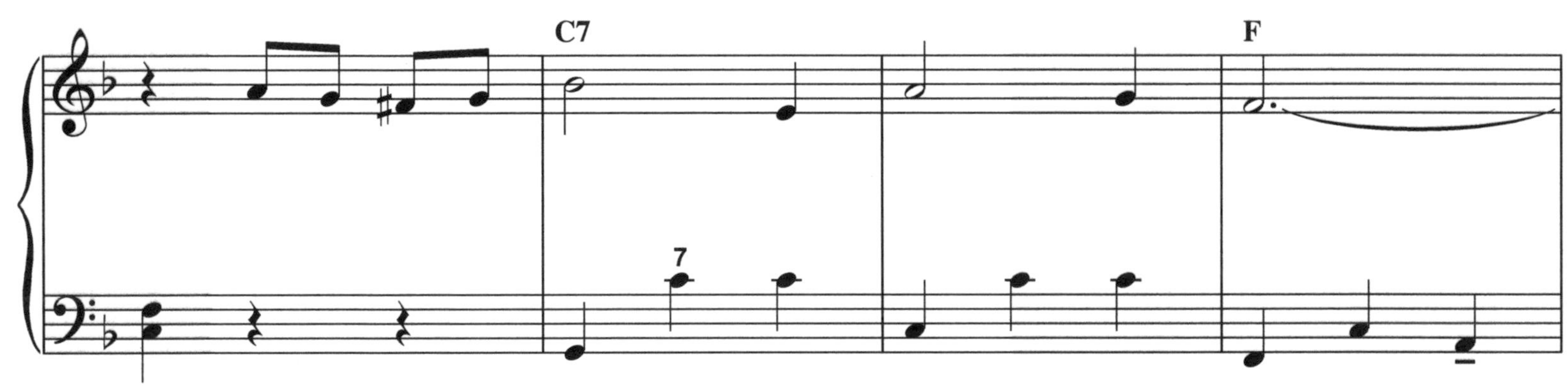

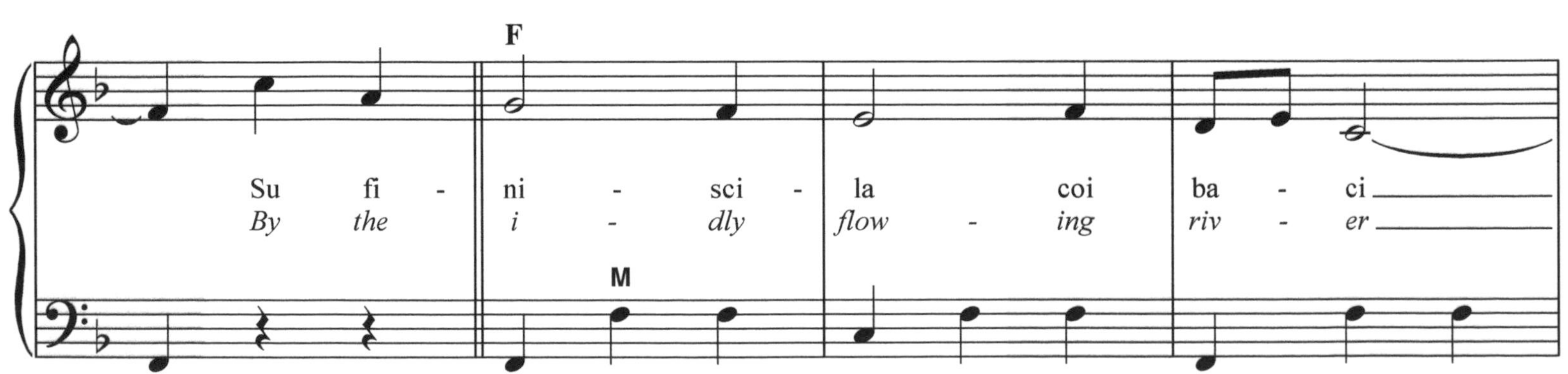

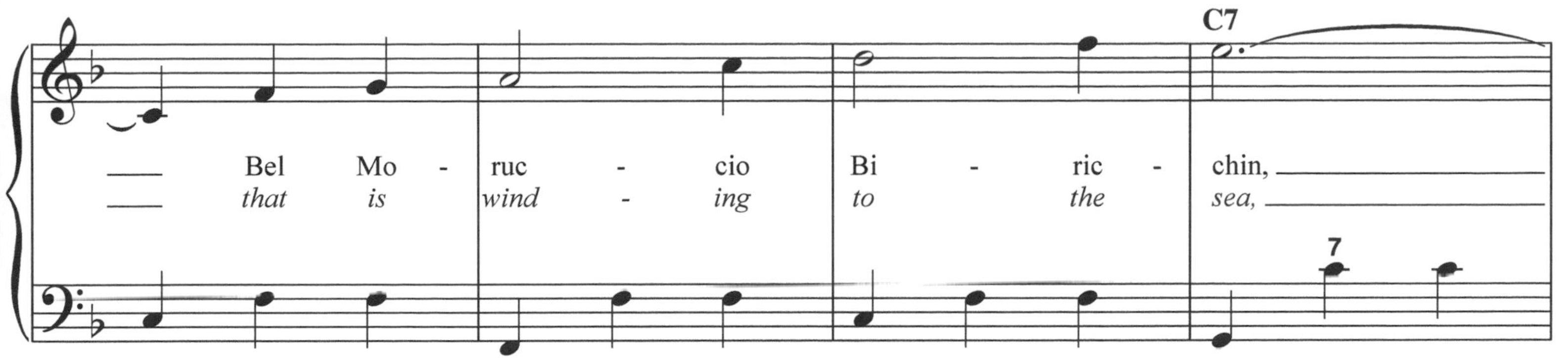
C7
Bel Mo - ruc - cio Bi - ric - chin,
that is wind - ing to the sea,
7

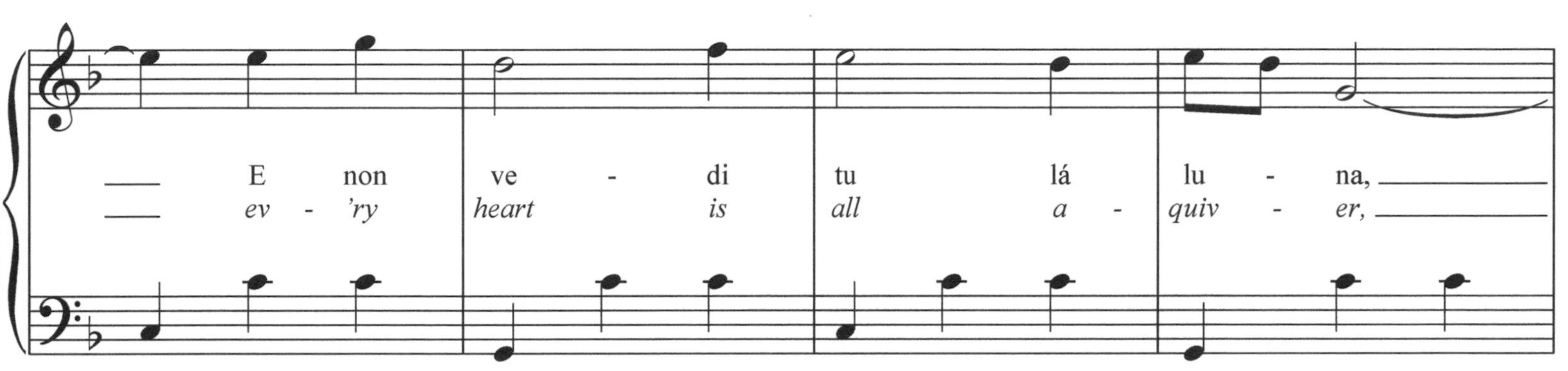
E non ve - di tu lá lu - na,
ev - 'ry heart is all a - quiv - er,

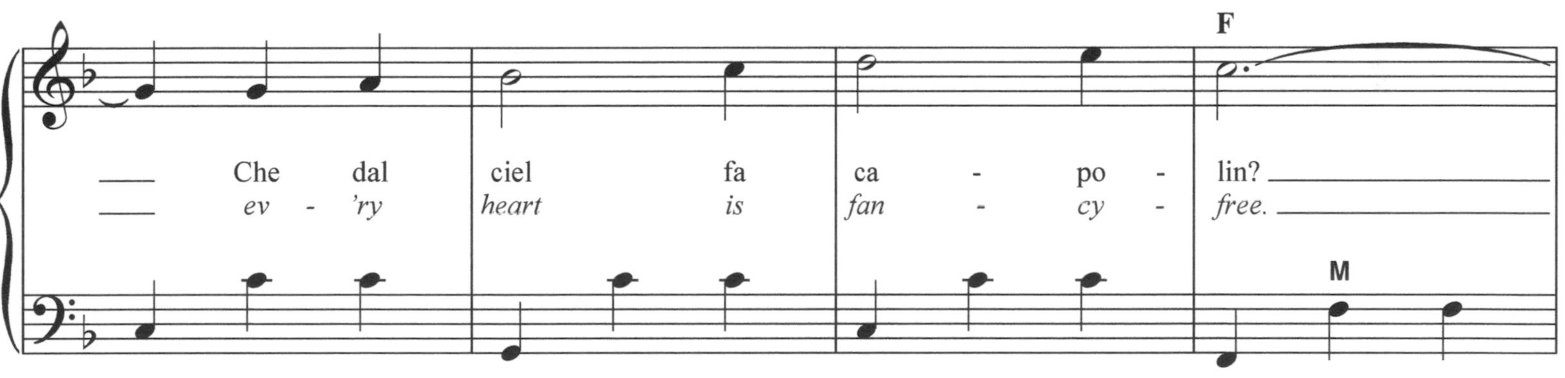
F
Che dal ciel fa ca - po - lin?
ev - 'ry heart is fan - cy - free.
M

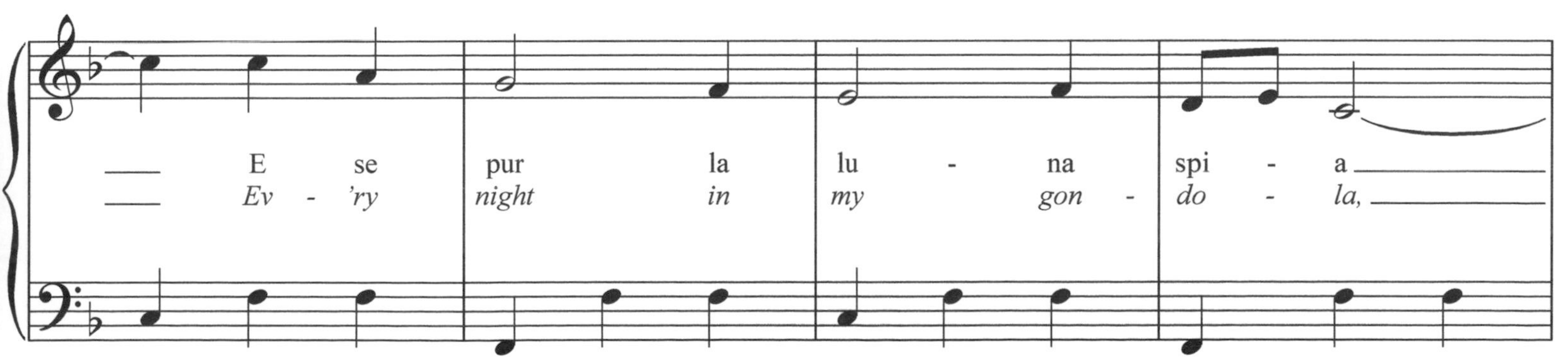
E se pur la lu - na spi - a
Ev - 'ry night in my gon - do - la,

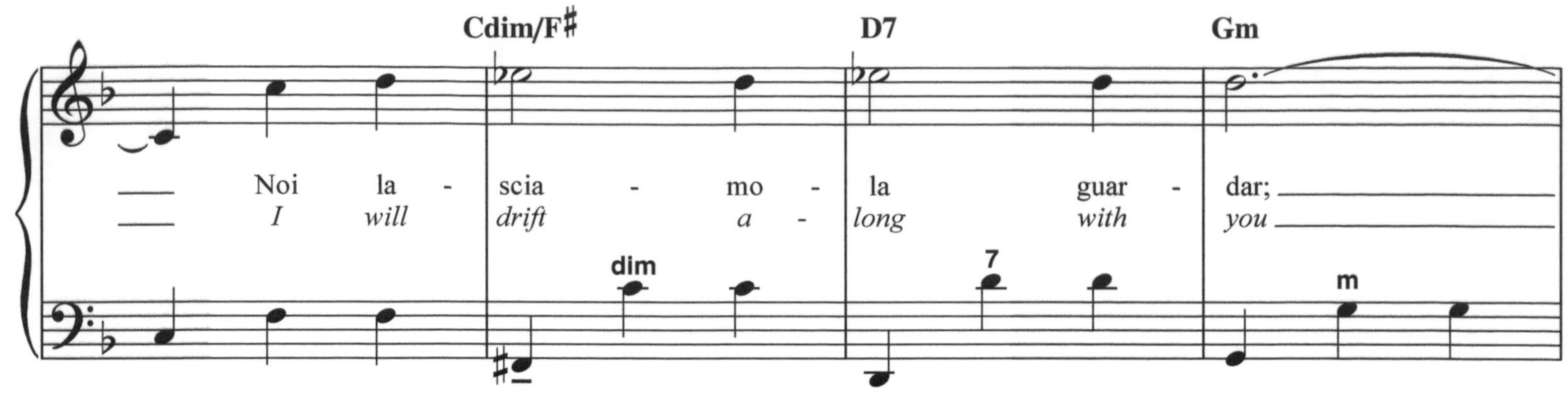
Cdim/F♯
D7
Gm
Noi la - scia - mo - la guar - dar;
I will drift a - long with you
dim
7
m

C7
F
An - zi il pal - li - do suo rag - gio
till we find a hap - py har - bor
7
M

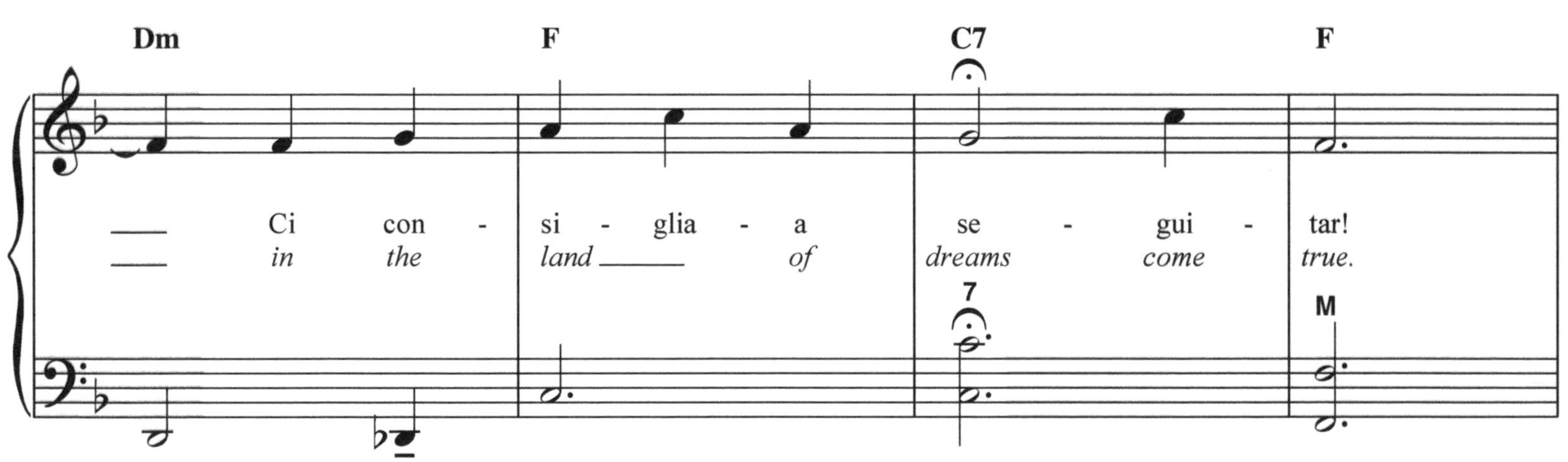
Dm
F
C7
F
Ci con - si - glia - a se - gui - tar!
in the land of dreams come true.
7
M

Dm
A7
Ma poi, chi - za? Co - sa di - ra?
My love and I let care go by;
m
7

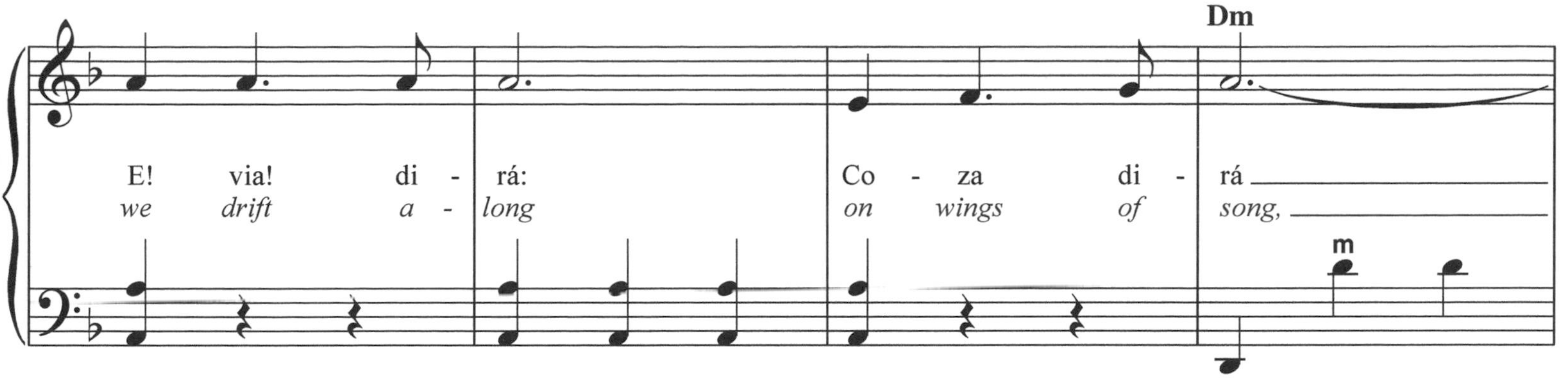
Dm
E! via! di - rá: Co - za di - rá
we drift a - long on wings of song,
m

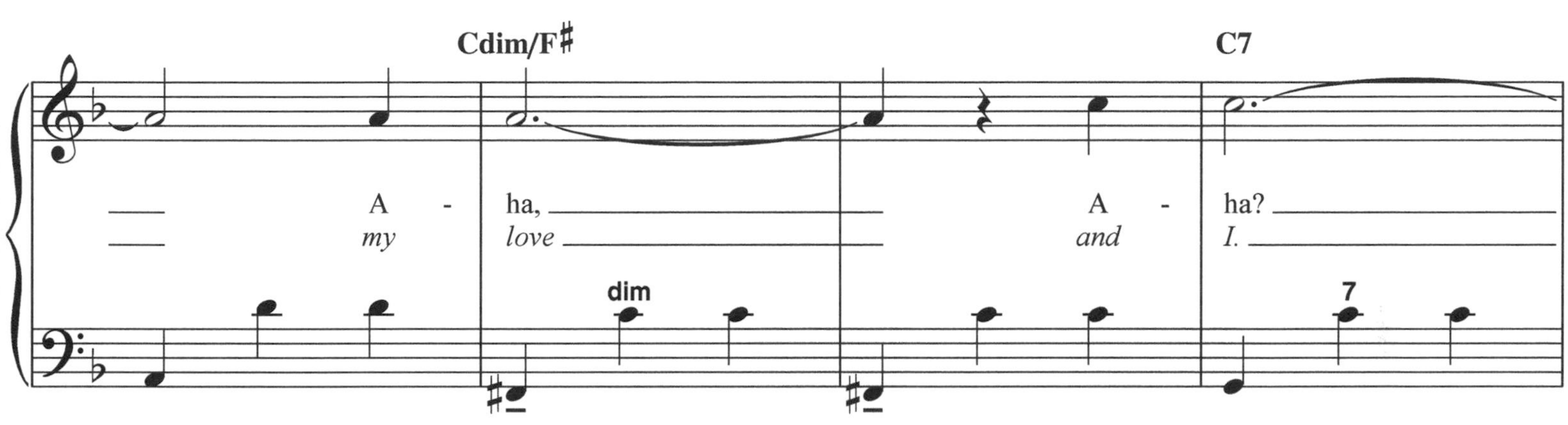
Cdim/F♯
C7
A - ha, A - ha?
my love and I.
dim
7

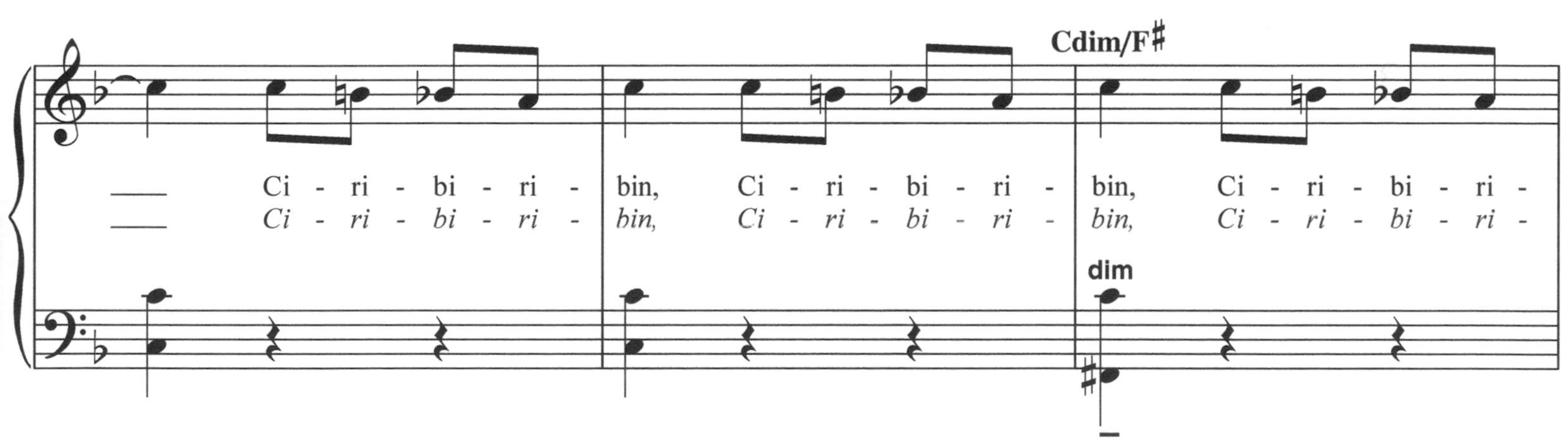
Cdim/F♯
Ci - ri - bi - ri - bin, Ci - ri - bi - ri - bin, Ci - ri - bi - ri -
Ci - ri - bi - ri - bin, Ci - ri - bi - ri - bin, Ci - ri - bi - ri -
dim

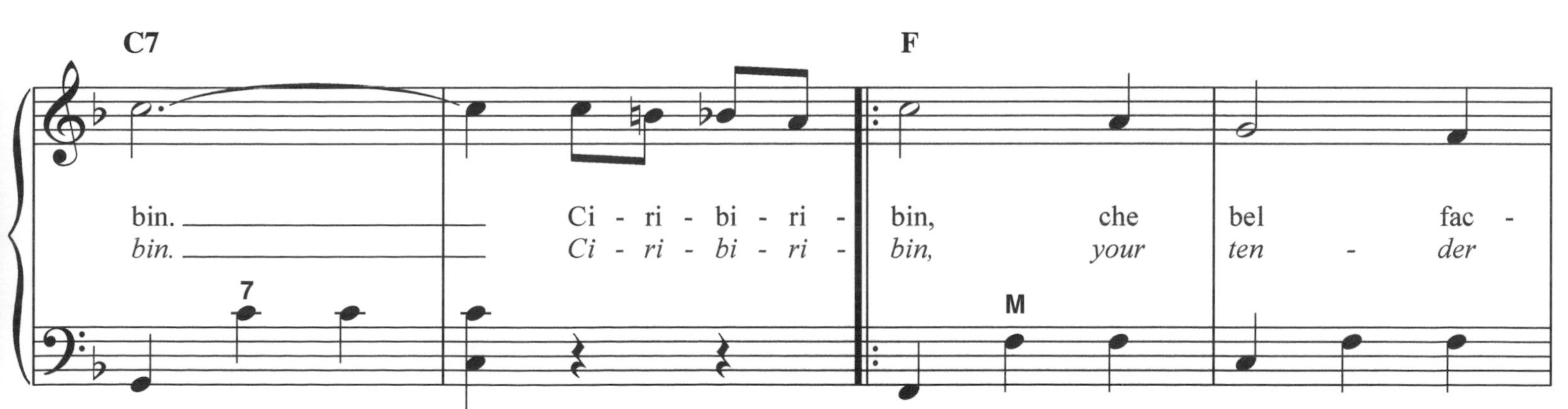
C7
F
bin. Ci - ri - bi - ri - bin, che bel fac -
bin. Ci - ri - bi - ri - bin, your ten - der
7
M

cin, Che squar - do dol - ce ed as - sas -
glance turns dark - est night to bright - est

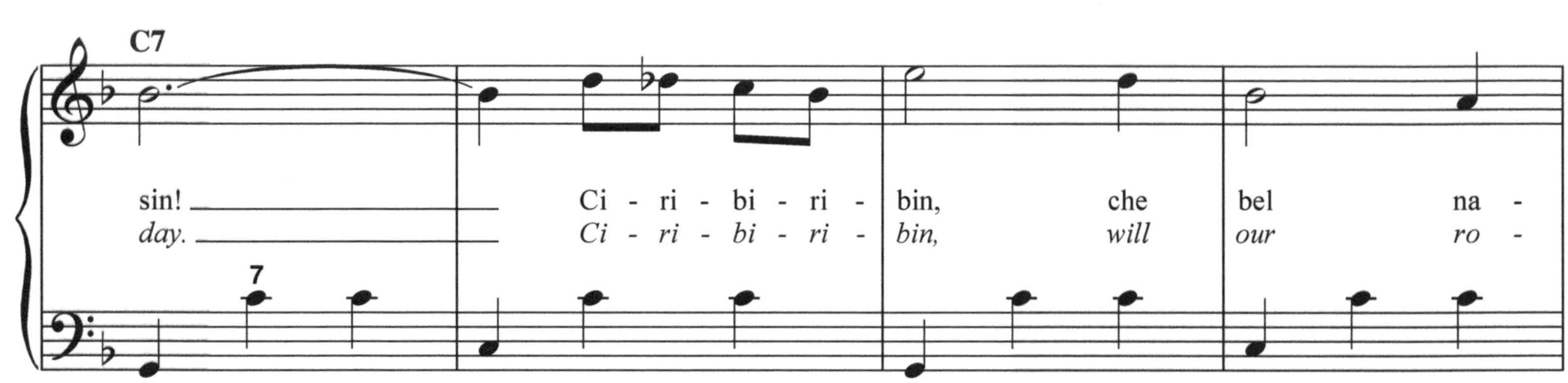
C7
sin! Ci - ri - bi - ri - bin, che bel na -
day. Ci - ri - bi - ri - bin, will our ro -
7

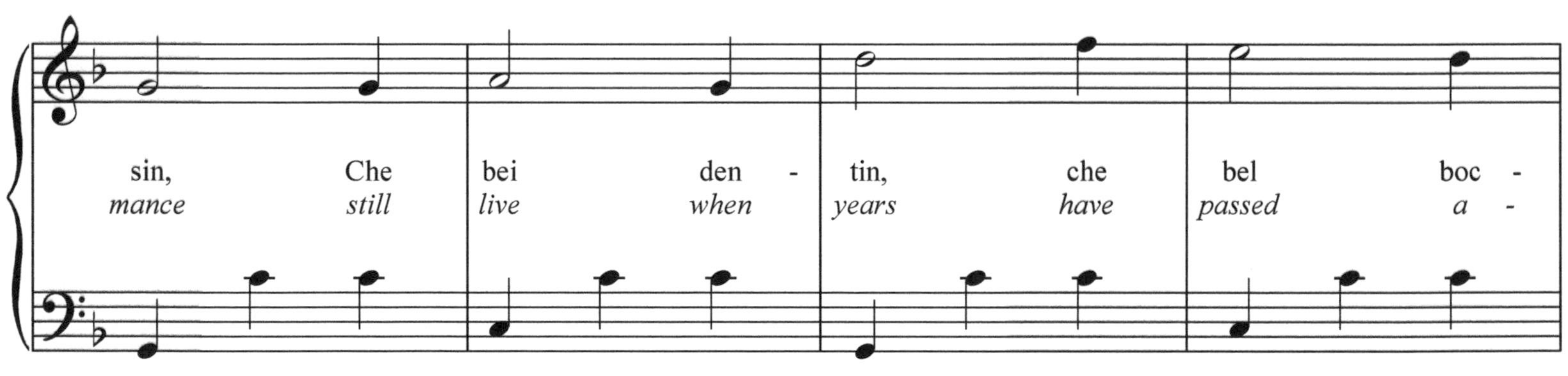
sin, Che bei den - tin, che bel boc -
mance still live when years have passed a -

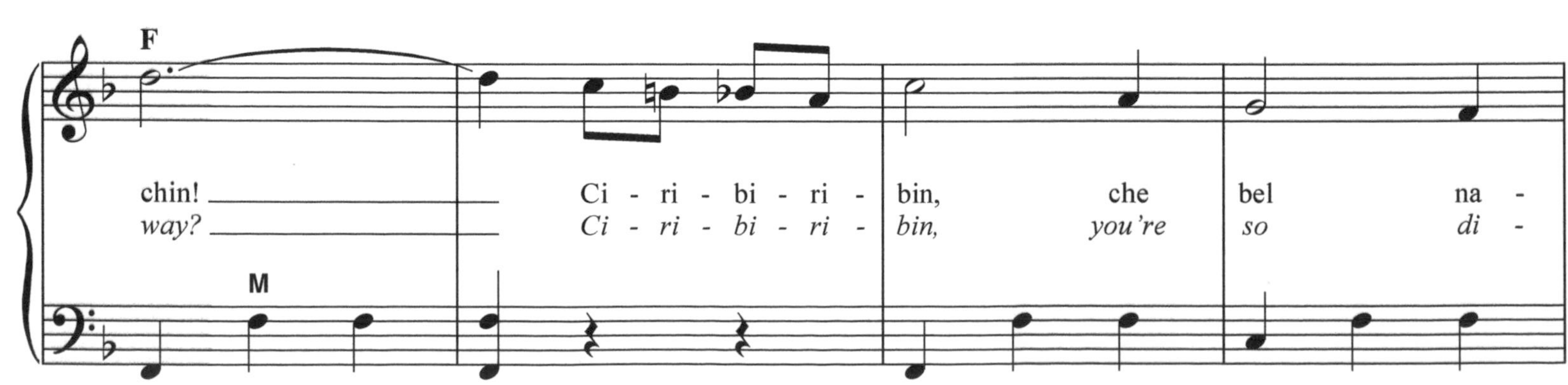
F
chin! Ci - ri - bi - ri - bin, che bel na -
way? Ci - ri - bi - ri - bin, you're so di -
M

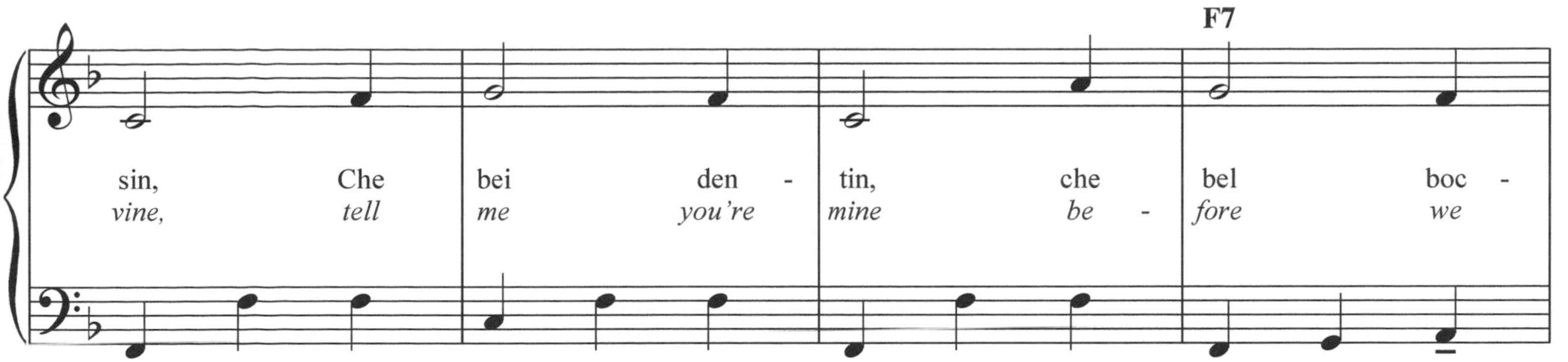
F7
sin, Che bei den - tin, che bel boc -
vine, tell me you're mine be - fore we

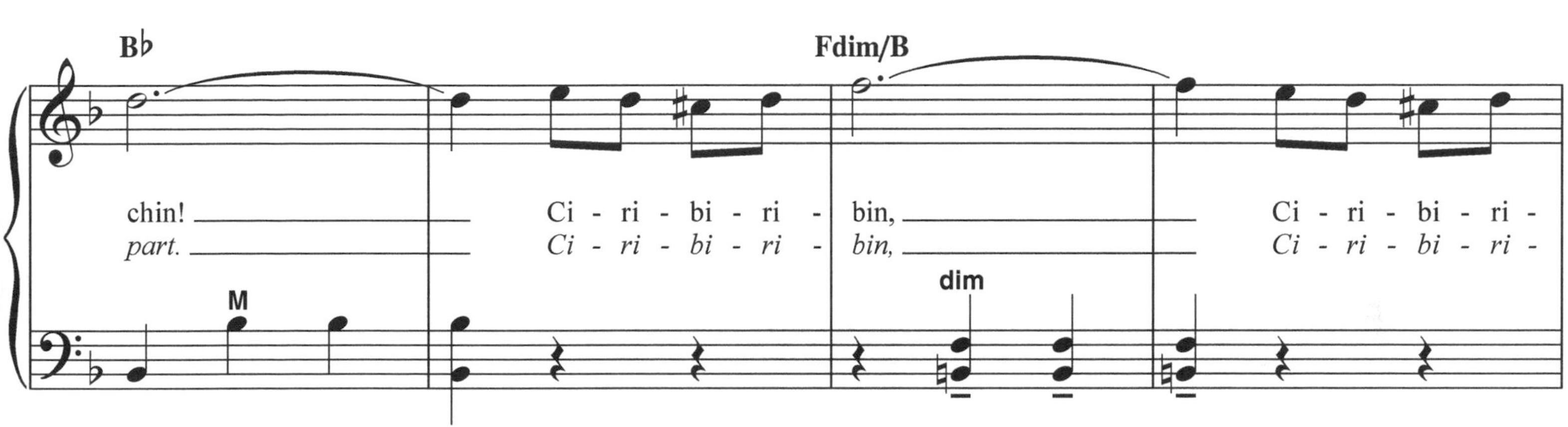
B♭
Fdim/B
chin! Ci - ri - bi - ri - bin, Ci - ri - bi - ri -
part. Ci - ri - bi - ri - bin, Ci - ri - bi - ri -
M
dim

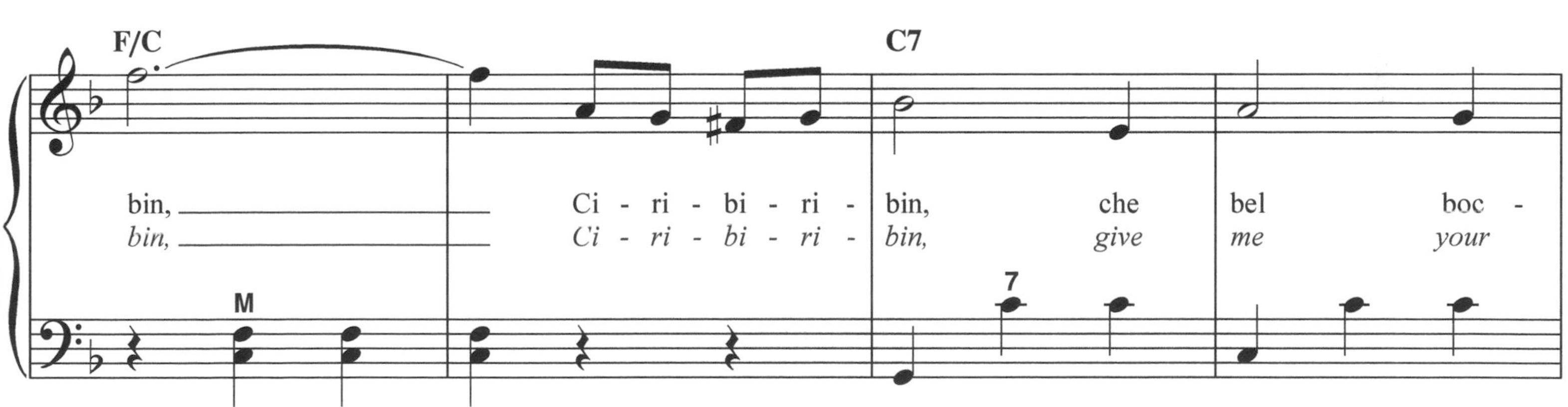
F/C
C7
bin, Ci - ri - bi - ri - bin, che bel boc -
bin, Ci - ri - bi - ri - bin, give me your
M
7

1.
2.
F
F
chin! Ci - ri - bi - ri - chin!
heart. Ci - ri - bi - ri - heart.

EDELWEISS

from THE SOUND OF MUSIC

Lyrics by OSCAR HAMMERSTEIN II
Music by RICHARD RODGERS

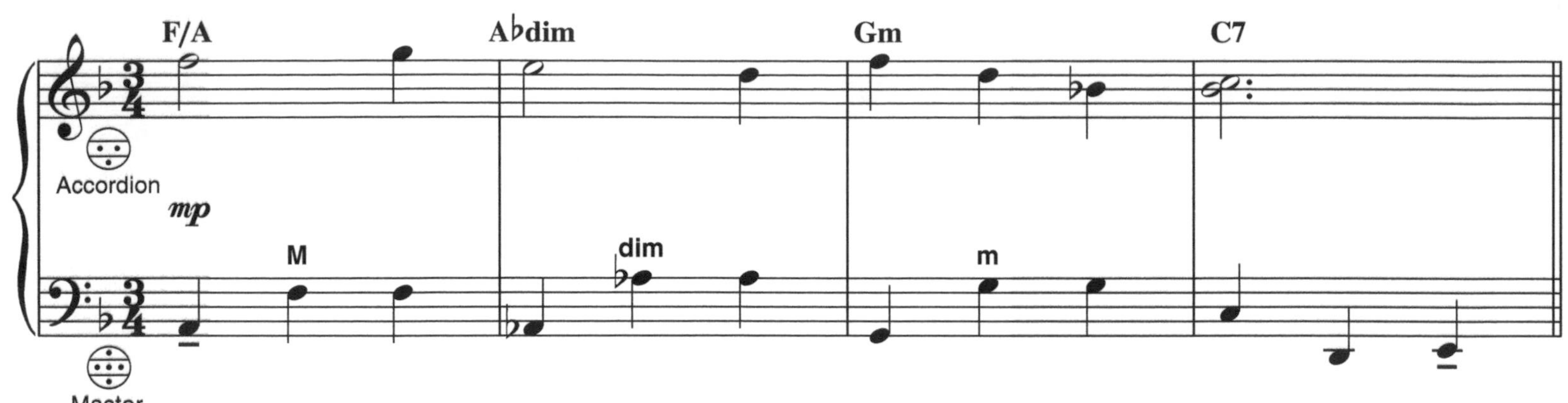

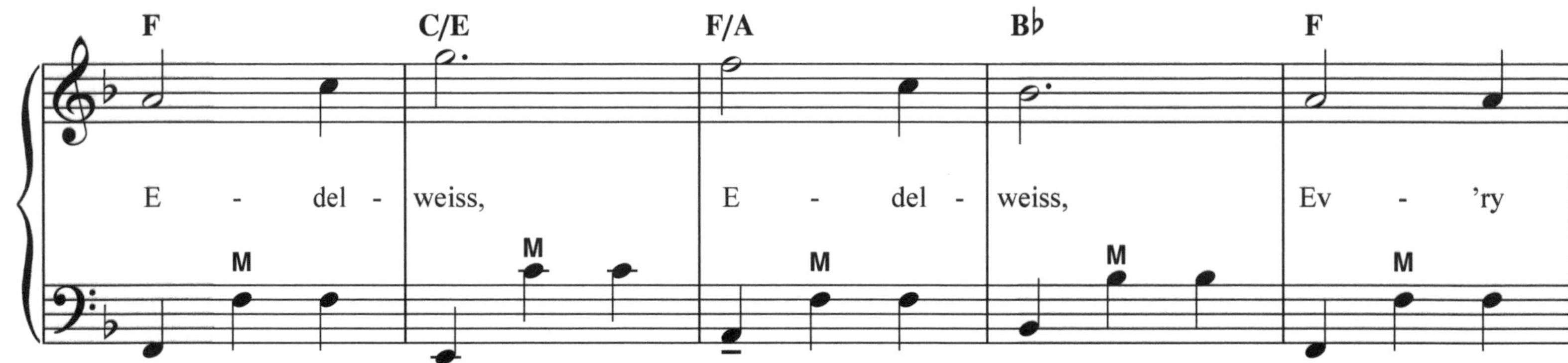

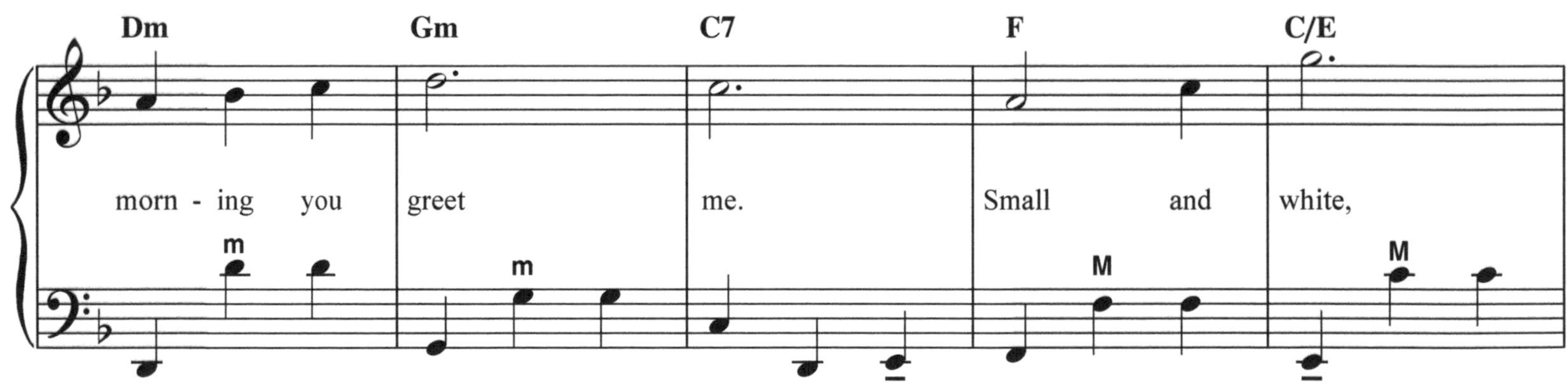

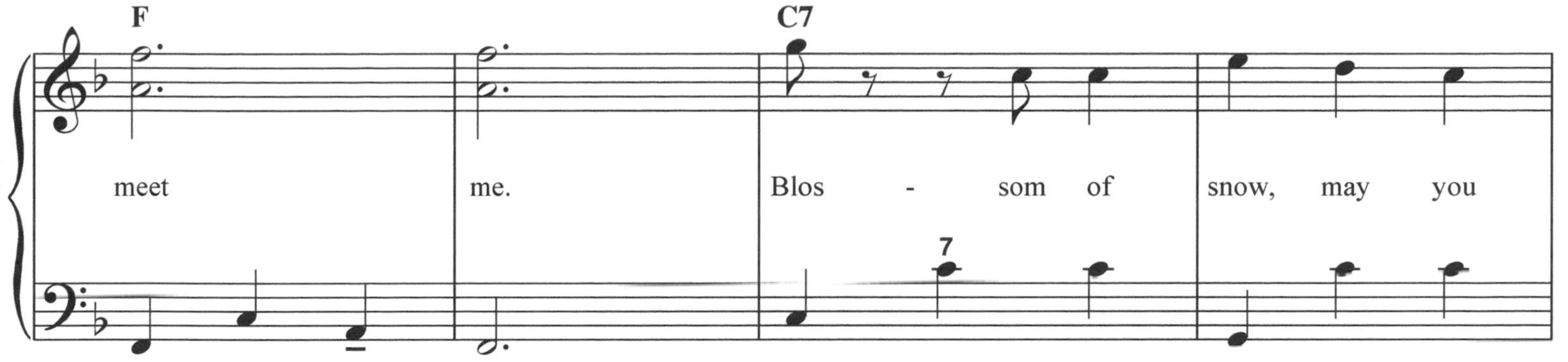
F
C7
meet
me.
Blos - som of
snow, may you
7

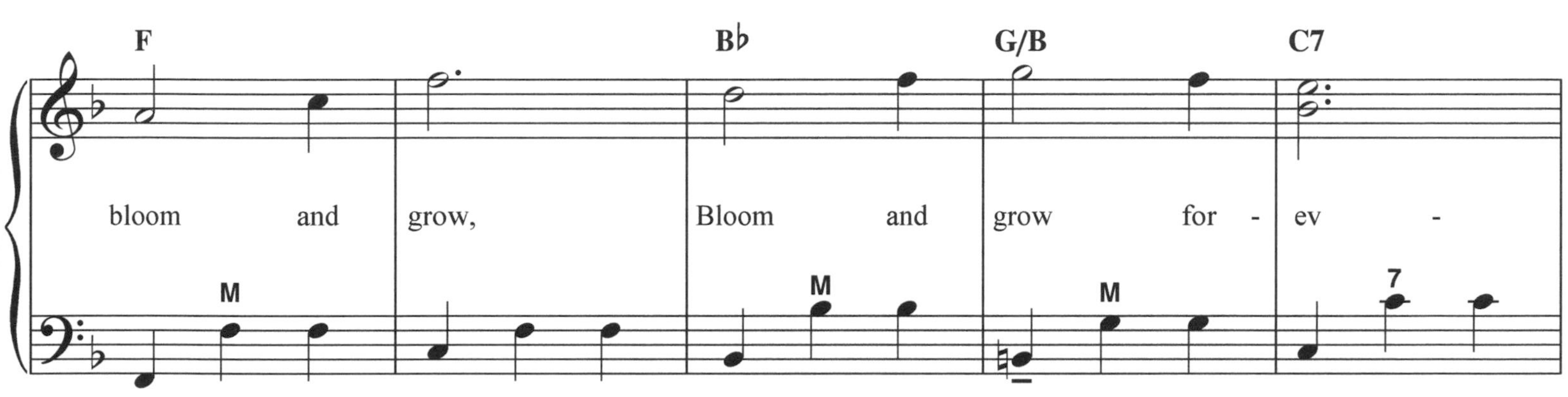
F
B♭
G/B
C7
bloom and
grow,
Bloom and
grow for - ev -
M
M
M
7

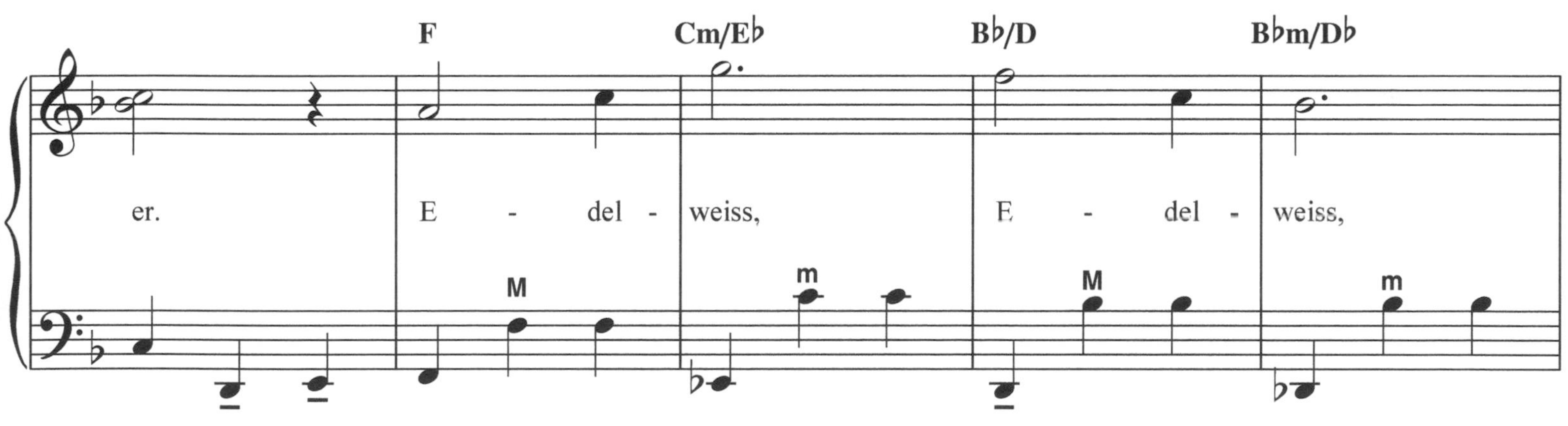
F
Cm/E♭
B♭/D
B♭m/D♭
er.
E - del -
weiss,
E - del -
weiss,
M
m
M
m

F/C
C7
F
Bless my
home - land for -
ev -
er.
M
7

THE GODFATHER WALTZ

from the Paramount Pictures THE GODFATHER, GODFATHER II and GODFATHER III

By NINO ROTA

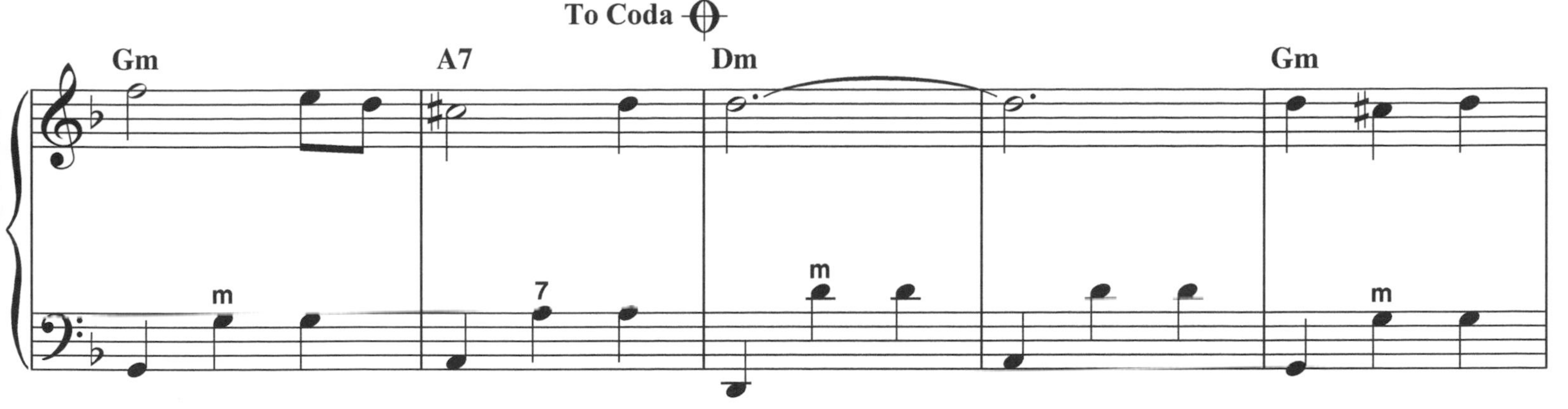
To Coda
Gm
A7
Dm
Gm
m
7
m
m

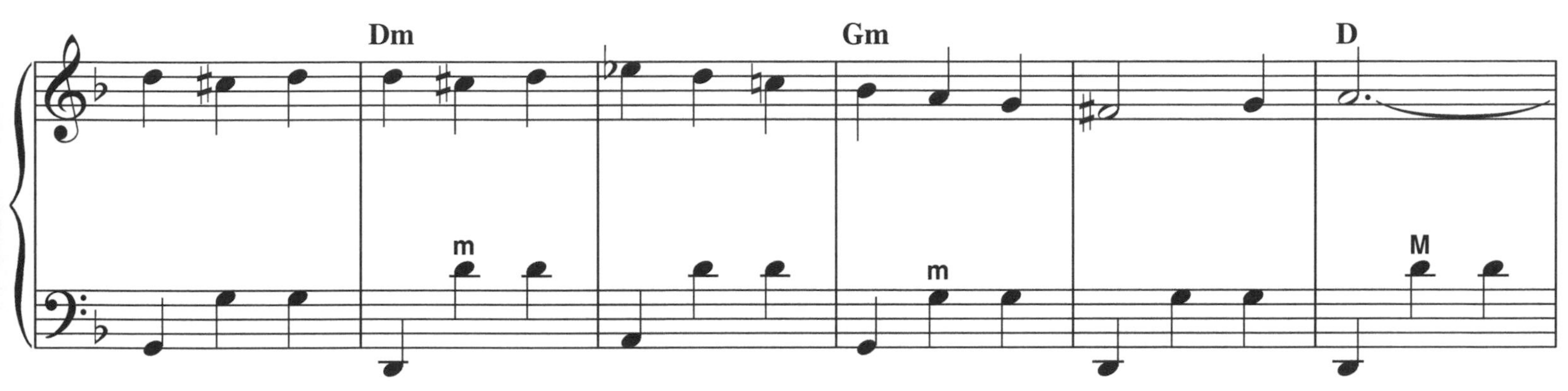
Dm
Gm
D
m
m
M

Gm
Dm
Am
m
m
m

E7
Am
D.C. al Coda
7
m

CODA
Dm

HAVA NAGILA
(Let's Be Happy)

Lyrics by MOSHE NATHANSON
Music by ABRAHAM Z. IDELSOHN

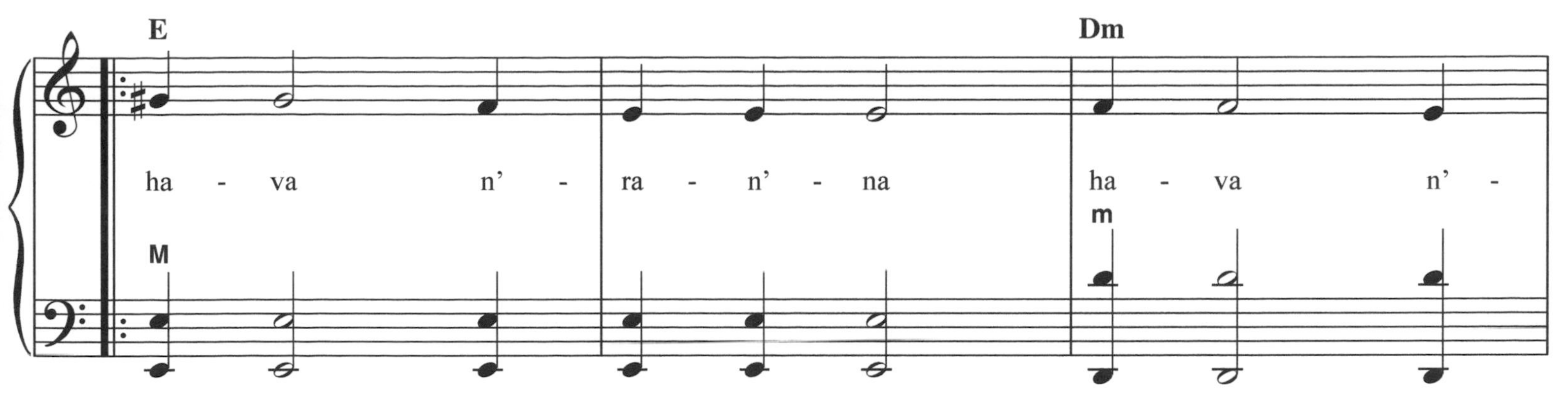
E
Dm
ha - va n' - ra - n' - na ha - va n' -
M
m

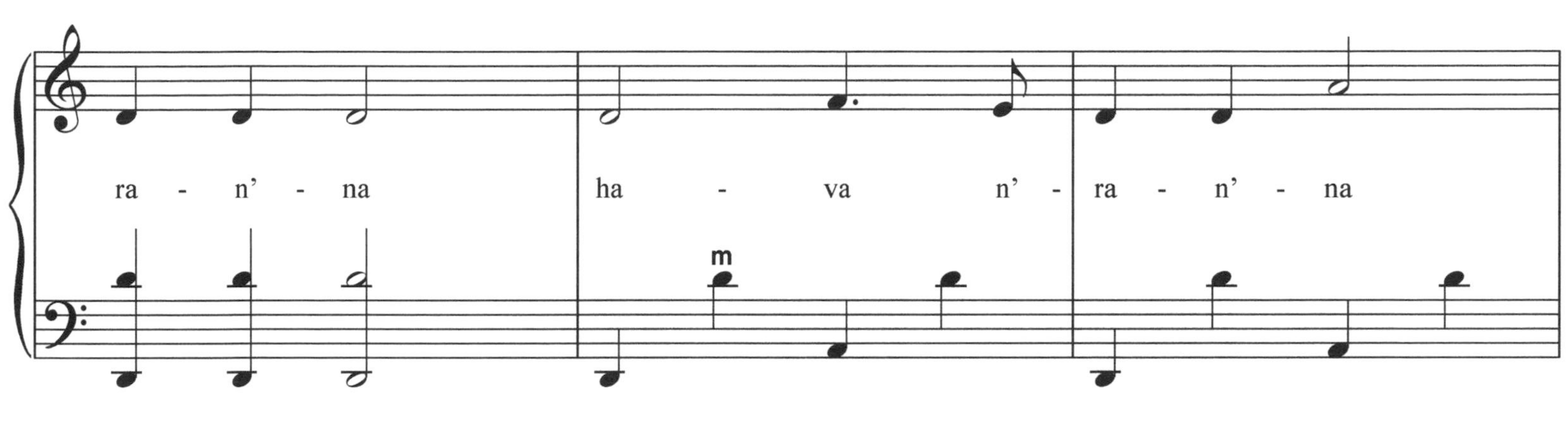
ra - n' - na ha - va n' - ra - n' - na
m

1.
2.
E
u' - nis - m' - cha cha
M

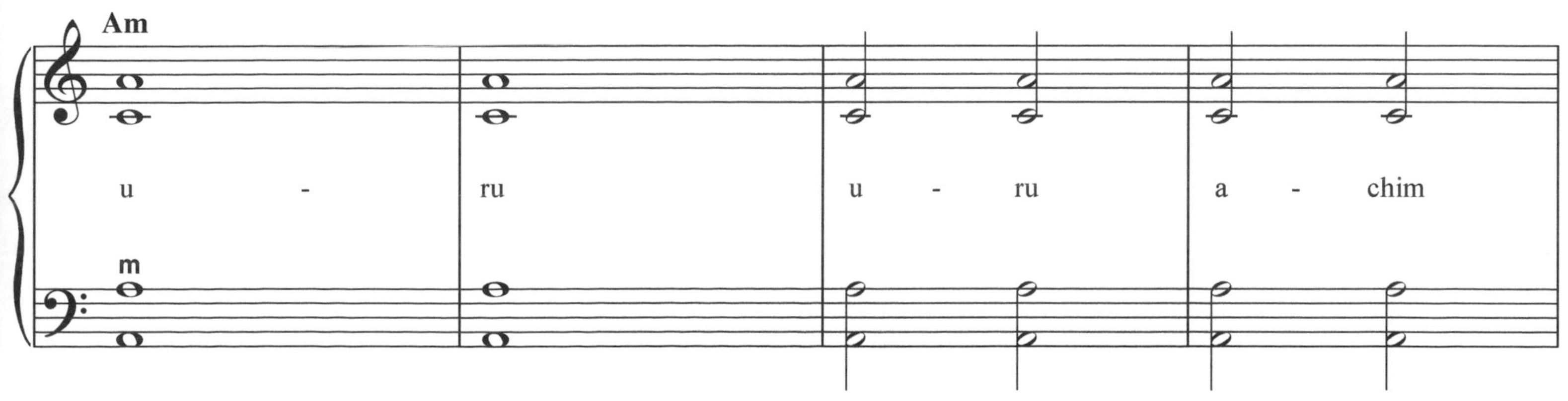
Am
u - ru u - ru a - chim
m

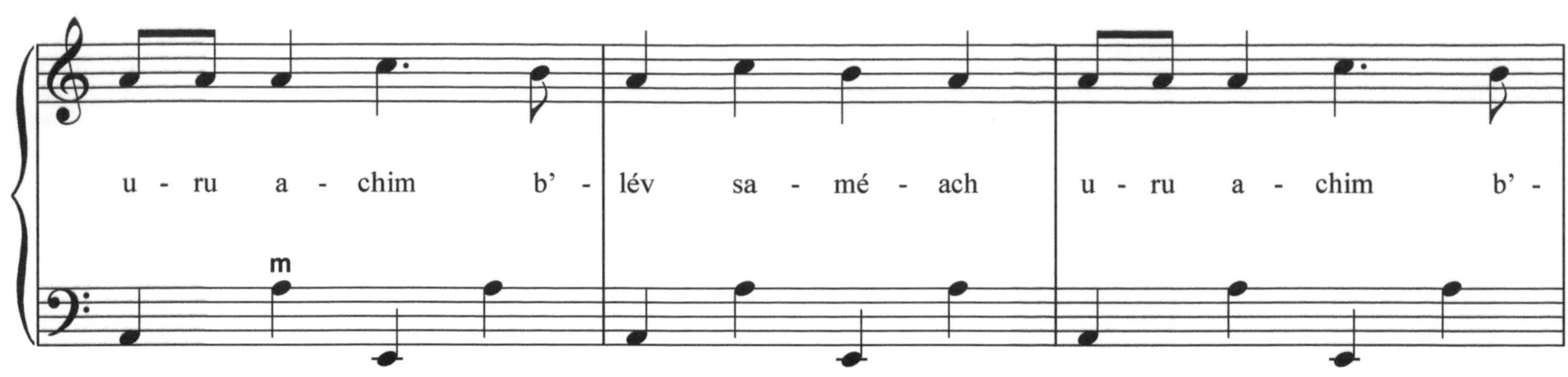
u - ru a - chim b' - lév sa - mé - ach u - ru a - chim b' -
m

E
lév sa - mé - ach u - ru a - chim b' - lév sa - mé - ach
M

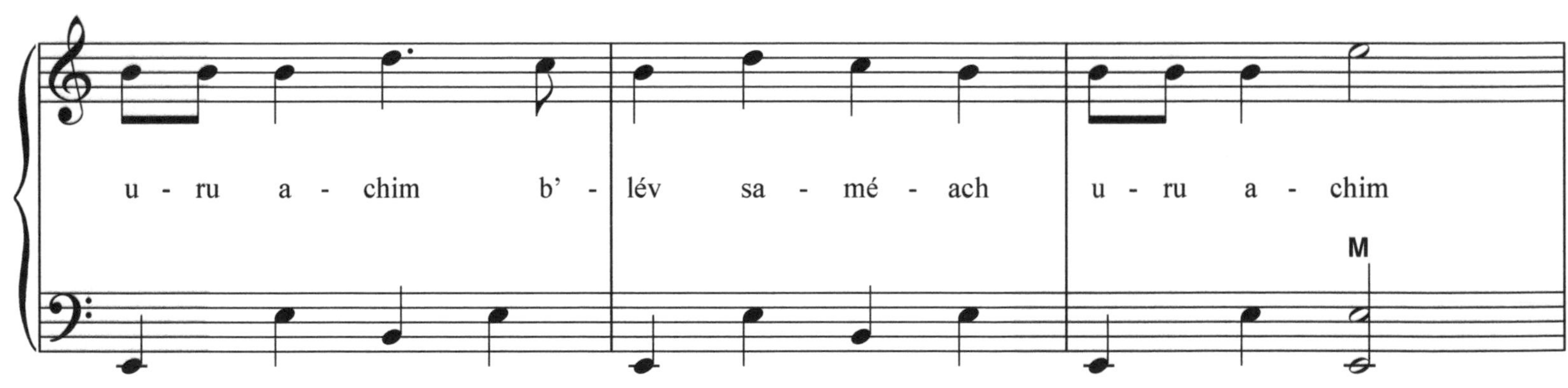
u - ru a - chim b' - lév sa - mé - ach u - ru a - chim
M

Am
u - ru a - chim b' - lév sa - mé - ach.
m

HELLO, DOLLY!

from HELLO, DOLLY!

Music and Lyric by
JERRY HERMAN

G7
tell,
Dol - ly, you're still
glow - in', you're still
crow - in', you're still
7

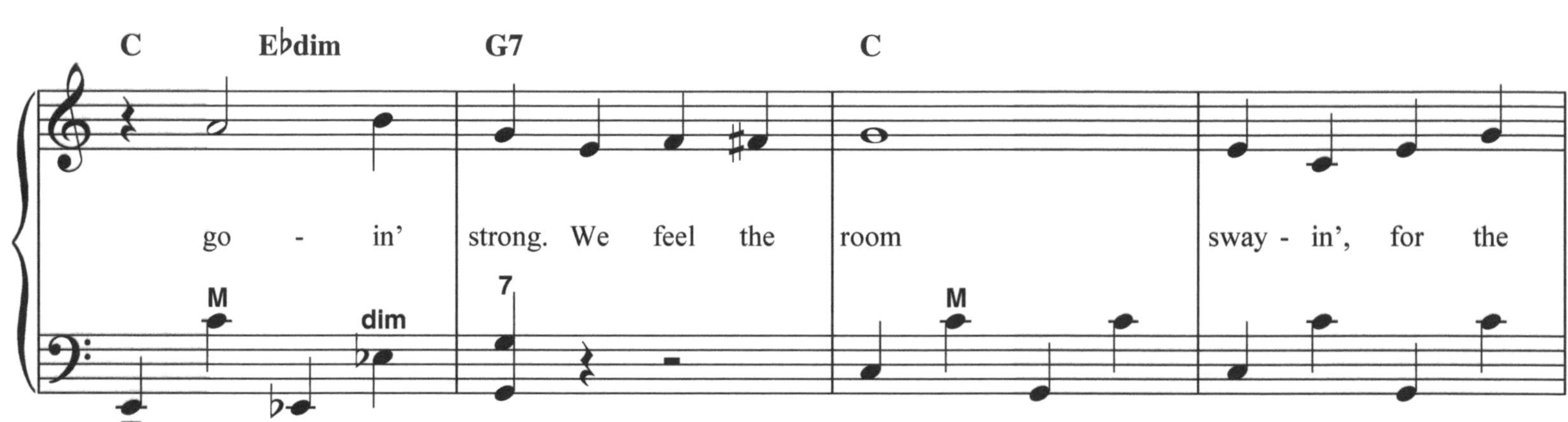
C
E♭dim
G7
C
go - in'
strong. We feel the
room
sway - in', for the
M
dim
7
M

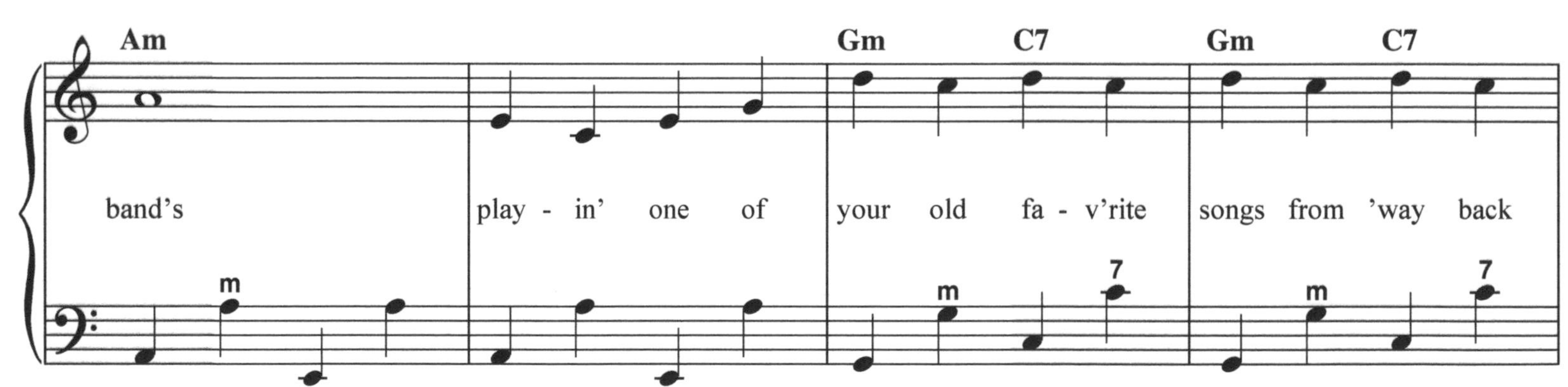
Am
Gm
C7
Gm
C7
band's
play - in' one of
your old fa - v'rite
songs from 'way back
m
m
7
m
7

F
E7
Am
Em
when.
So,
take her
gol - ly
wrap, fel - las,
gee, fel - las,
M
7
m
m

Am
Em
D7
find her an emp - ty
find her a va - cant
lap, fel - las.
knee, fel - las.
Dol - ly 'll nev - er
m
m
7

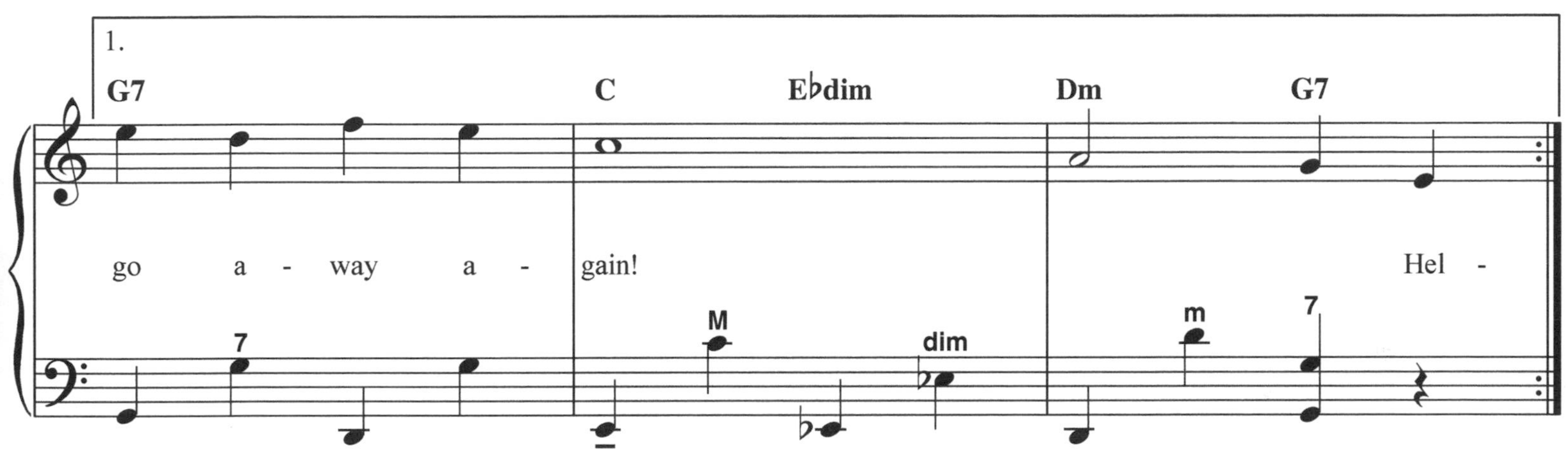
1.
G7
C
E♭dim
Dm
G7
go a - way a -
gain!
Hel -
7
M
dim
m
7

2.
G7
D7
G7
go a - way,
Dol - ly 'll nev - er
go a - way,
7
7
7

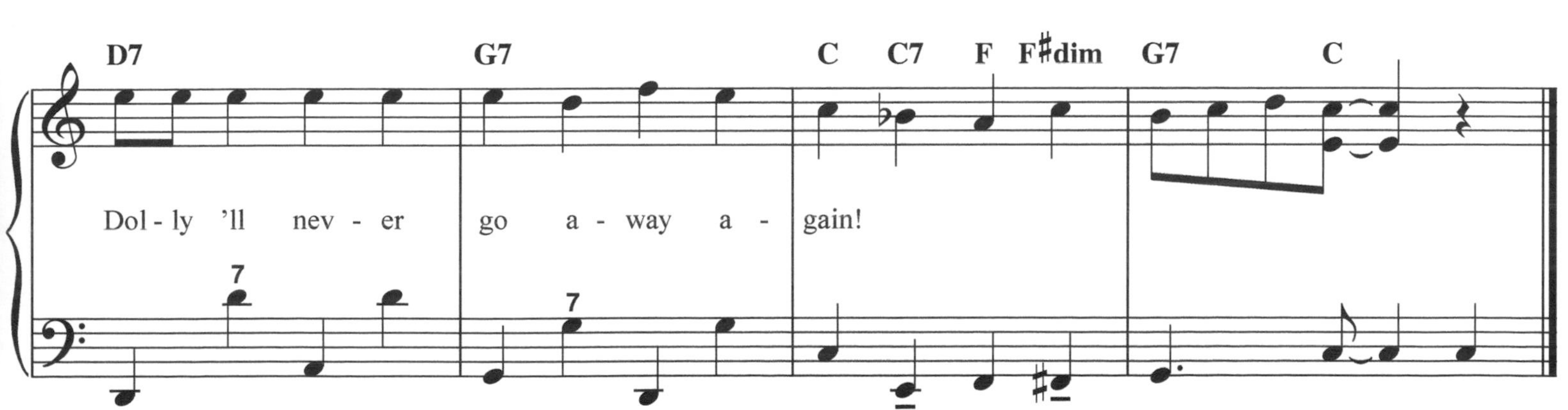
D7
G7
C C7 F F♯dim
G7
C
Dol - ly 'll nev - er
go a - way a -
gain!
7
7

HERNANDO'S HIDEAWAY

from THE PAJAMA GAME

Words and Music by RICHARD ADLER
and JERRY ROSS

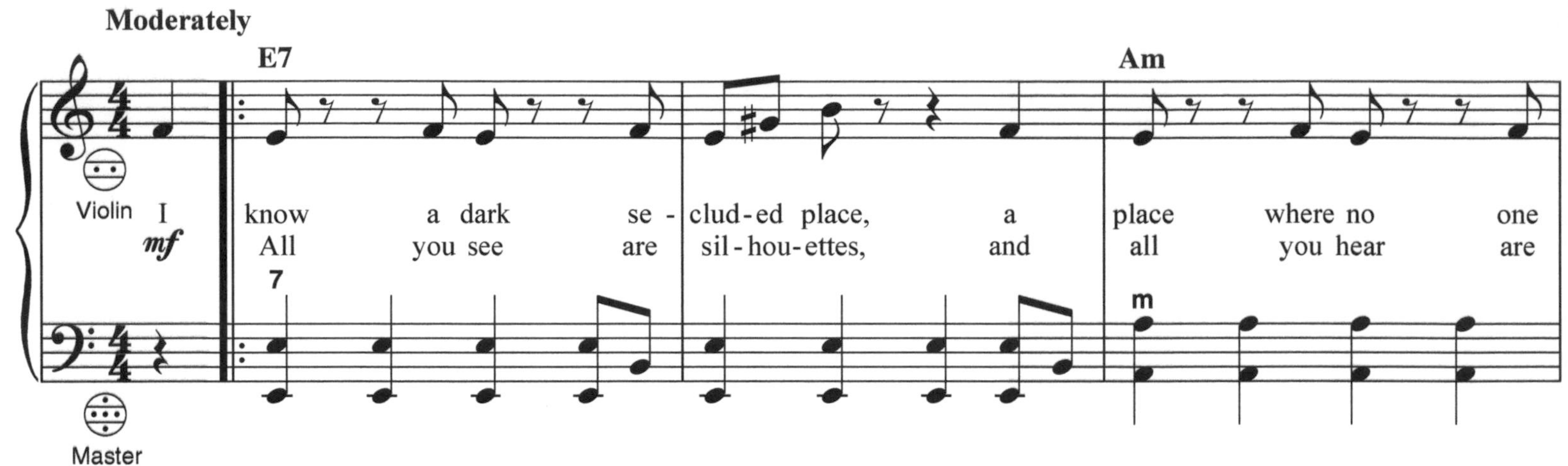

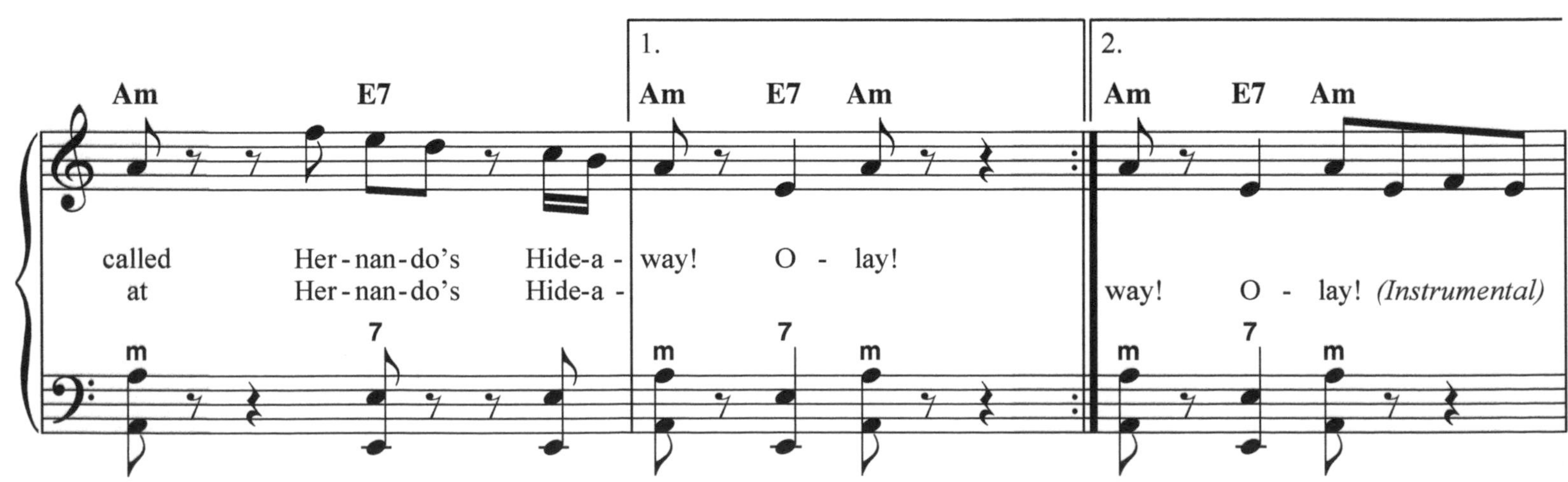

E7
Am
At the Gold - en Fin - ger - bowl or
7
m

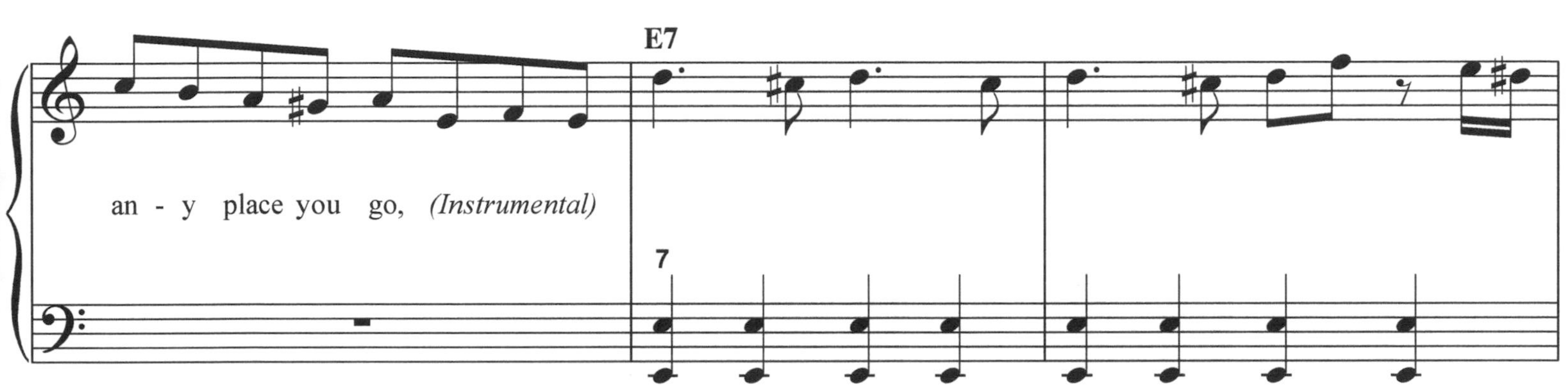
E7
an - y place you go, (Instrumental)
7

Am
A7
You will meet your Un - cle Max and
ev - 'ry - one you know. (Instrumental)
m
7

Dm
But if you go to the spot that
I am think - ing of,
m
m

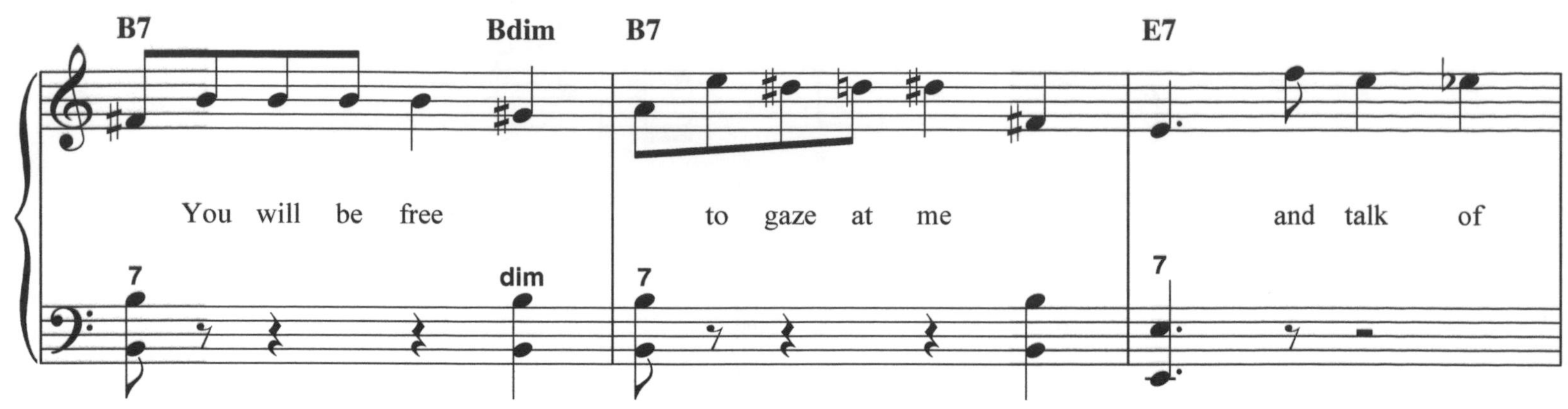
B7
Bdim
B7
E7
You will be free
to gaze at me
and talk of
7
dim
7
7

E7
Dm
E7
love! Just
knock three times and
whis - per low that
m
7

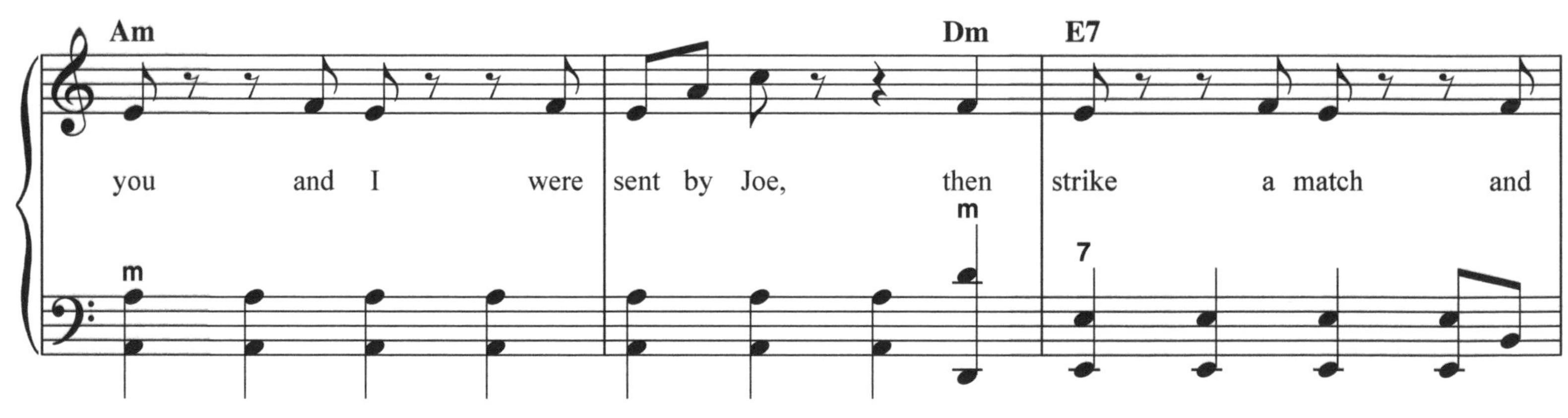
Am
Dm
E7
you and I were
sent by Joe, then
strike a match and
m
m
7

Am
E7
Am
E7
Am
you will know you're
in Her - nan - do's Hide-a -
way! O - lay!
m
7
m
7
m

JAMBALAYA
(On the Bayou)

Words and Music by
HANK WILLIAMS

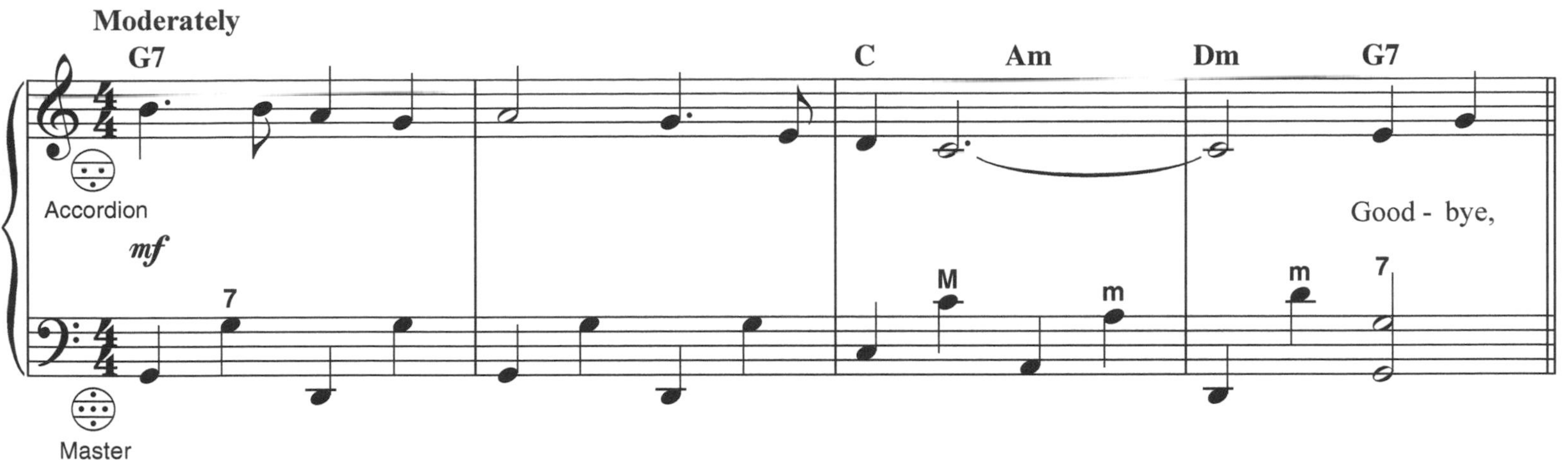

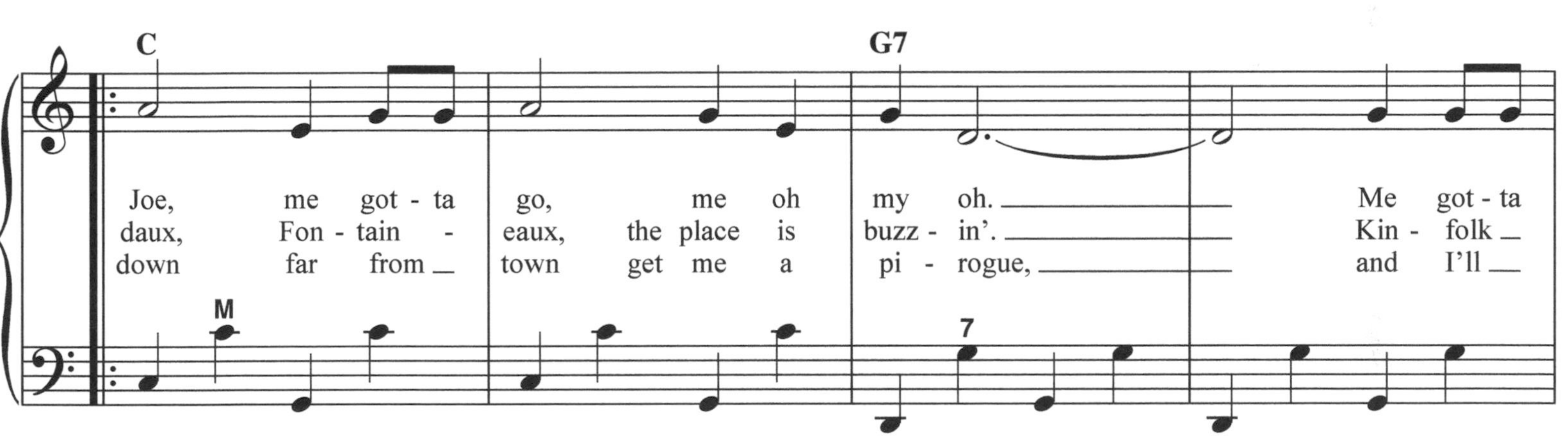

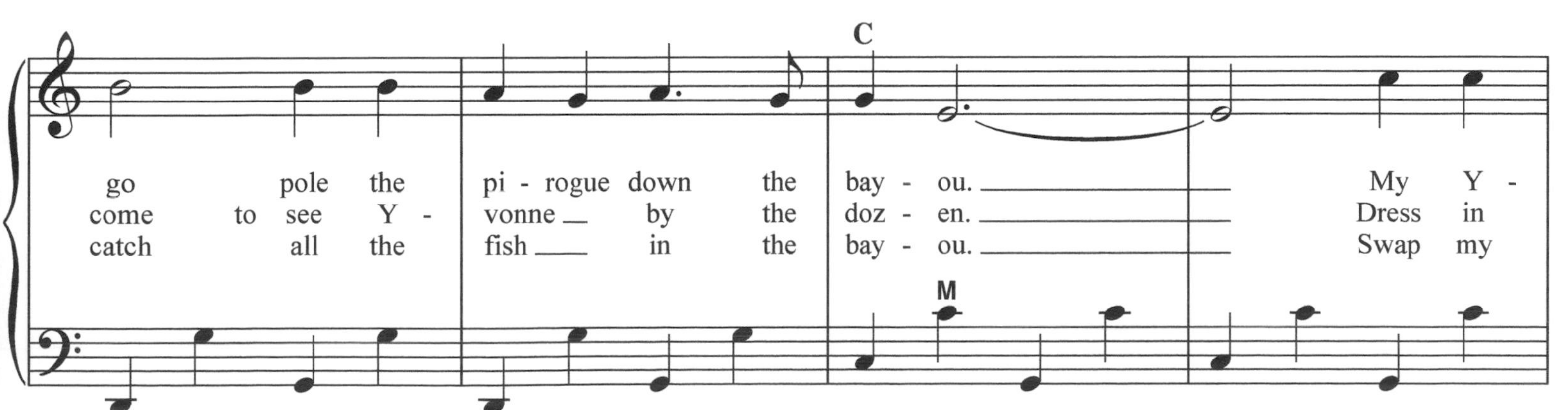

C♯dim
G7
vonne, the sweet - est one, me oh my oh.
style and go hog - wild, me oh my oh.
mon to buy Y - vonne what we need - o.
7

Son of a gun, we'll have big fun on the

C
bay - ou. Jam - ba - la - ya and a craw - fish
M

G7
pie and fi - lé gum - bo, 'cause to -
7

C C/B
night I'm gon - na see my ma cher a - mi - o.
M

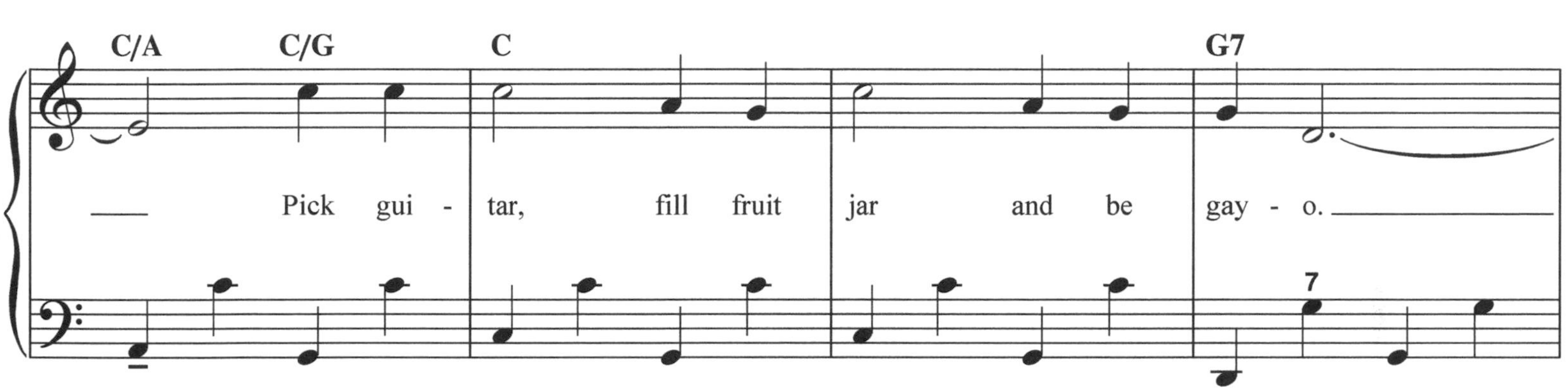
C/A C/G C G7
Pick gui - tar, fill fruit jar and be gay - o.
7

Son of a gun, we'll have big fun on the

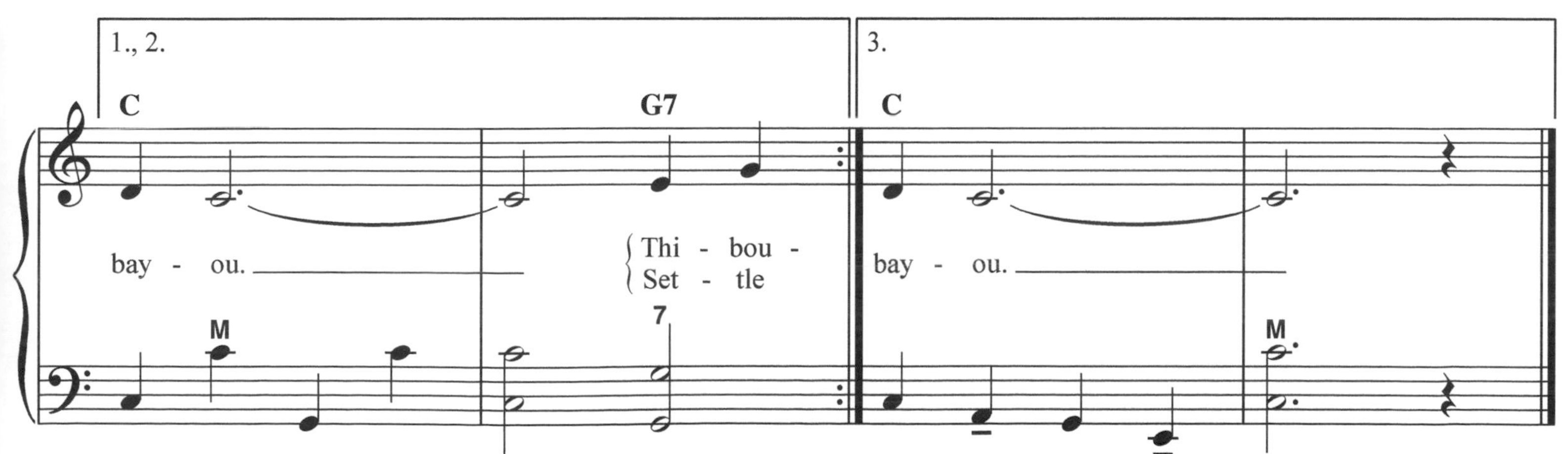
1., 2. 3.
C G7 C
bay - ou.
Thi - bou -
Set - tle
bay - ou.
M 7 M

JUST BECAUSE

Words and Music by BOB SHELTON,
JOE SHELTON and SID ROBIN

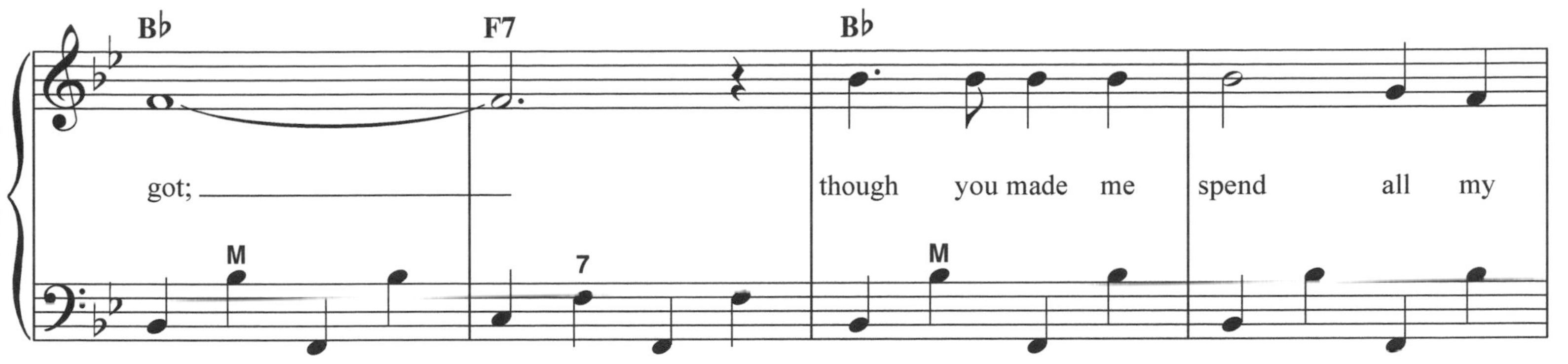
B♭ F7 B♭
got; ___ though you made me spend all my
M 7 M

B♭7
mon - ey, ___ you laughed and called me old San - ta
7

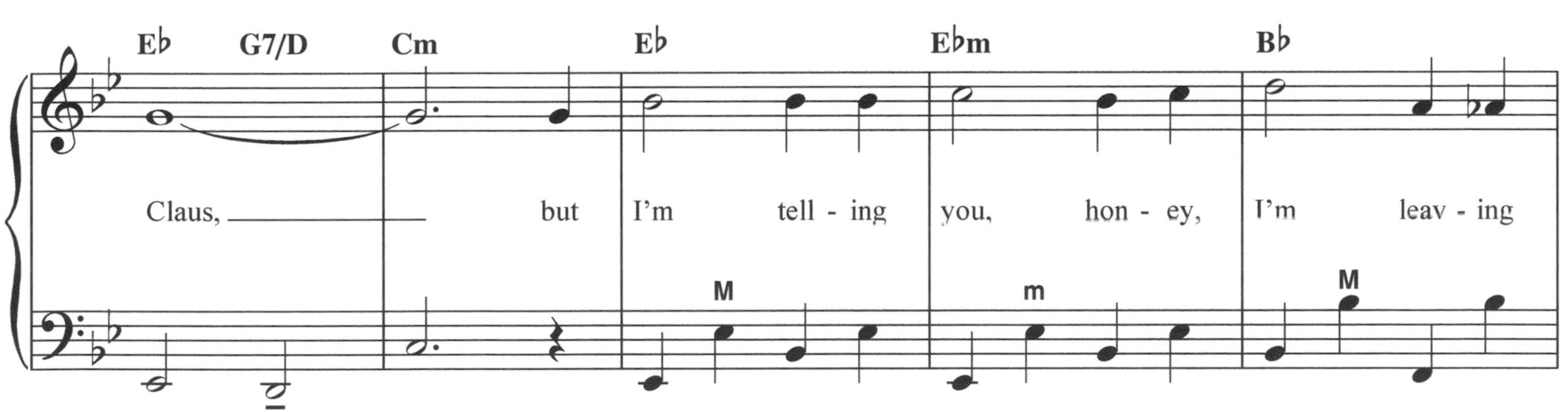
E♭ G7/D Cm E♭ E♭m B♭
Claus, ___ but I'm tell - ing you, hon - ey, I'm leav - ing
M m M

G7 C7 F7 B♭
you be - cause, just be - cause. ___
7 7 7

LA CUMPARSITA

(The Masked One)

Words and Music by GERARDO MATOS RODRIQUEZ,
PASCUAL CONTURSI and ENRIQUE PEDRO MORONI

D7
Gm
D7
Can it be that love's flame has seared your heart?
Is love's flame not smoul - der - ing in your heart?
7
m
7

1.
2.
Gm
D7
Gm
Gm
D7
Gm
Fine
Gm
Fling a - way your black dis -
m
7
m
m
7
m
m

D7
guise. __ Your love - ly feat - ures now un - cov - er,
7

and to your lov - er, show your sweet eyes. Come on, beau - ti -

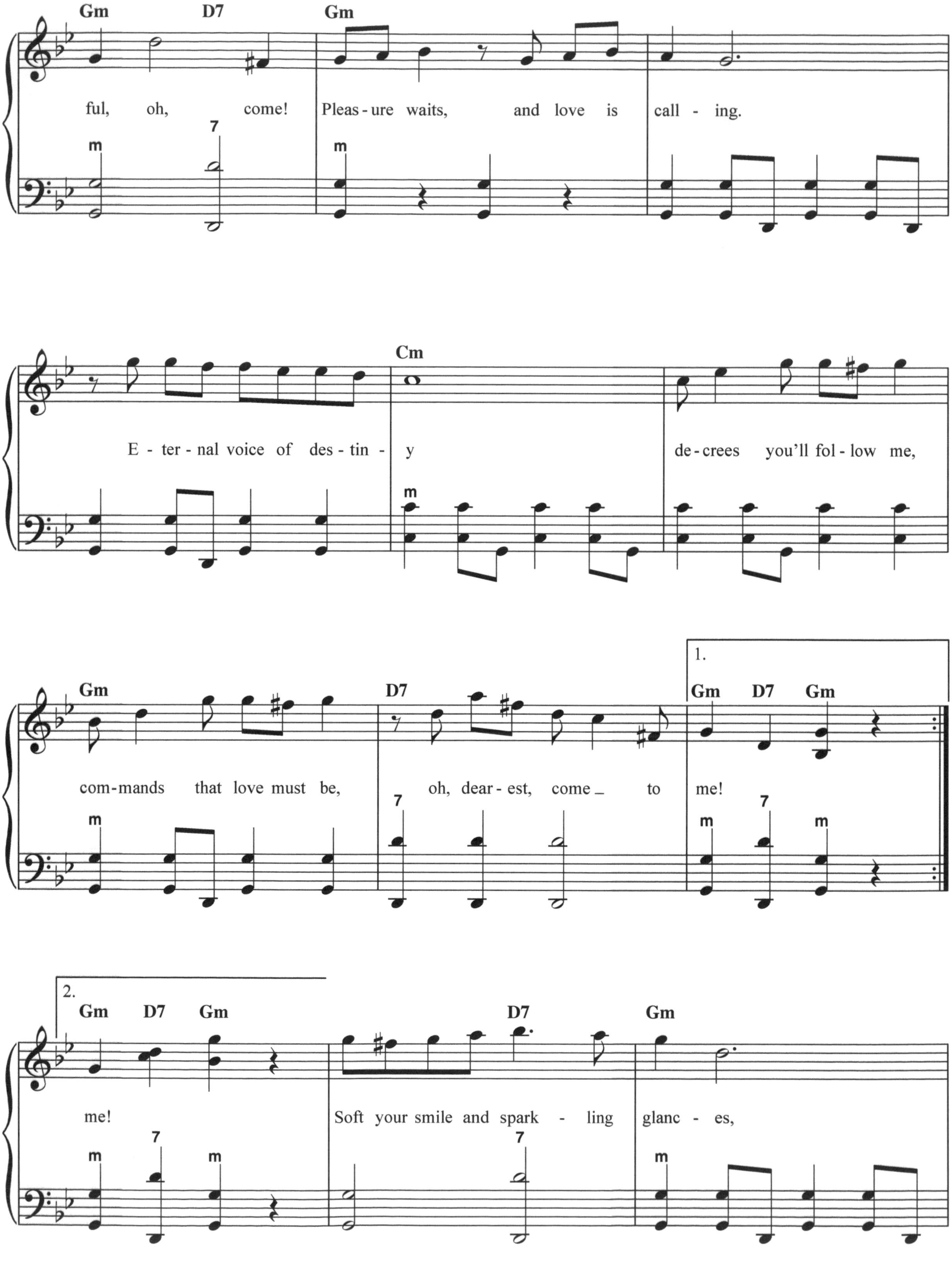

Cm

E - ter - nal voice of des - tin - y decrees you'll fol - low me,

m

Gm D7 | 1. Gm D7 Gm

com-mands that love must be, oh, dear-est, come_ to me!

m 7 m 7 m

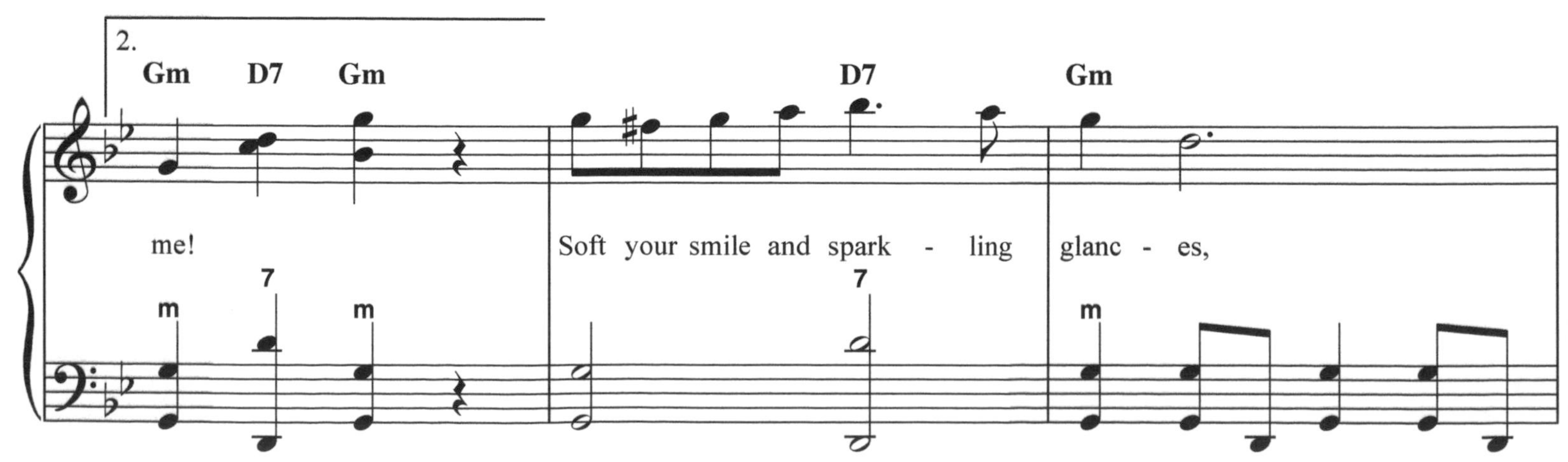

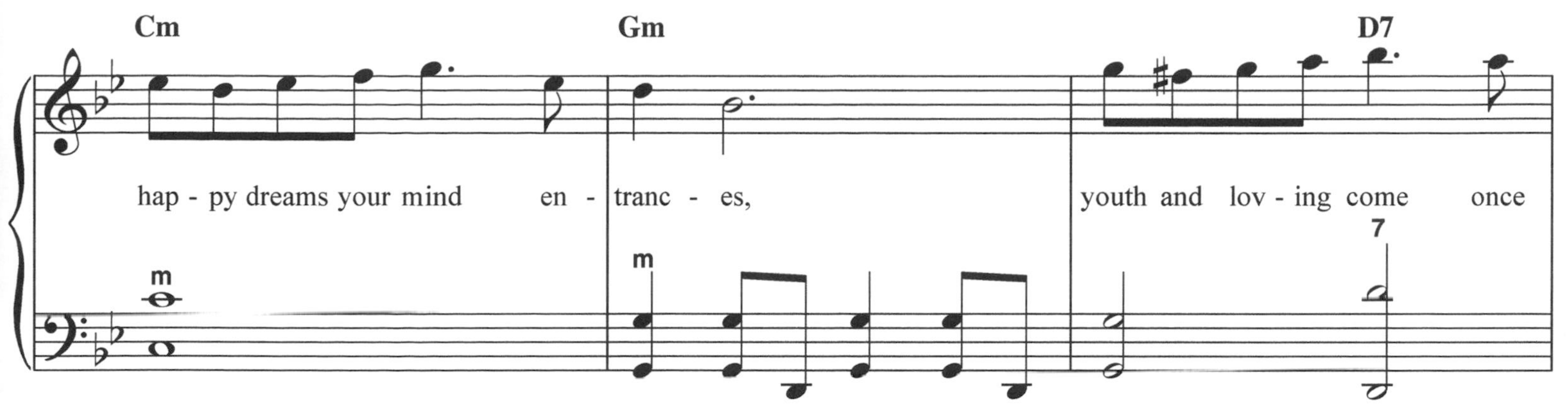
Cm
Gm
D7
hap - py dreams your mind en - tranc - es,
youth and lov - ing come once
m
m
7

Gm
Cm
Gm
on - ly,
love will pass and leave you lone - ly.
m
m
m

D7
Gm
Re - fuse not joy and pleas - ure.
Why dance with me no meas - ure,
7
m

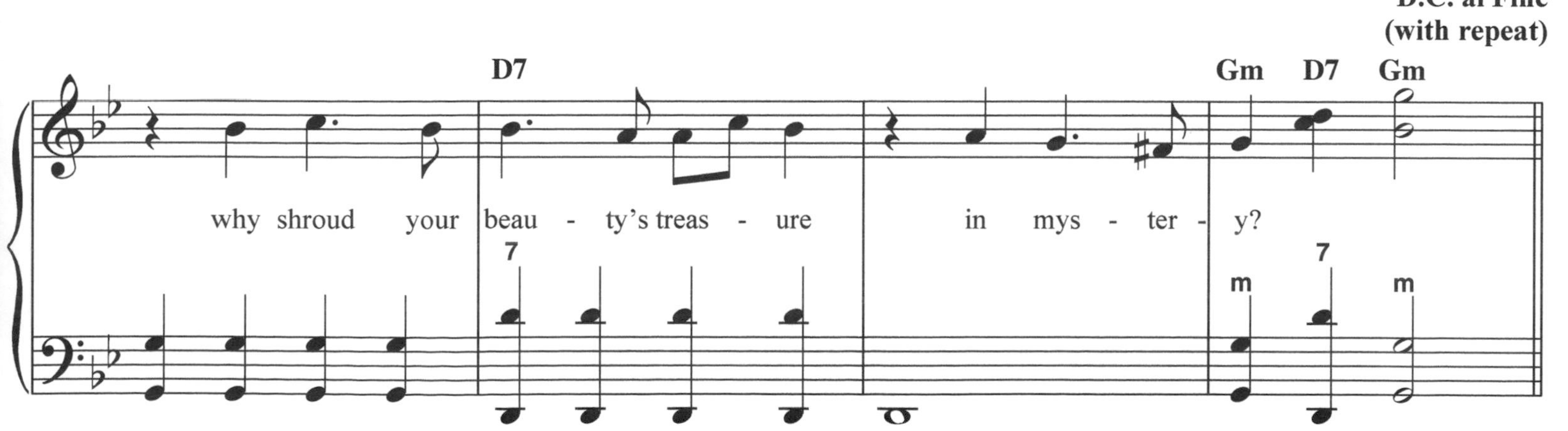
D.C. al Fine
(with repeat)
D7
Gm D7 Gm
why shroud your beau - ty's treas - ure in mys - ter - y?
7
m 7 m

LA MARSEILLAISE

Words and Music by
CLAUDE ROUGET DE LISLE

D Gm D7
dats? Ils vien - nent jus - que dans nos bras, É - gor-
M m 7

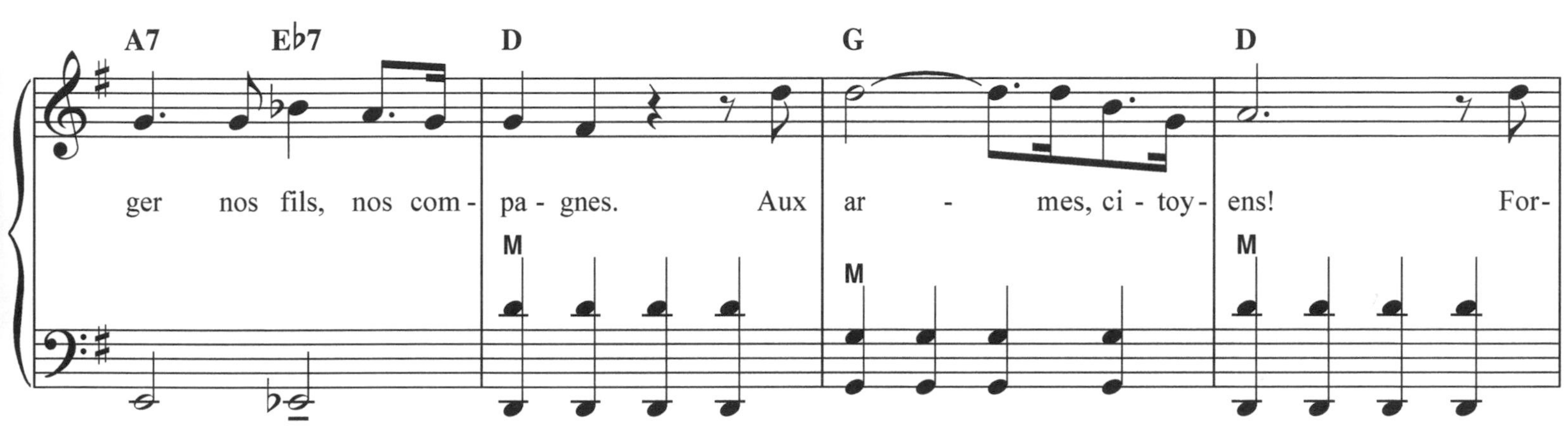
A7 E♭7 D G D
ger nos fils, nos com - pa - gnes. Aux ar - mes, ci - toy - ens! For-
M M M

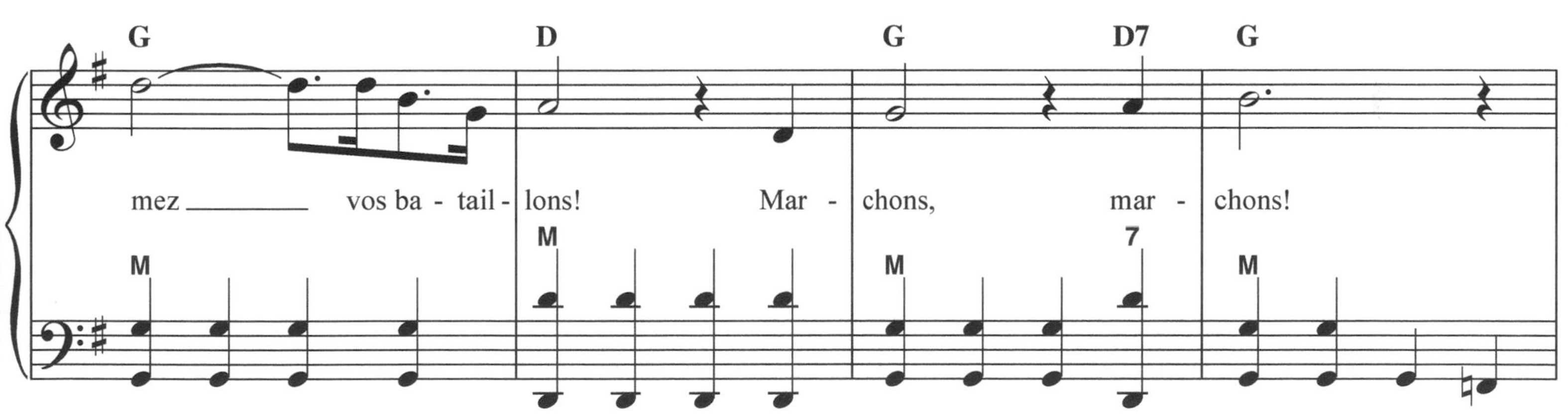
G D G D7 G
mez vos ba - tail - lons! Mar - chons, mar - chons!
M M M 7 M

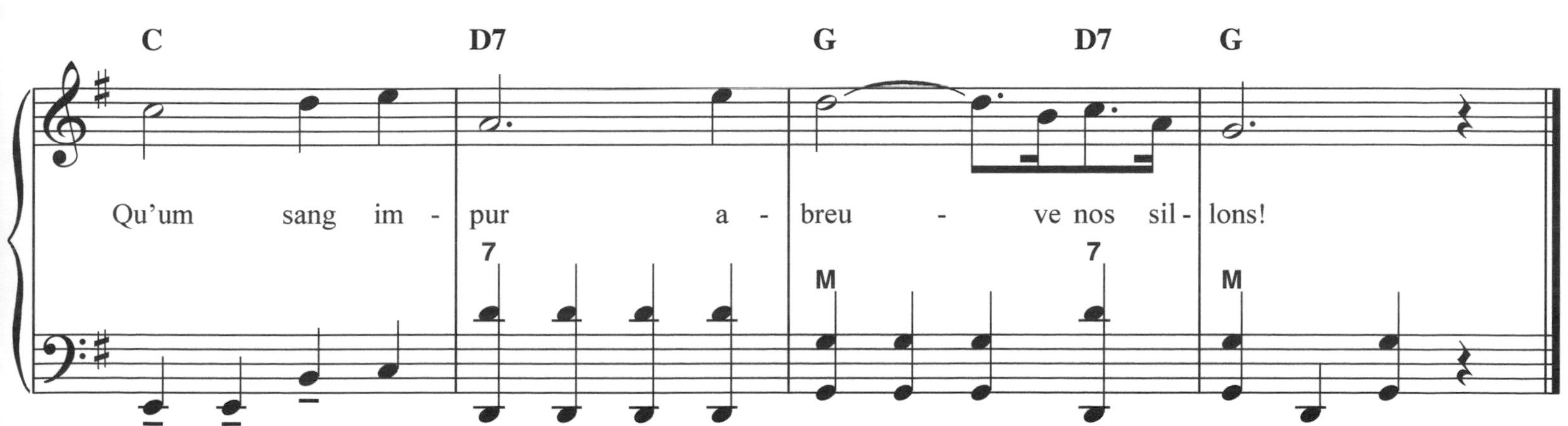
C D7 G D7 G
Qu'um sang im - pur a - breu - ve nos sil - lons!
7 M 7 M

LA PALOMA BLANCA

from MEXICAN SONG SETTINGS

Mexican Folk Song
Arranged by EDWARD KILENYI

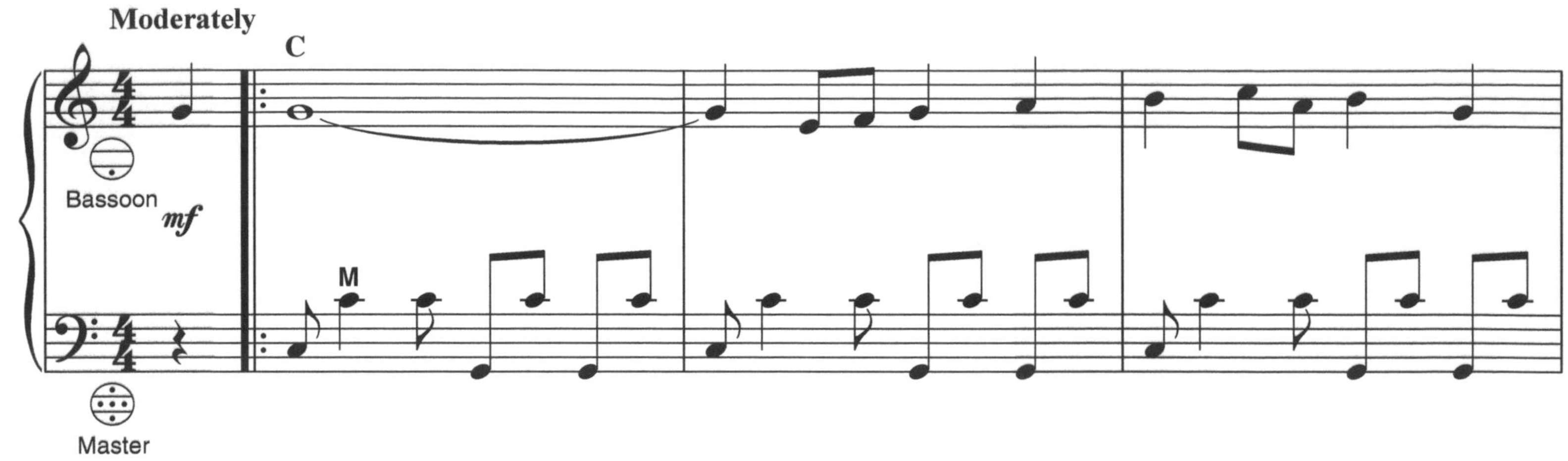

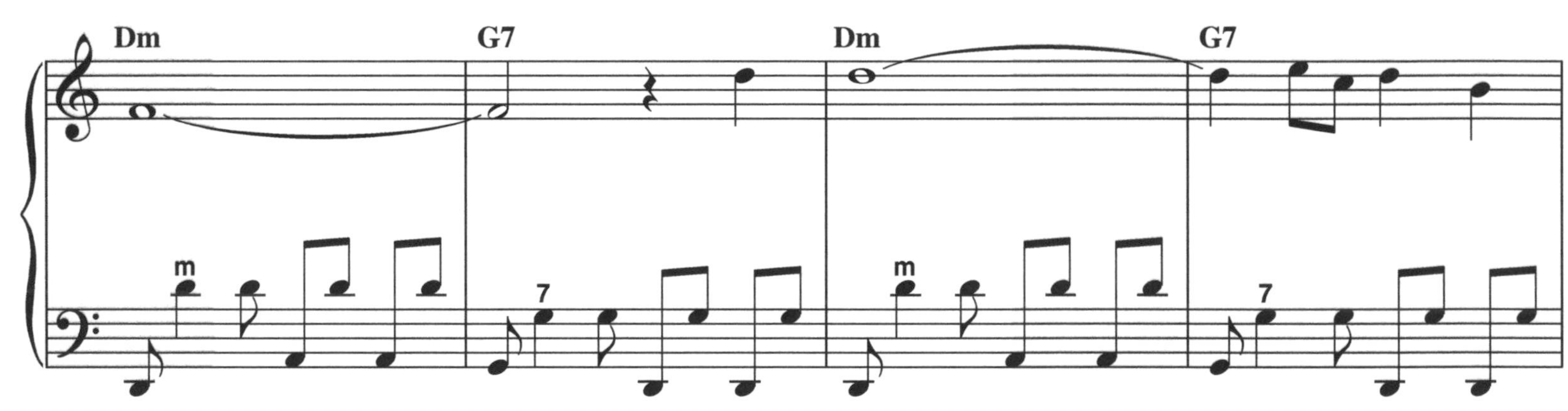

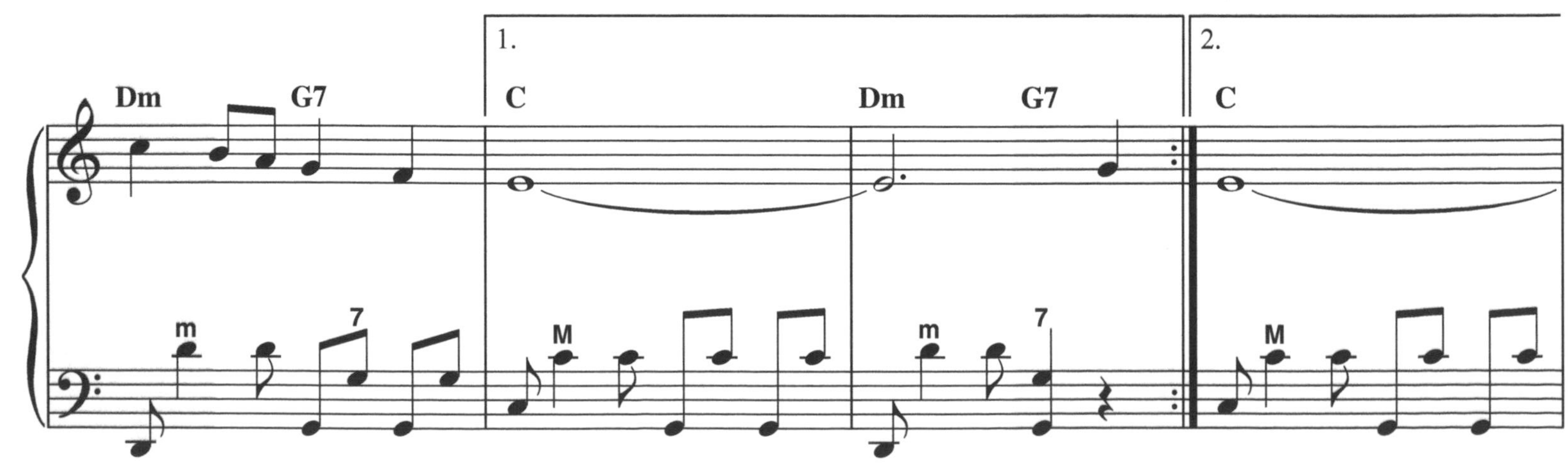

Dm
G7
C
C/E
E♭dim
G7
m
7
M
dim
7
1.
C
M
Dm
G7
2.
C
m
7
M
G7
7

C
M
G7
7
C
M
G7
7
C
M

LIBERTANGO

By ASTOR PIAZZOLLA

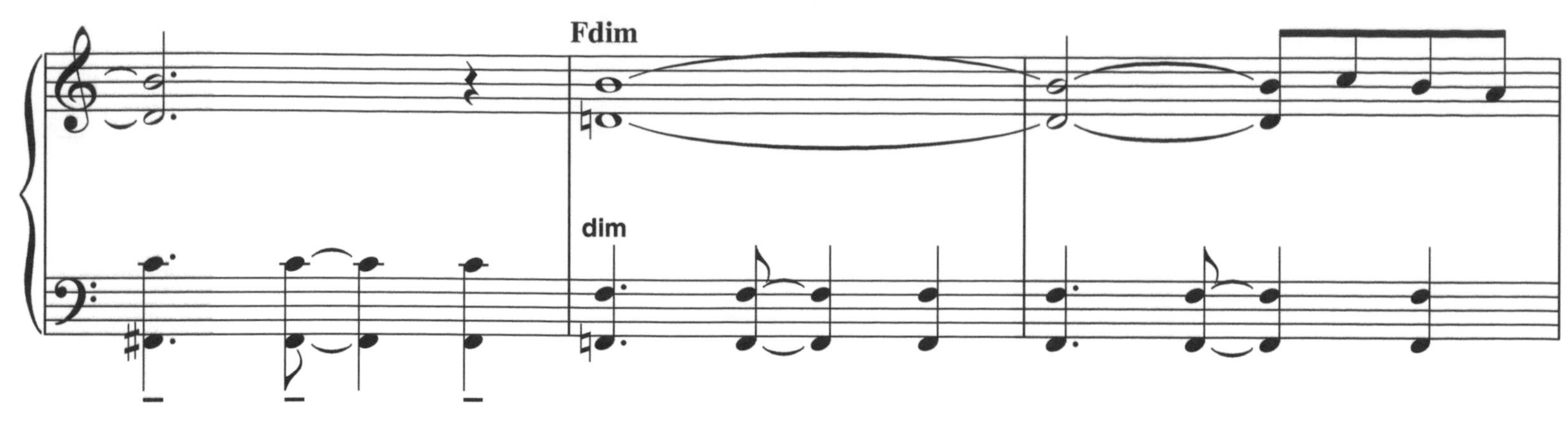
Fdim
dim

1.
E7
7
2.
E7
7

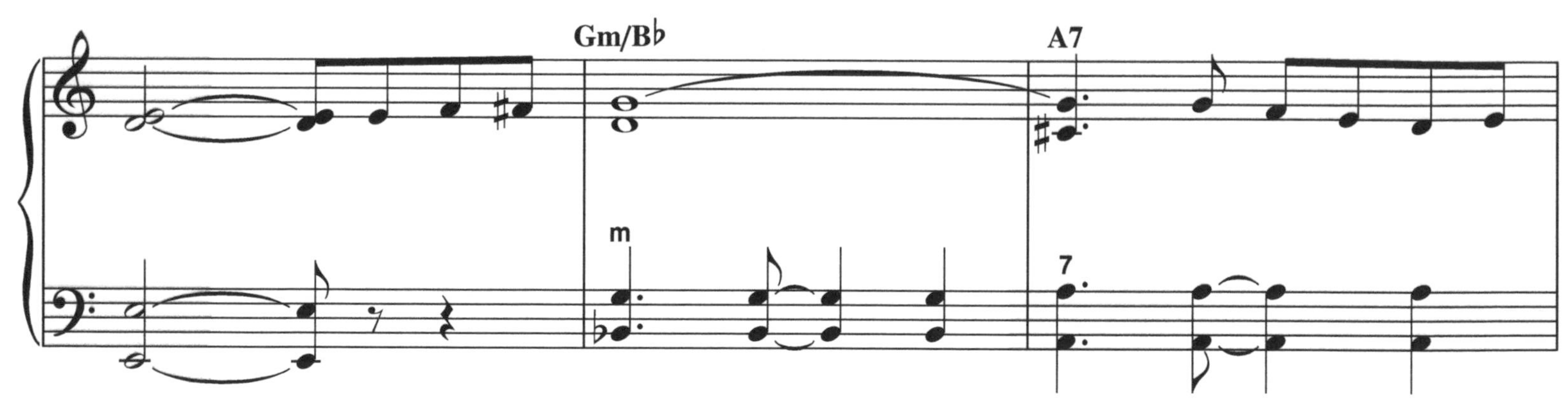
Gm/B♭
m
A7
7

Dm
m
3
Fm/A♭
m

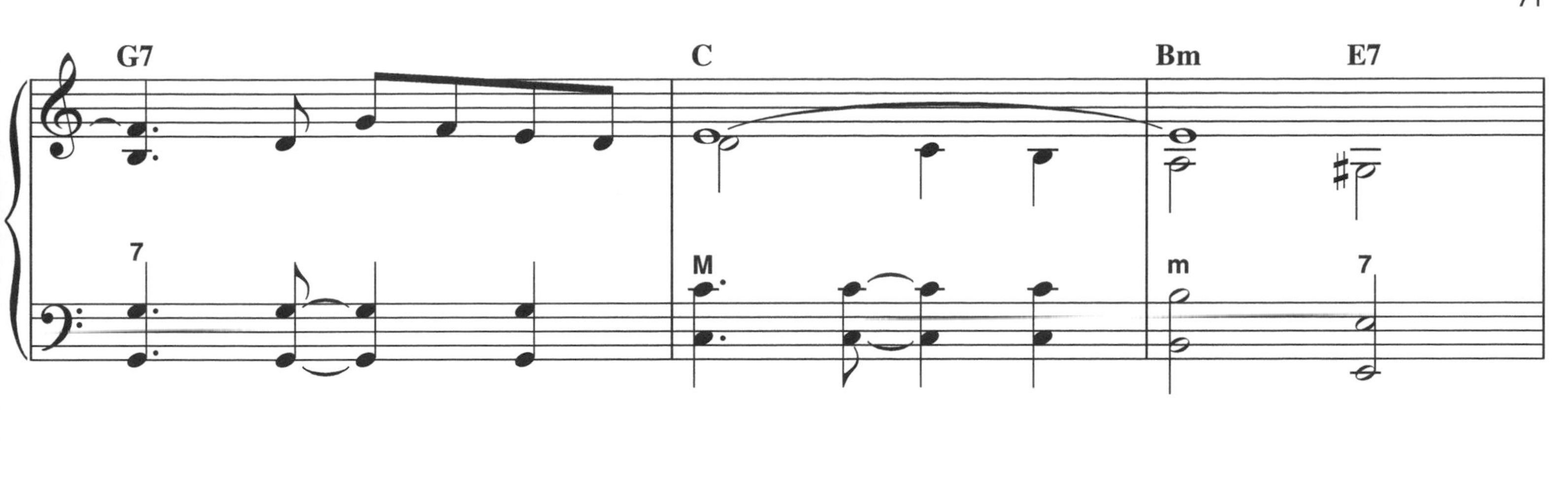
G7
C
Bm
E7
7
M
m
7

Am
B/A
m
M

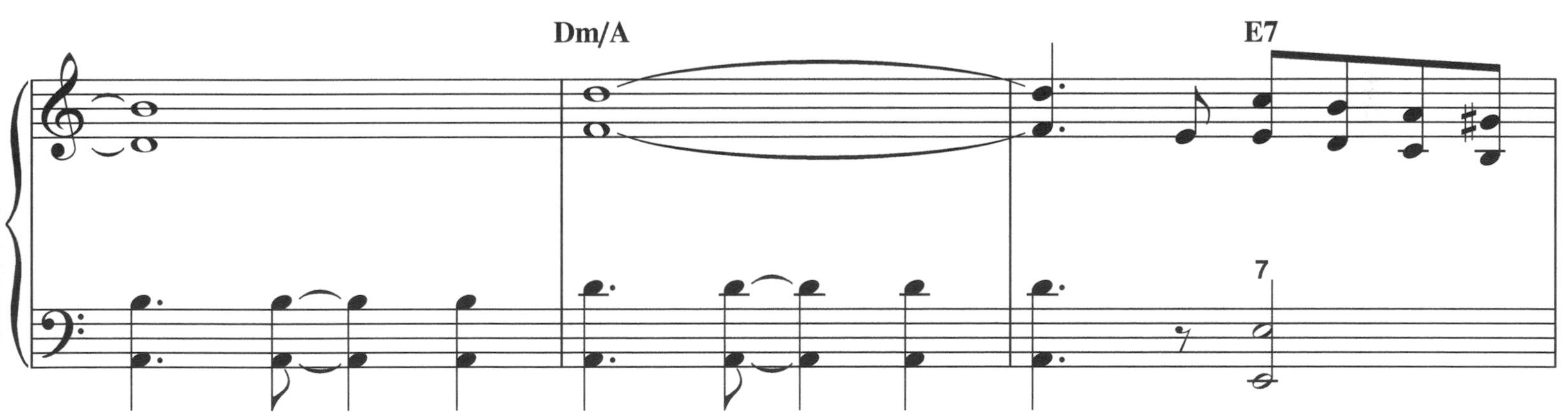
Dm/A
E7
7

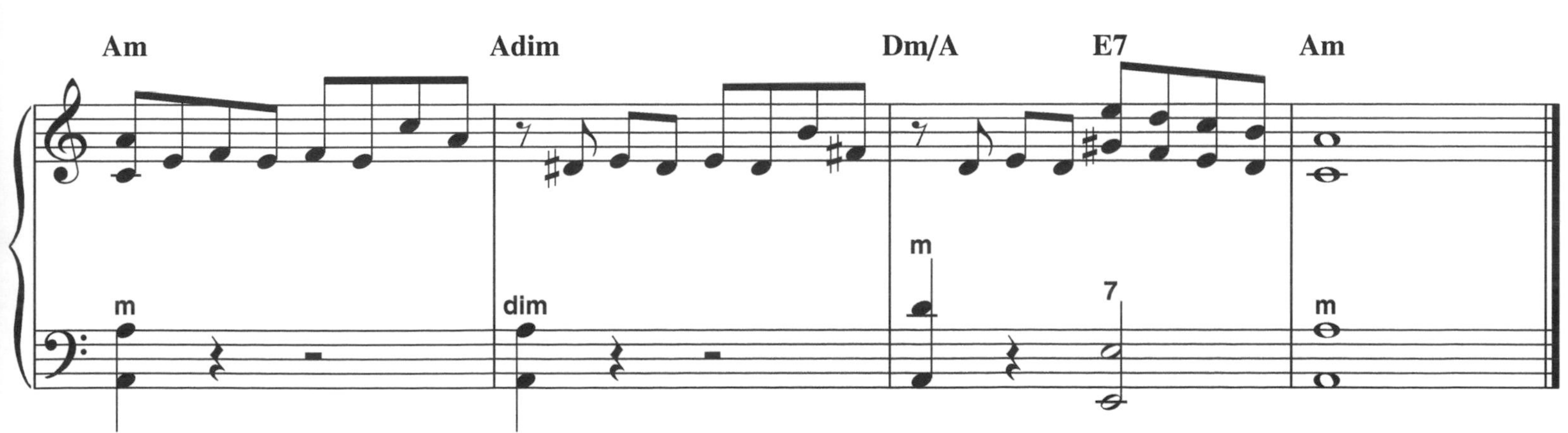
Am
Adim
Dm/A
E7
Am
m
dim
m
7
m

LA VIE EN ROSE
(Take Me to Your Heart Again)

Original French Lyrics by ÉDITH PIAF
Music by LUIS GUGLIELMI
English Lyrics by MACK DAVID

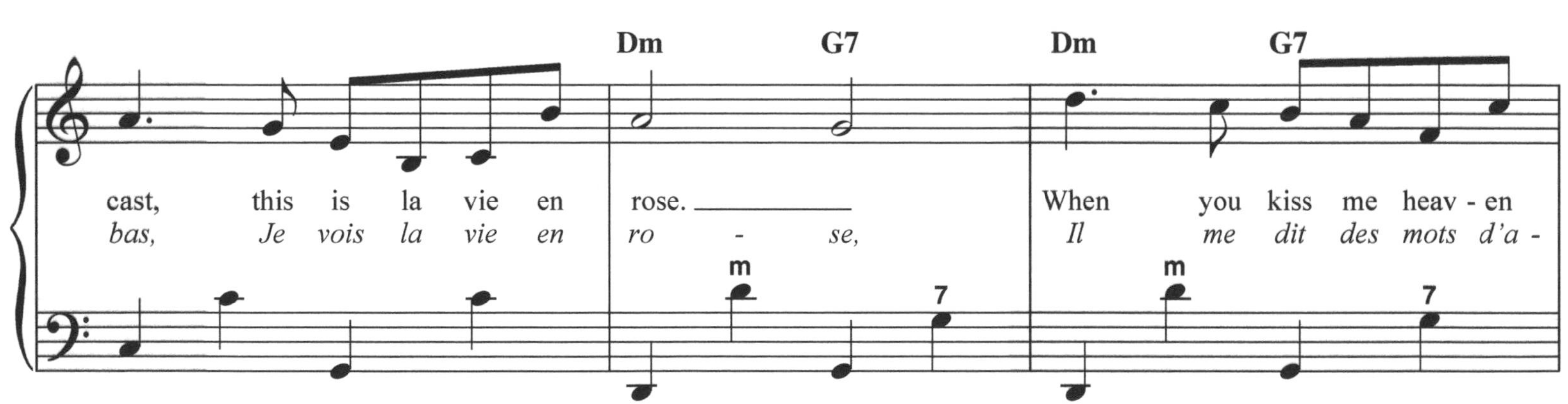

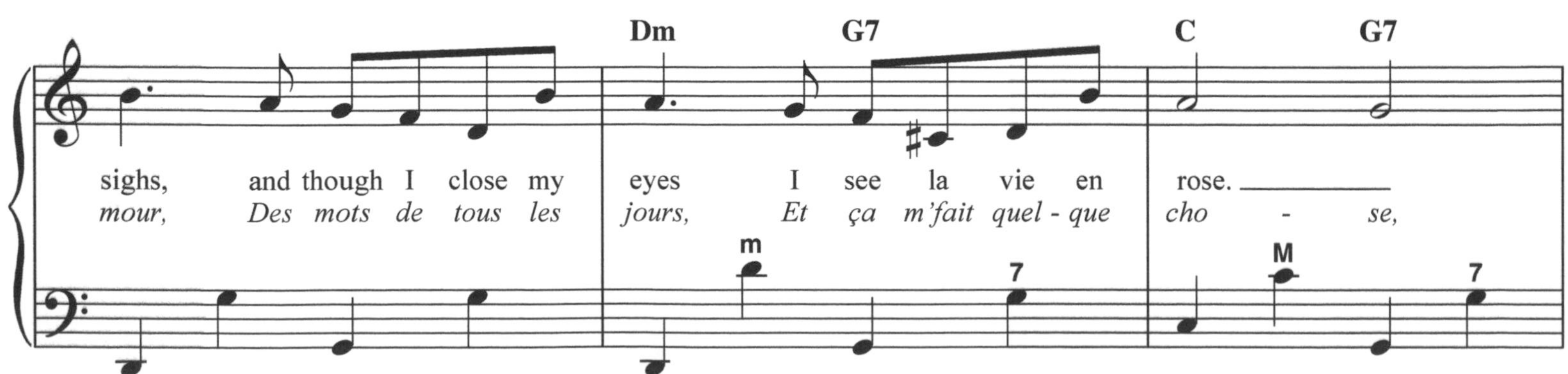

C
C7
When you press me to your heart I'm in a world a - part, a world where ro - ses
Il est en - tré dans mon cœur. U - ne part de bon - heur, Dont je con - nais la
M
7

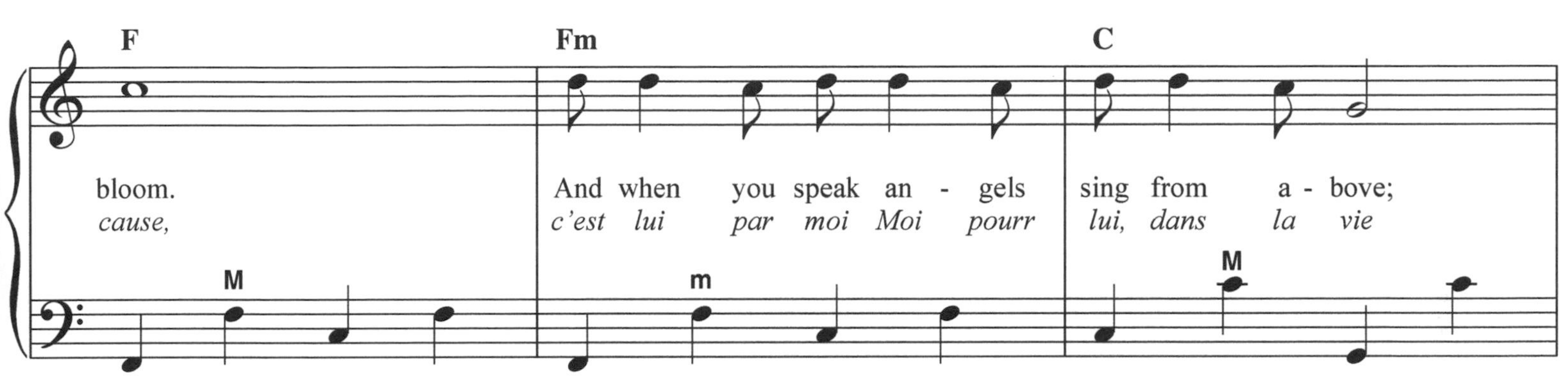
F
Fm
C
bloom. And when you speak an - gels sing from a - bove;
cause, c'est lui par moi Moi pourr lui, dans la vie
M
m
M

D7
Dm
G7
C
ev - 'ry - day words seem to turn in - to love songs. Give your heart and soul to
Il me l'a dit, l'a ju - ré pour la vi - e, Et dès que je l'a - per -
7
m
7
M

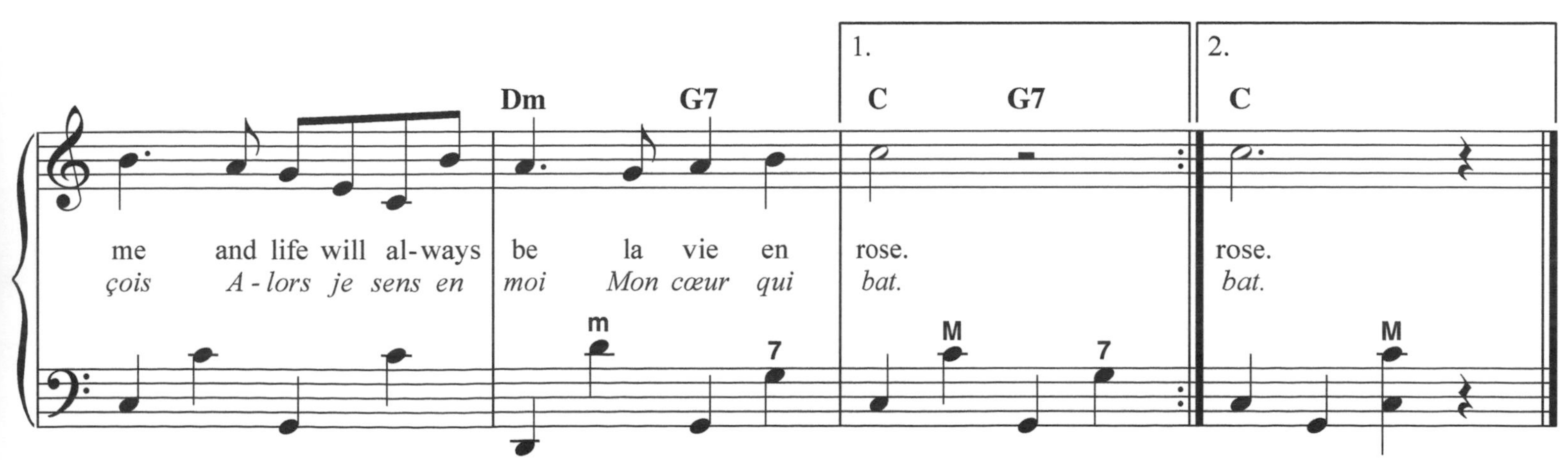
1.
2.
Dm
G7
C
G7
C
me and life will al-ways be la vie en rose. rose.
çois A - lors je sens en moi Mon cœur qui bat. bat.
m
7
M
7
M

LADY OF SPAIN

Words by ERELL REAVES
Music by TOLCHARD EVANS

C
Right from the night I first saw you,
Why should my lips be con - ceal - ing.
M
A7
My heart has been yearn - ing for you;
All that my eyes are re - veal - ing?
7
Dm
m
1.
D7
what else could an - y heart
7
Fm
do?
m
G7
7
2.
D7
La - dy of
G7
Spain, I love
7
C
Fm
you.
M
m
C
M

MILORD

Lyrics by JOSEPH MUSTACCHI
Music by MARGUERITE MONNOT

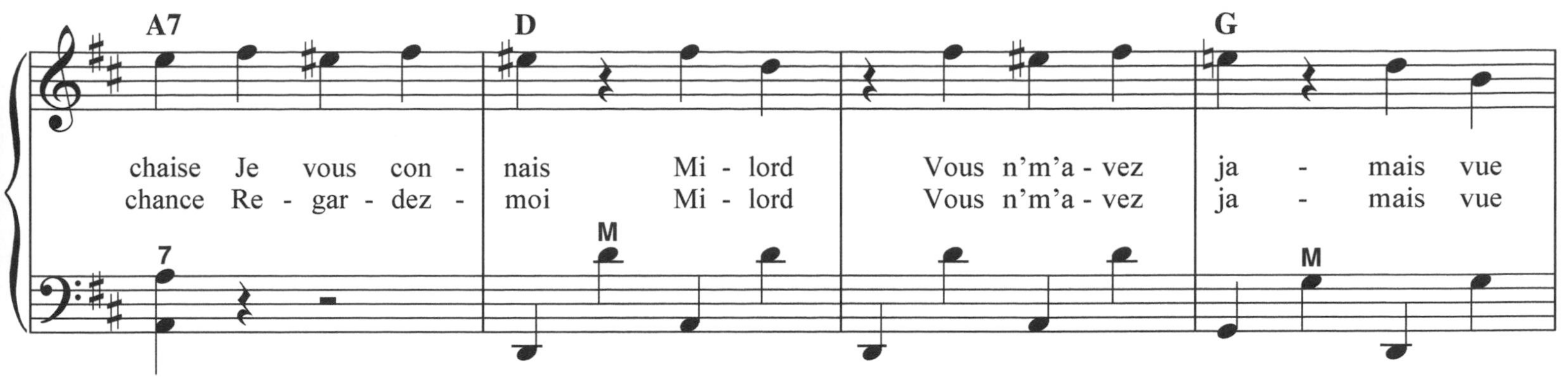
A7
D
G
chaise Je vous con - nais Mi - lord Vous n'm'a - vez ja - mais vue
chance Re - gar - dez - moi Mi - lord Vous n'm'a - vez ja - mais vue
7
M
M

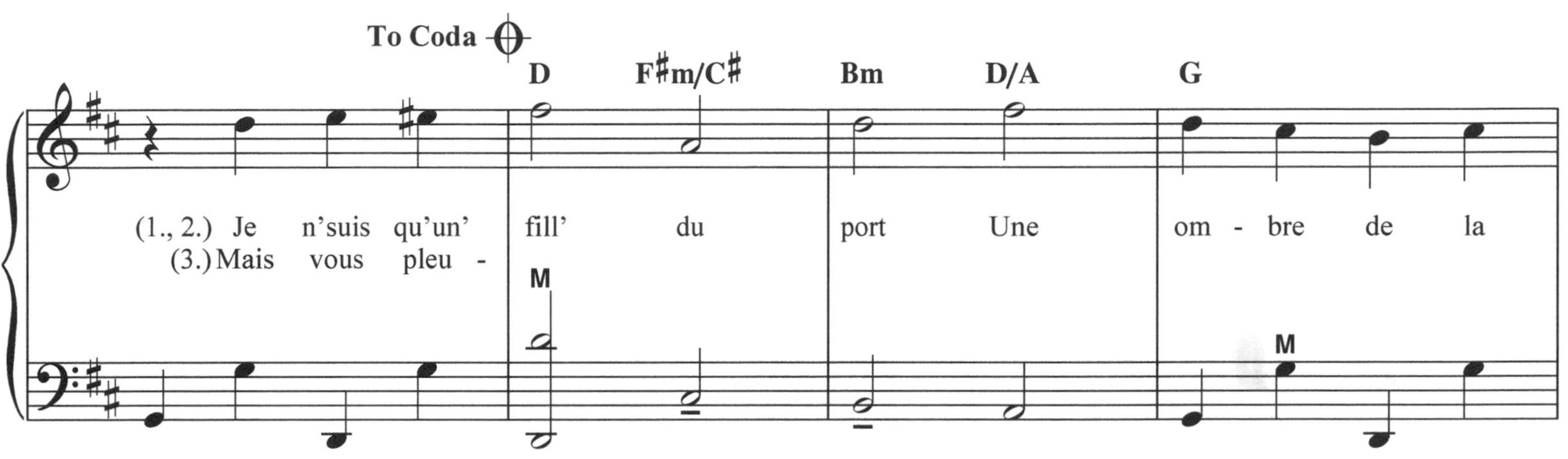
To Coda
D
F♯m/C♯
Bm
D/A
G
(1., 2.) Je n'suis qu'un' fill' du port Une om - bre de la
(3.) Mais vous pleu -
M
M

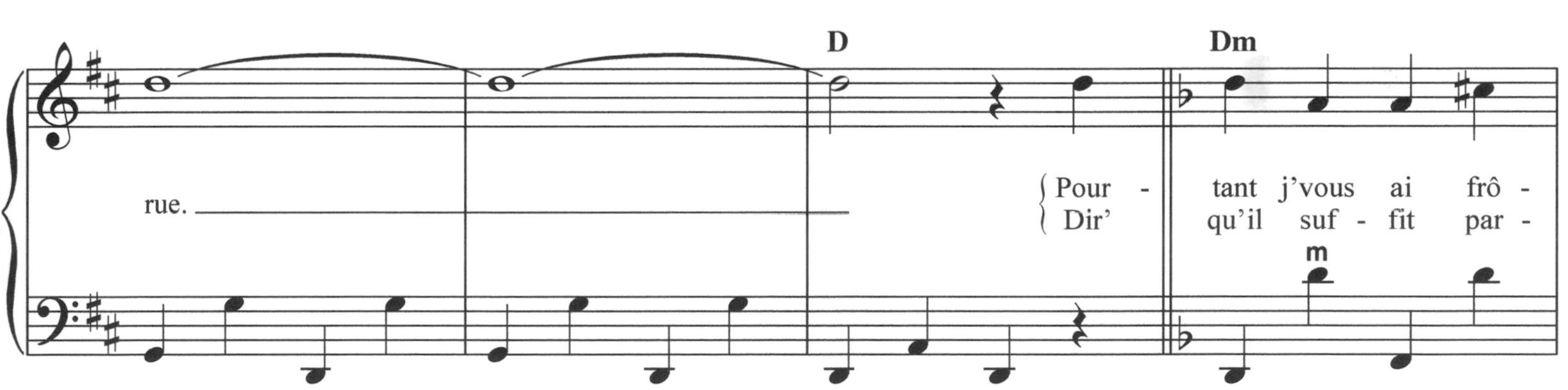
D
Dm
rue.
Pour - tant j'vous ai frô -
Dir' qu'il suf - fit par -
m

lé Quand vous pas - siez hi - er Vous n'é - tiez pas peu
fois Qu'il y ait un na - vire Pour que tout se dé -

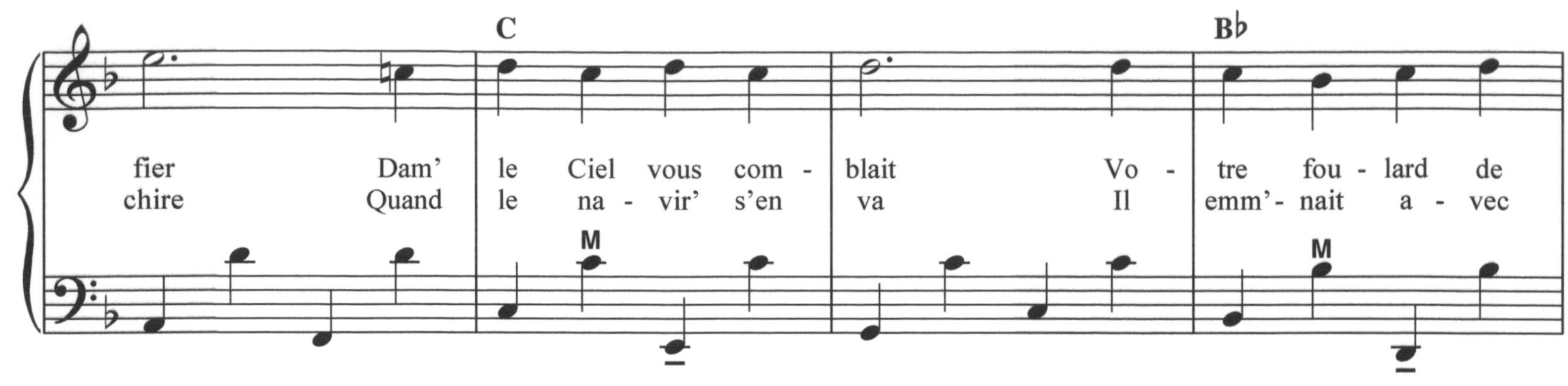
C
Bb
fier Dam' le Ciel vous com - blait Vo - tre fou - lard de
chire Quand le na - vir' s'en va Il emm' - nait a - vec
M
M

soie Flot - tant sur vos é - paules Vous a - viez le beau
lui La douce aux yeux si tendres Qui n'a pas su com -

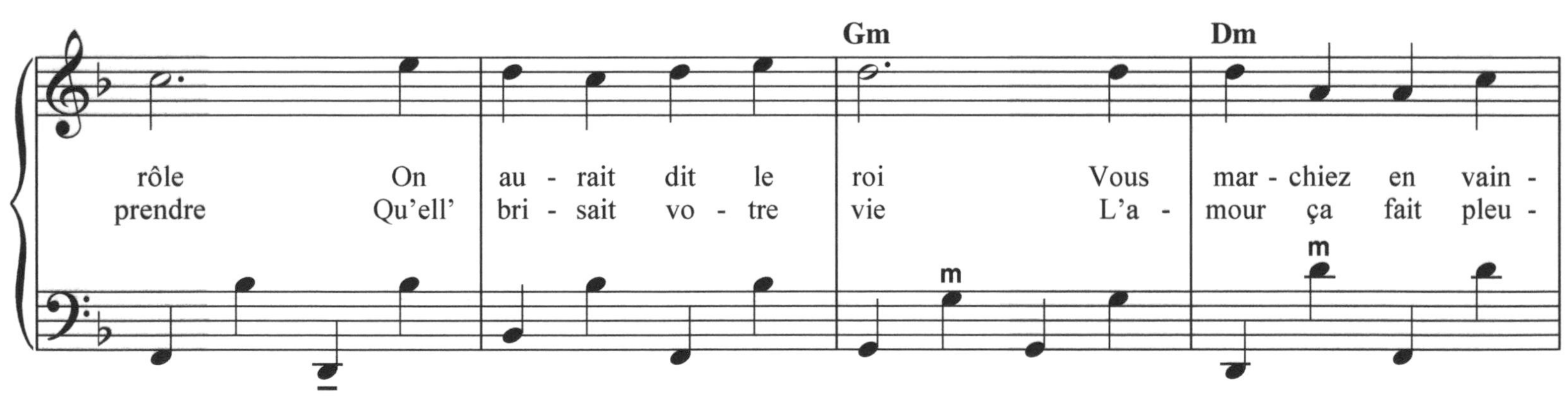
Gm
Dm
rôle On au - rait dit le roi Vous mar - chiez en vain -
prendre Qu'ell' bri - sait vo - tre vie L'a - mour ça fait pleu -
m
m

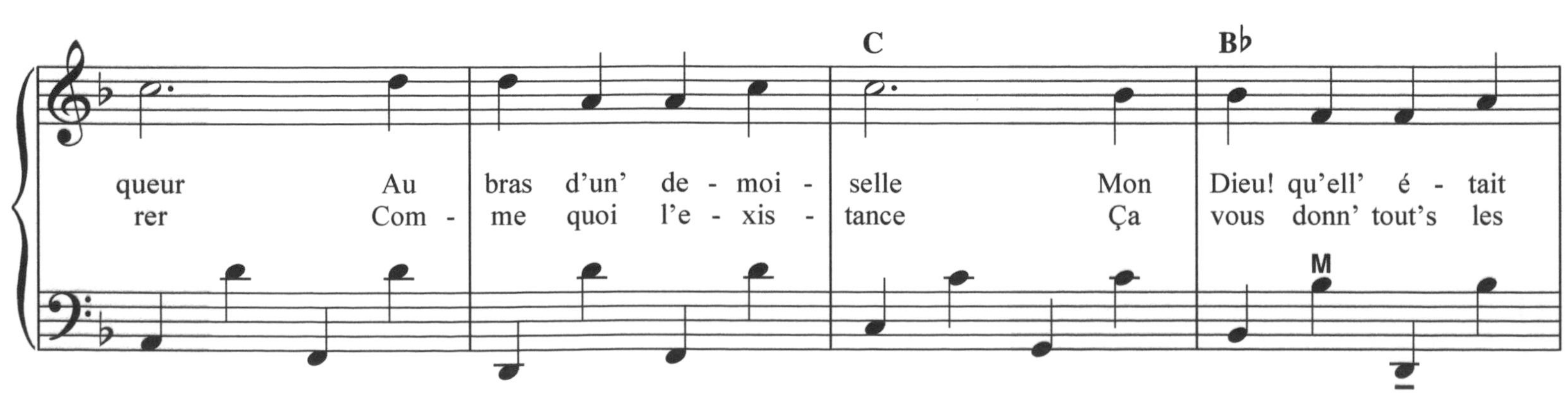
C
Bb
queur Au bras d'un' de - moi - selle Mon Dieu! qu'ell' é - tait
rer Com - me quoi l'e - xis - tance Ça vous donn' tout's les
M

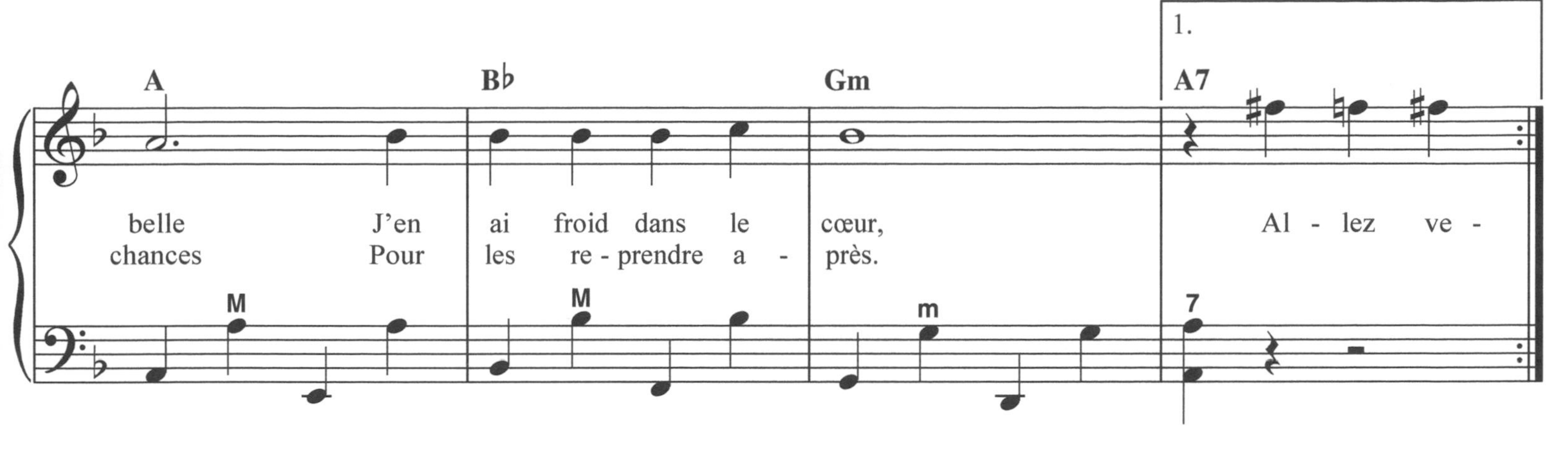
1.
A
B♭
Gm
A7
belle J'en ai froid dans le cœur, Al - lez ve -
chances Pour les re - prendre a - près.
M
M
m
7

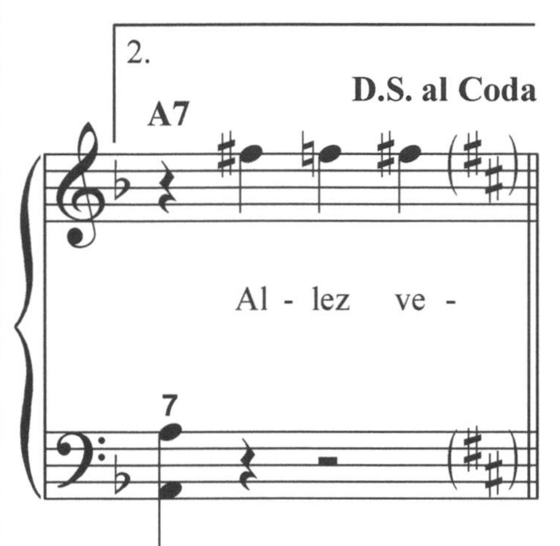
2.
A7
D.S. al Coda
Al - lez ve -
7

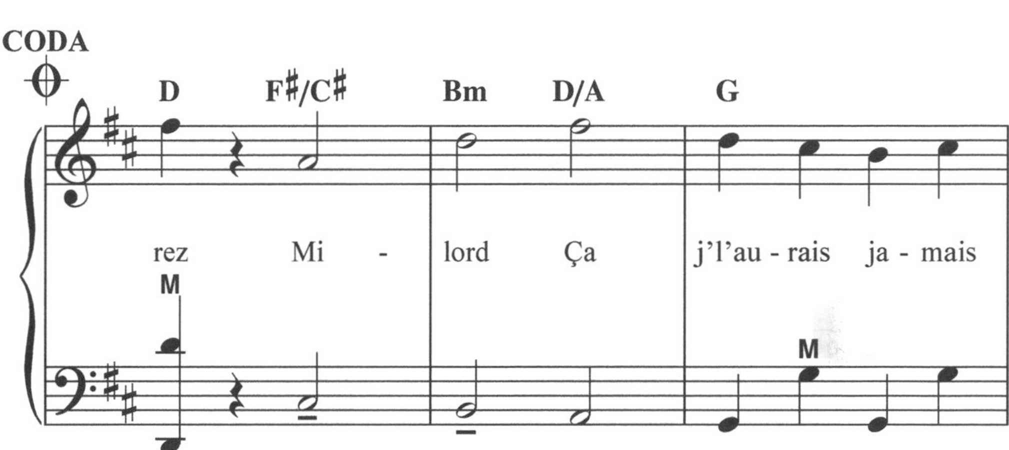
CODA
D
F♯/C♯
Bm
D/A
G
rez Mi - lord Ça j'l'au - rais ja - mais
M
M

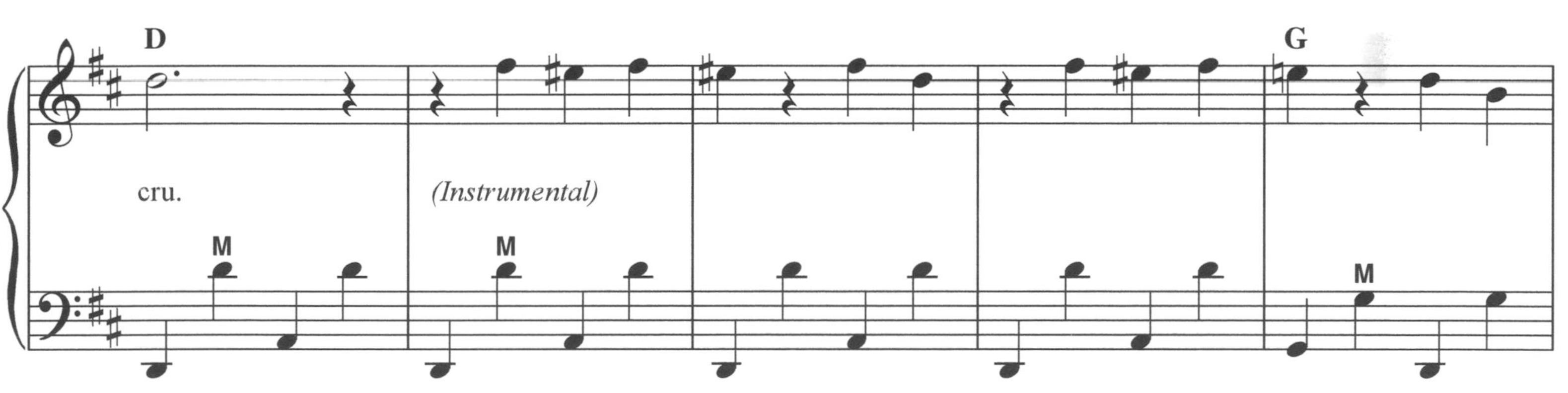
D
G
cru.
(Instrumental)
M
M
M

D
G
A7
D
M
M
7
M

MOON RIVER

from the Paramount Picture BREAKFAST AT TIFFANY'S

Words by JOHNNY MERCER
Music by HENRY MANCINI

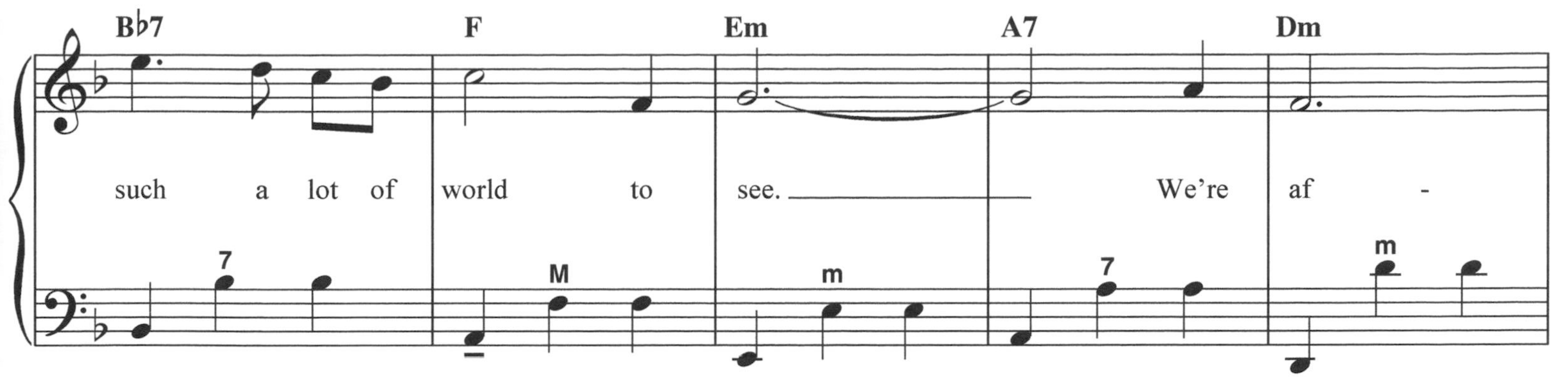

B♭7
F
Em
A7
Dm
such a lot of world to see. We're af -
7
M
m
7
m

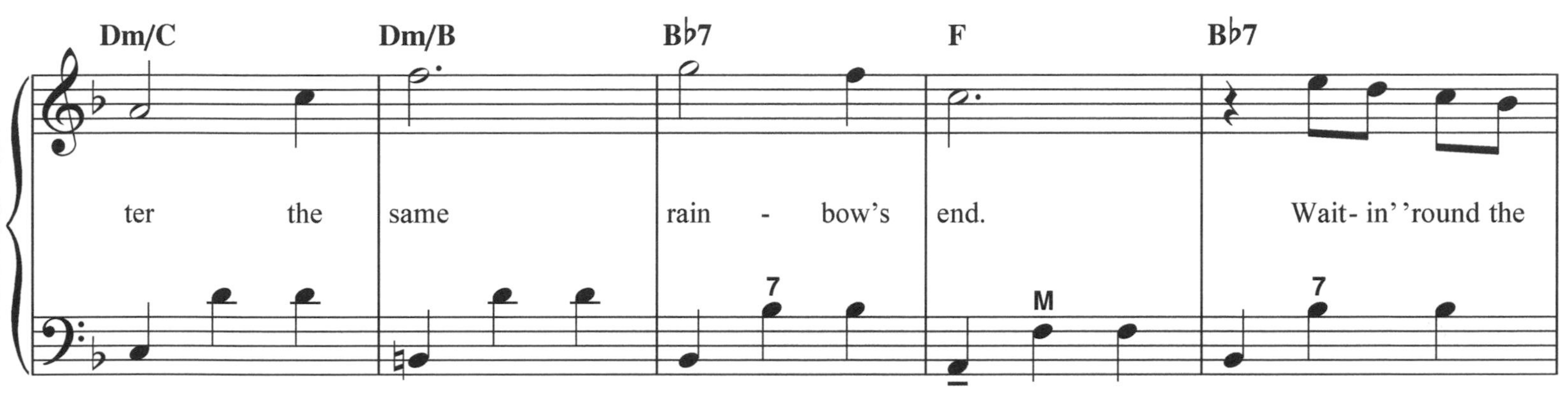

Dm/C
Dm/B
B♭7
F
B♭7
ter the same rain - bow's end. Wait- in' 'round the
7
M
7

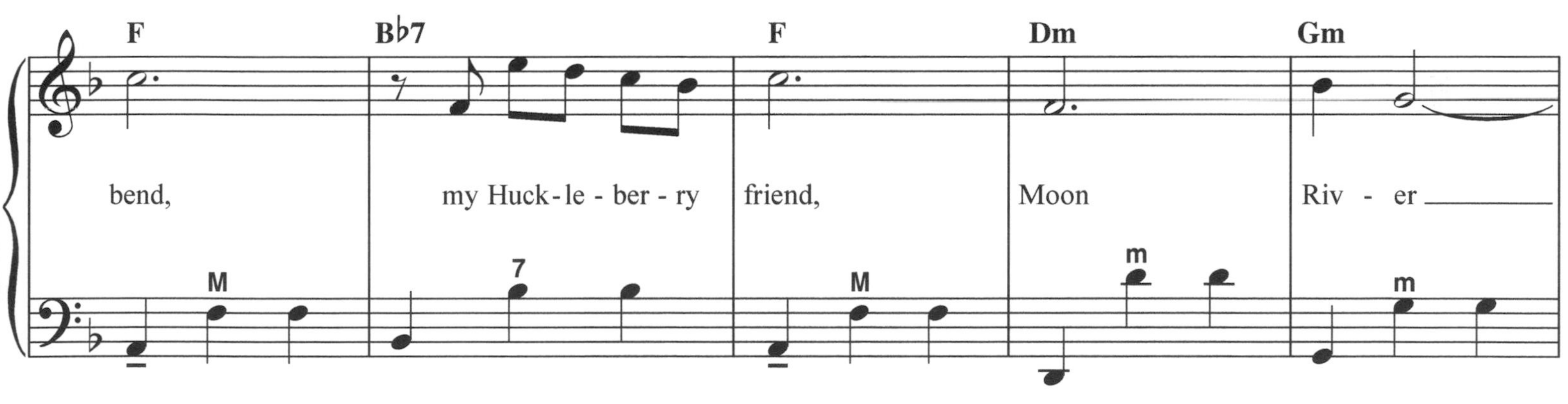

F
B♭7
F
Dm
Gm
bend, my Huck-le - ber - ry friend, Moon Riv - er
M
7
M
m
m

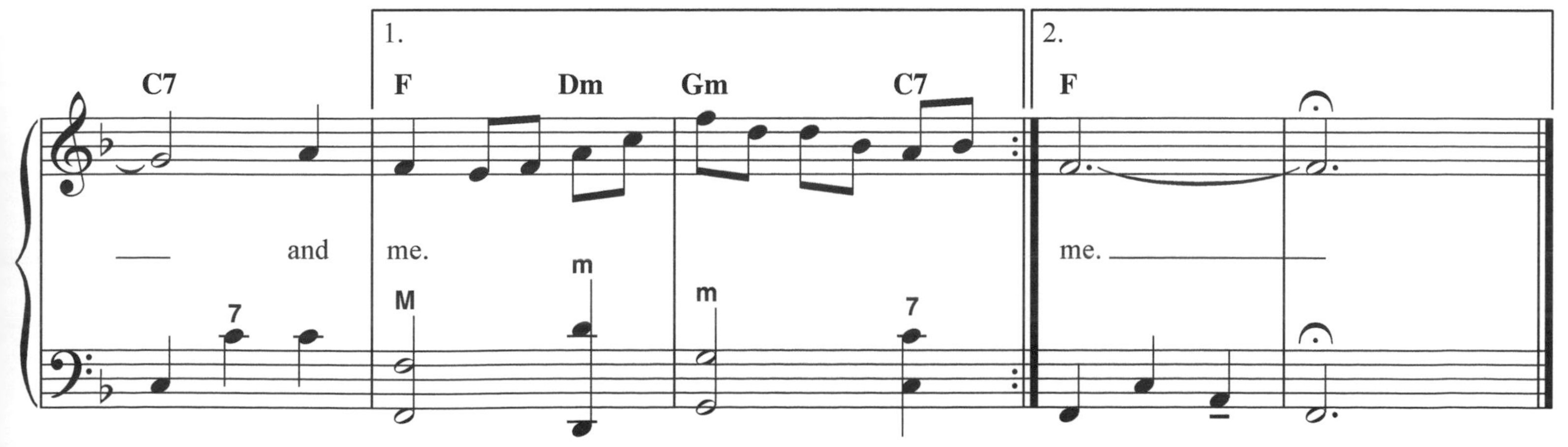

1.
2.
C7
F
Dm
Gm
C7
F
and me. me.
7
M
m
m
7

MORE
(Ti guarderò nel cuore)
from the film MONDO CANE

Music by NINO OLIVIERO and RIZ ORTOLANI
Italian Lyrics by MARCELLO CIORCIOLINI
English Lyrics by NORMAN NEWELL

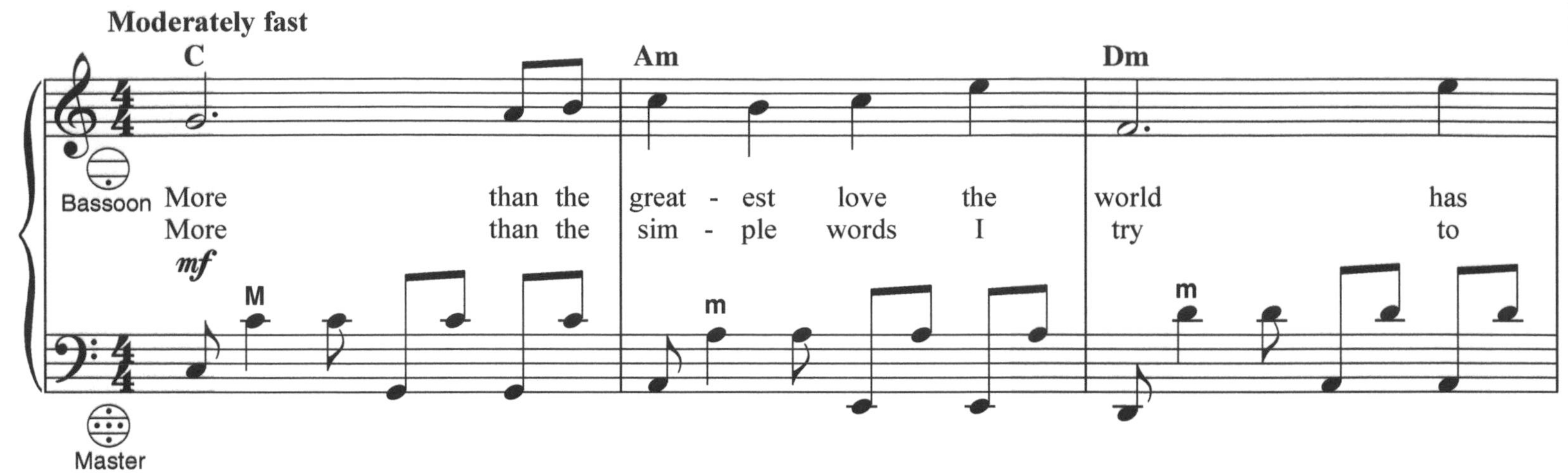

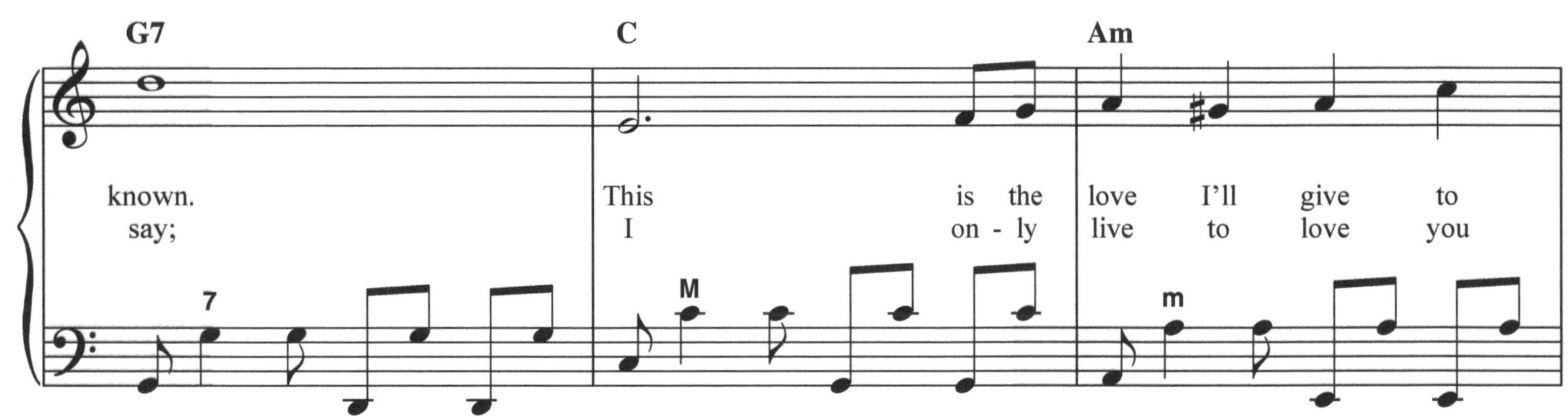

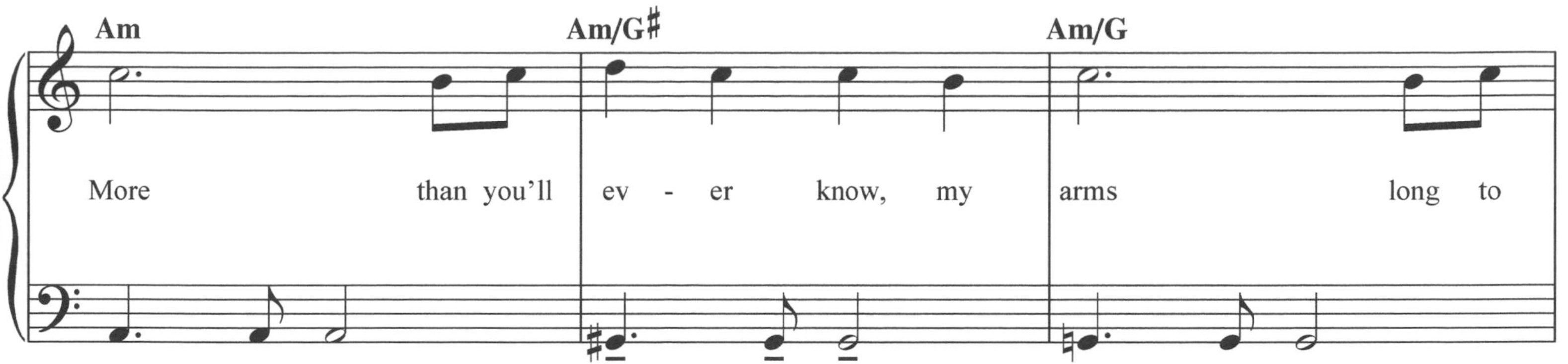
Am
Am/G♯
Am/G
More than you'll ev - er know, my arms long to

Am/F♯
F
F/E
D7
hold you so, my life will be in your keep - ing,
7

G7
D♭7
C
wak - ing, sleep - ing, laugh - ing, weep - ing. Long - er than
7
M

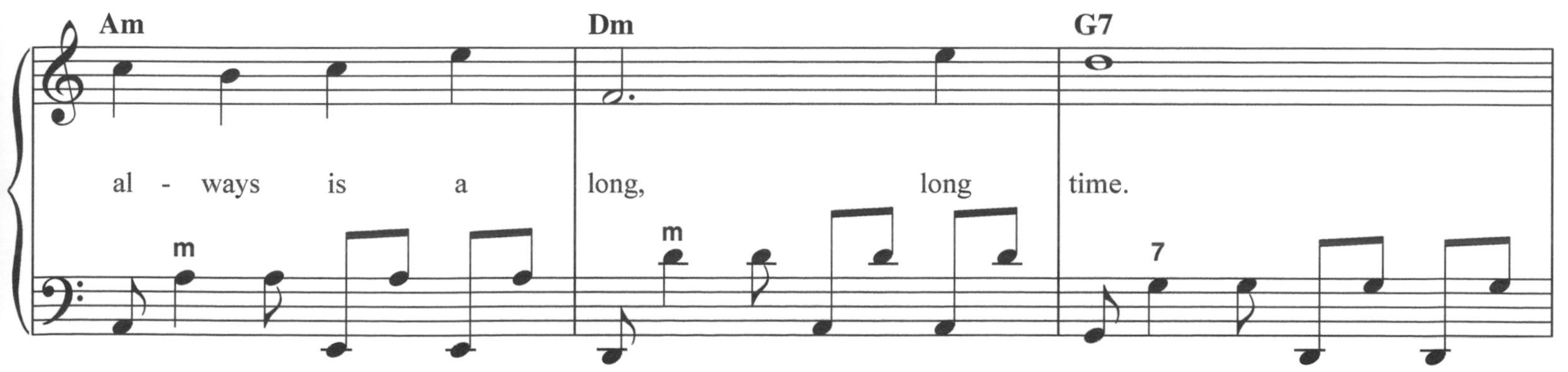
Am
Dm
G7
al - ways is a long, long time.
m
m
7

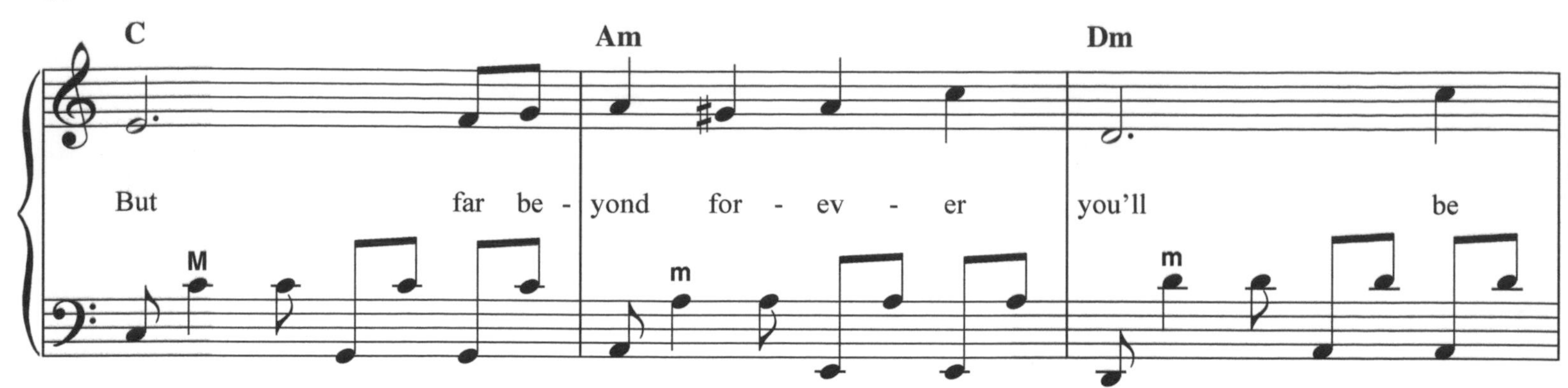
C
Am
Dm
But far be - yond for - ev - er you'll be
M
m
m

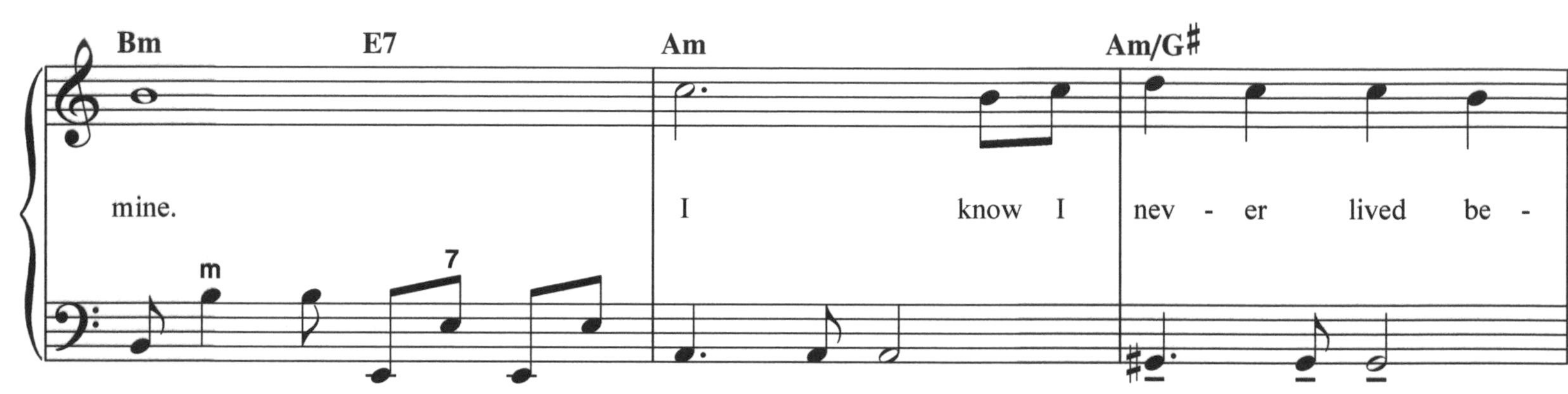
Bm
E7
Am
Am/G♯
mine.
I know I nev - er lived be -
m
7

Am/G
Am/F♯
F
F/E
fore and my heart is ver - y sure no one

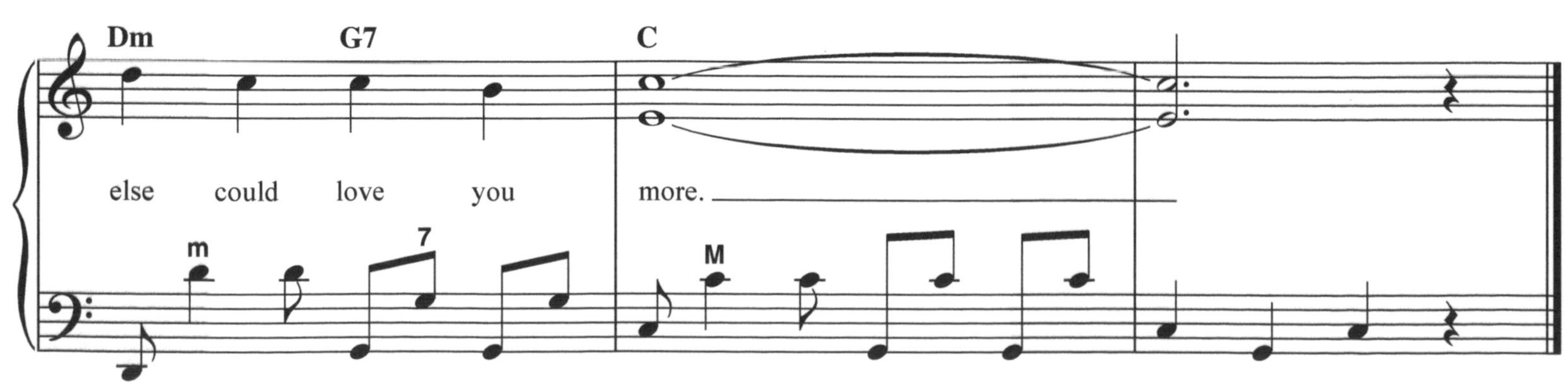
Dm
G7
C
else could love you more.
m
7
M

NEVER ON SUNDAY

from Jules Dassin's Motion Picture NEVER ON SUNDAY

Words by BILLY TOWNE
Music by MANOS HADJIDAKIS

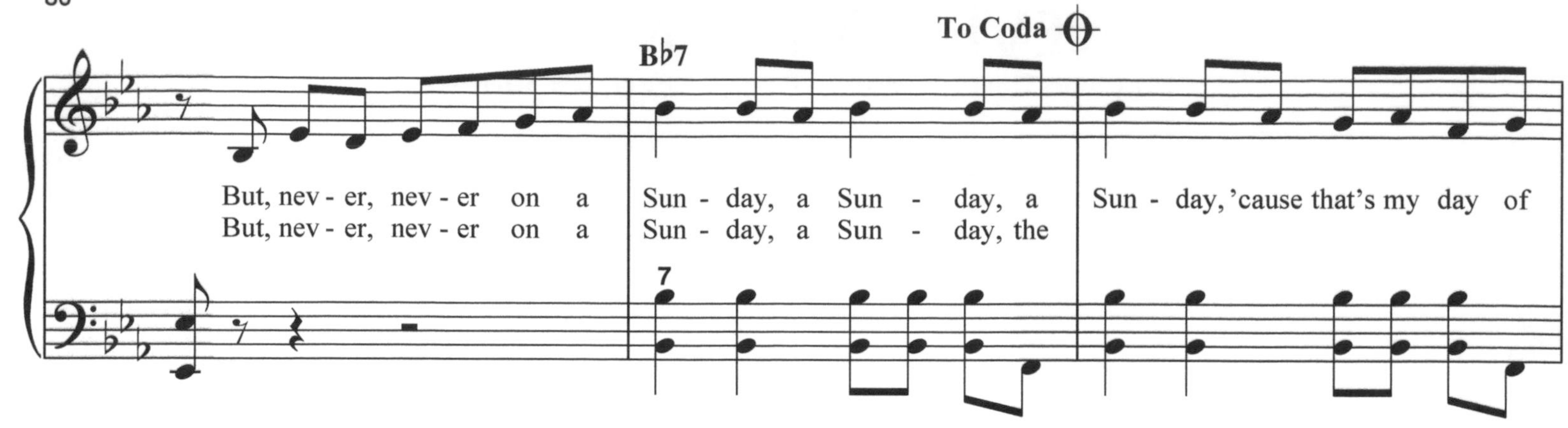
To Coda
B♭7
But, never, never on a
But, nev - er, nev - er on a
Sun - day, a Sun - day, a
Sun - day, a Sun - day, the
Sun - day, 'cause that's my day of
7

E♭
E♭
rest.
Most an - y
day
M
M

B♭7
you can be my
guest.
An - y day you
7

Fm
B♭7
E♭
say,
but my day of
rest.
m
7
M

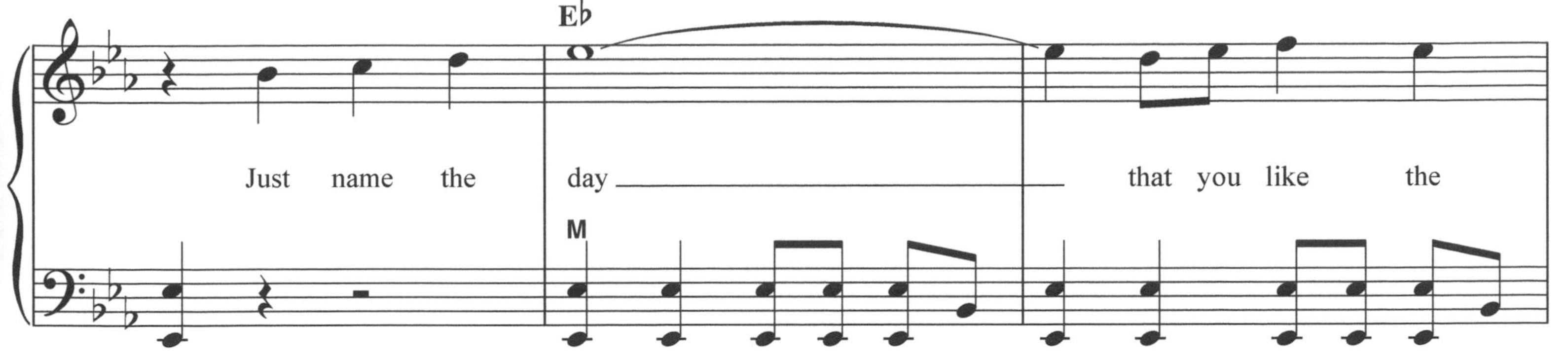
E♭
Just name the day that you like the
M

B♭7
Fm
best. On - ly, stay a - way
7
m

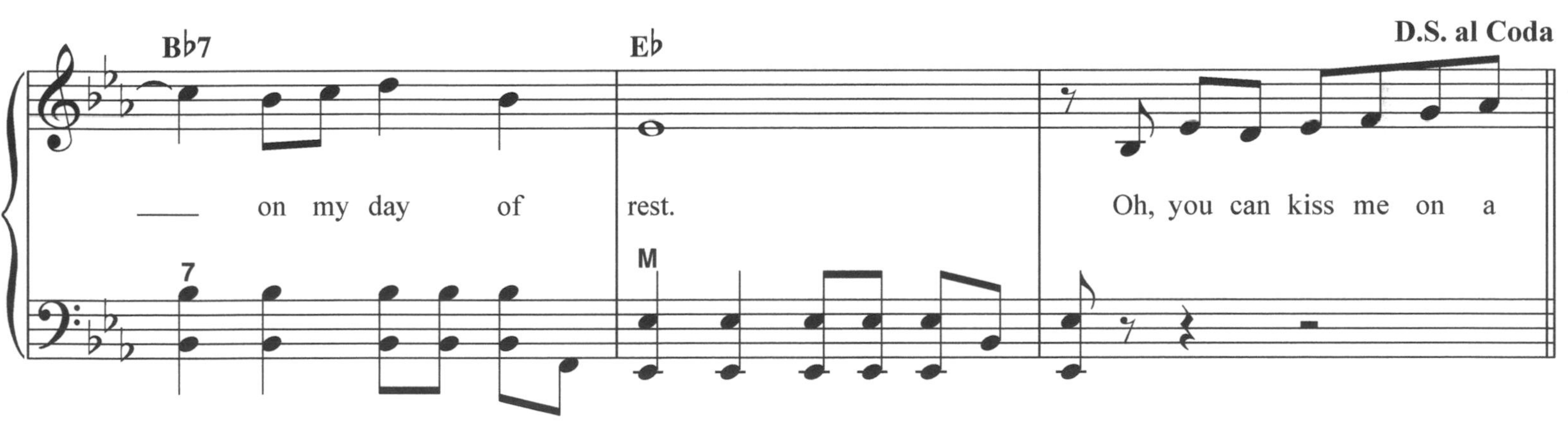
B♭7
E♭
D.S. al Coda
on my day of rest. Oh, you can kiss me on a
7
M

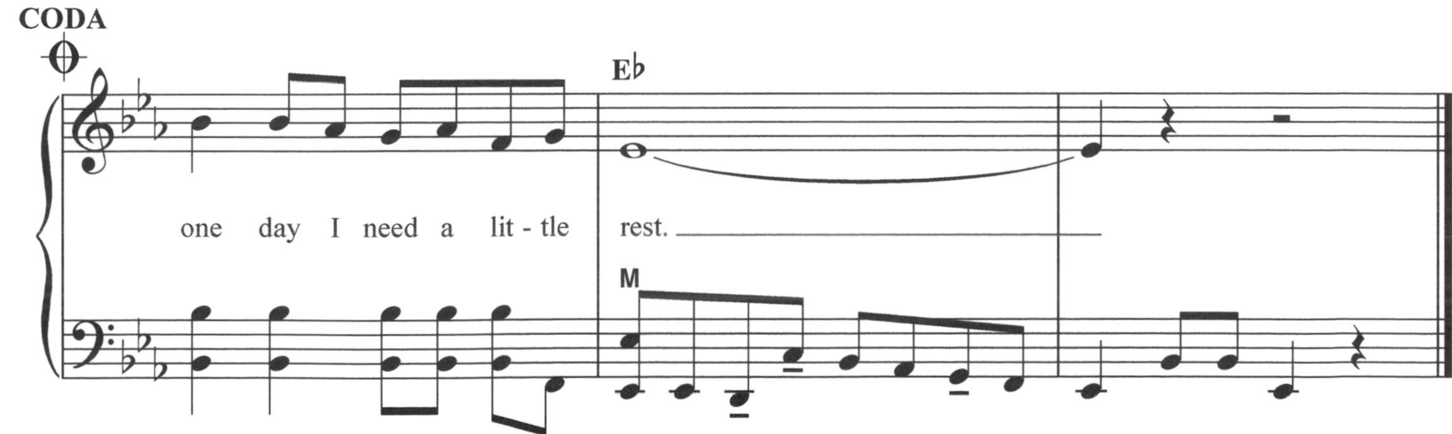
CODA
E♭
one day I need a lit - tle rest.
M

'O SOLE MIO

Words by GIOVANNI CAPURRO
Music by EDUARDO DI CAPUA

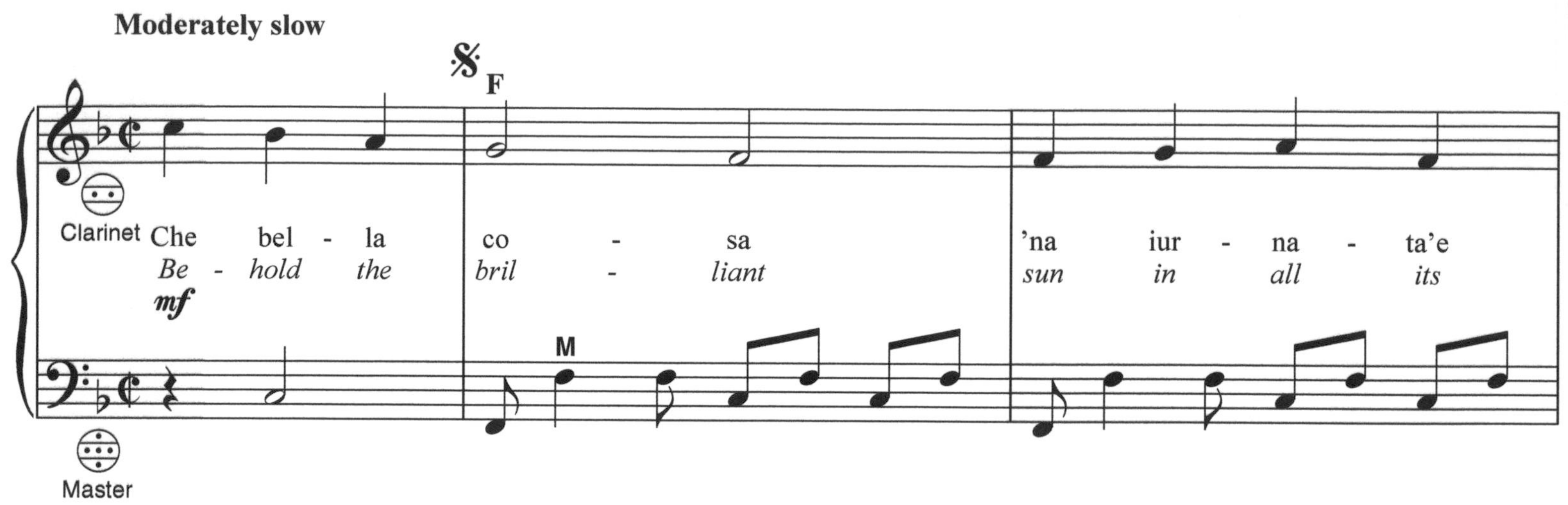

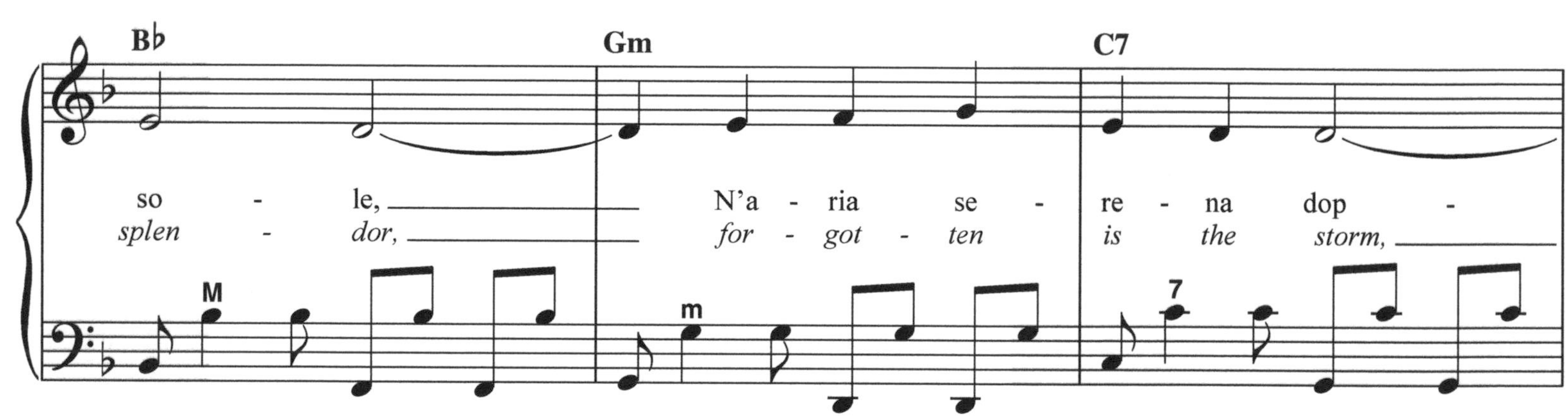

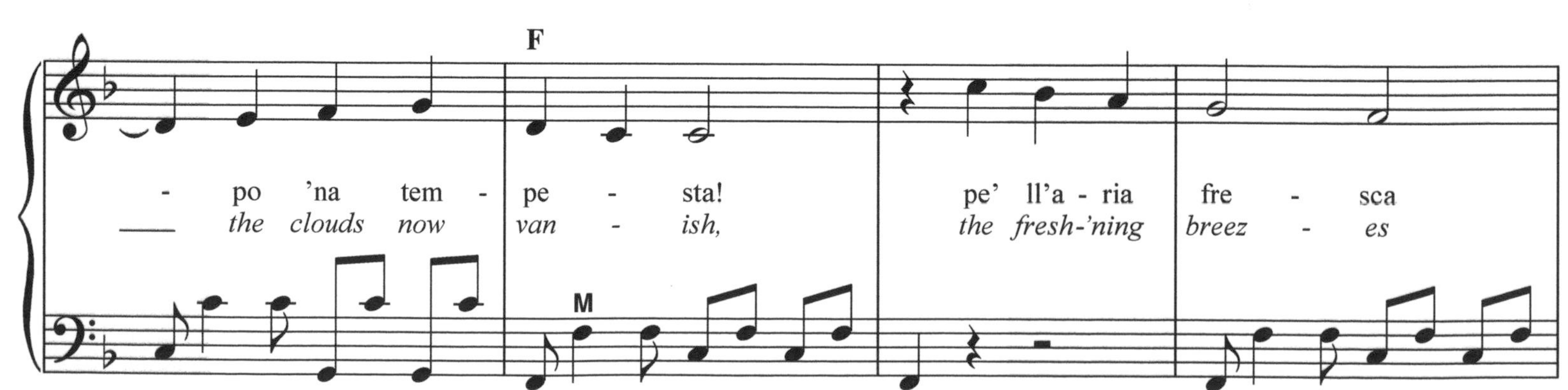

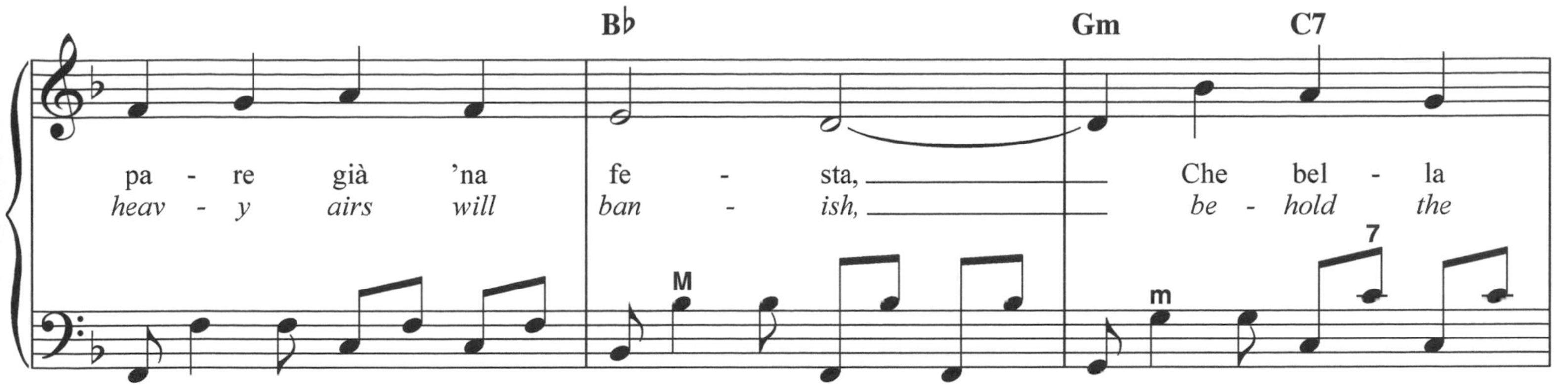
B♭
Gm
C7
pa - re già 'na fe - sta, Che bel - la
heav - y airs will ban - ish, be - hold the
M
m
7

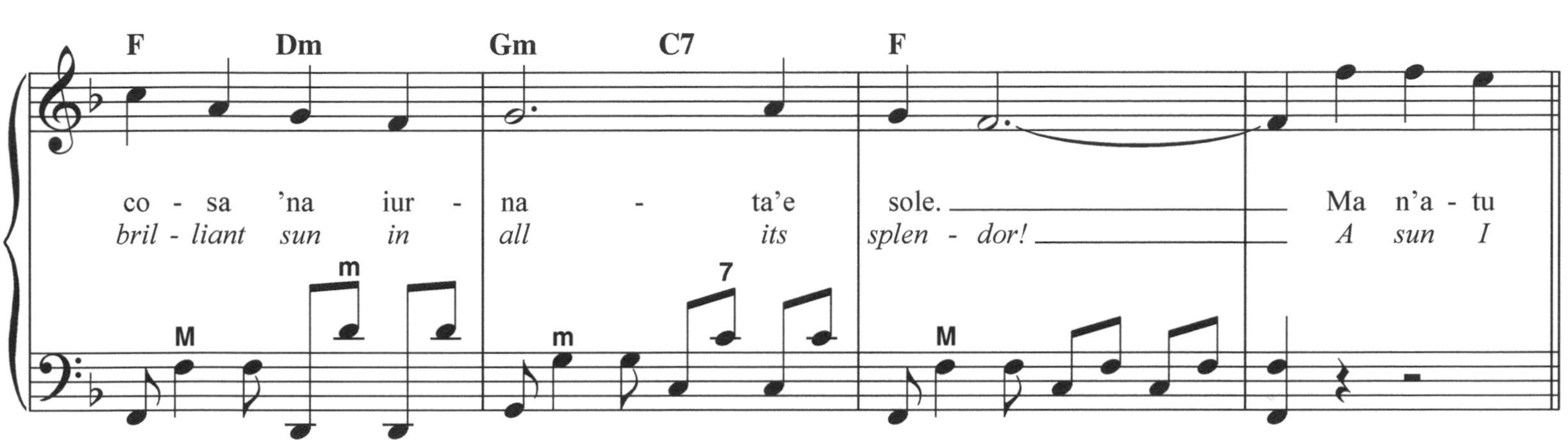
F
Dm
Gm
C7
F
co - sa 'na iur - na - ta'e sole. Ma n'a - tu
bril - liant sun in all its splen - dor! A sun I
M
m
m
7
M

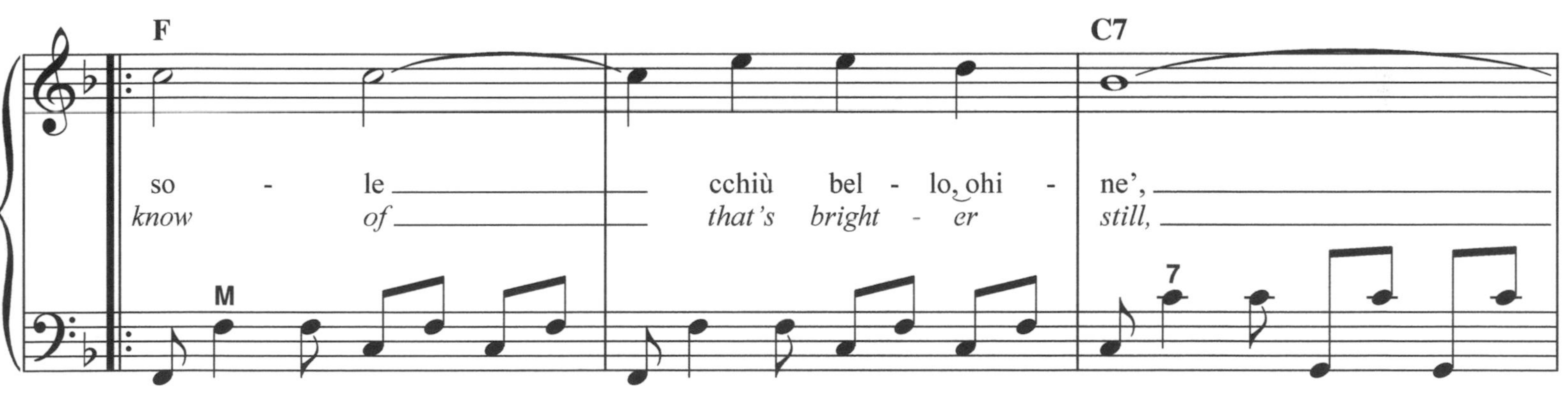
F
C7
so - le cchiù bel - lo, ohi - ne',
know of that's bright - er still,
M
7

'o so - le mi - o sta - nfron - te a
this sun, my dear - est, is naught but

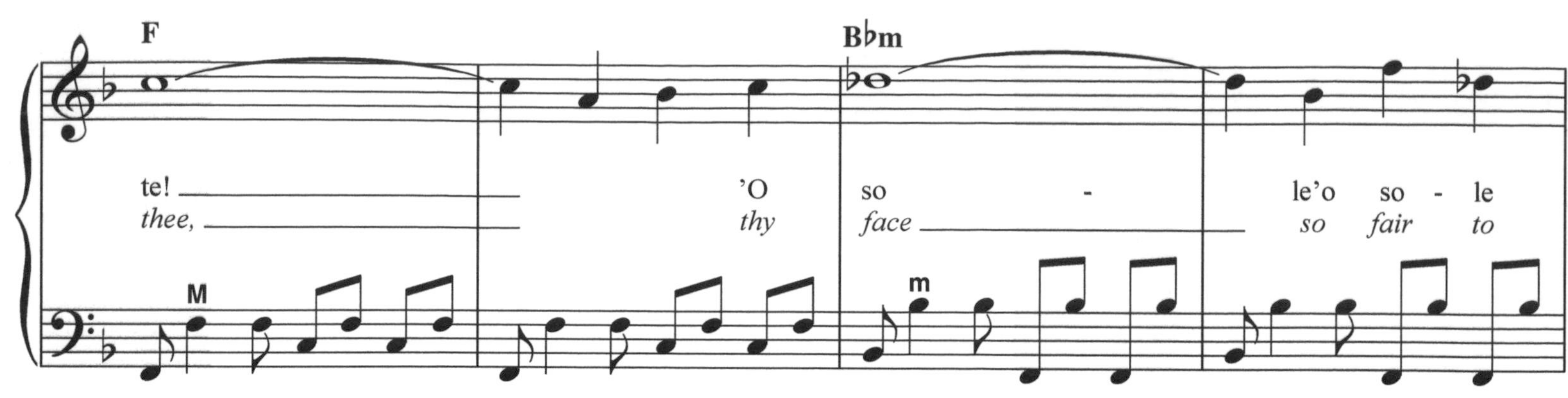
F
B♭m
te! 'O so - le'o so - le
thee, thy face so fair to
M
m

F
C7
mi - o sta - nfron - te'a te,
see, that shall now my sun
M
7

To Coda
1.
2.
F
F
F
sta - nfron - te a te! Ma n'a - tu te!
for - ev - er be! A sun I be!
M
M
M

D.S. al Coda
Che bel - la
Be - hold the

CODA
F
te!
be!
M

PIGALLE

English Lyric by CHARLES NEWMAN
French Lyric by GEO KOGER,
GEORGES ULMER and GUY LUYPAERTS
Music by GEORGES ULMER and GUY LUYPAERTS

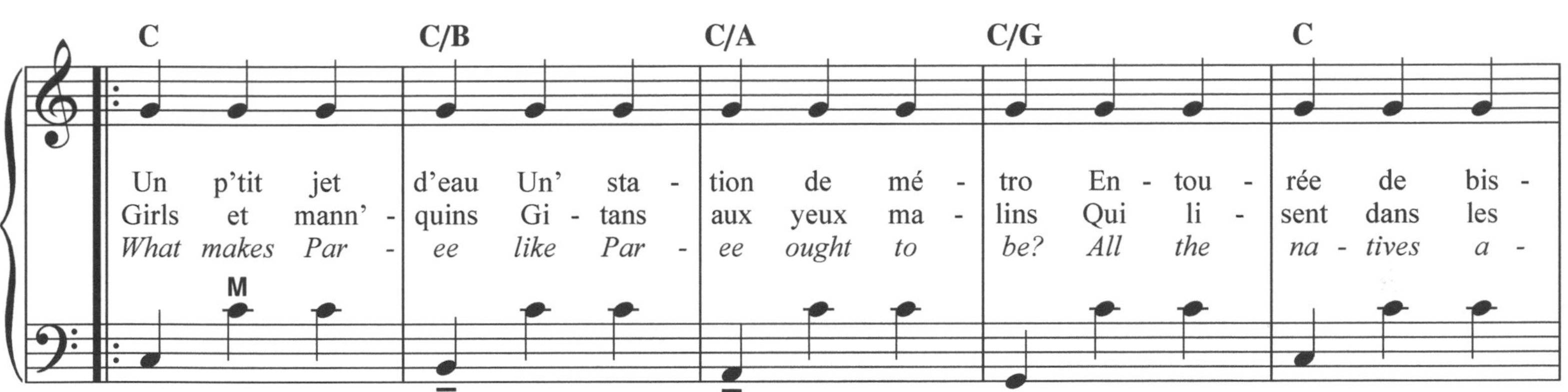

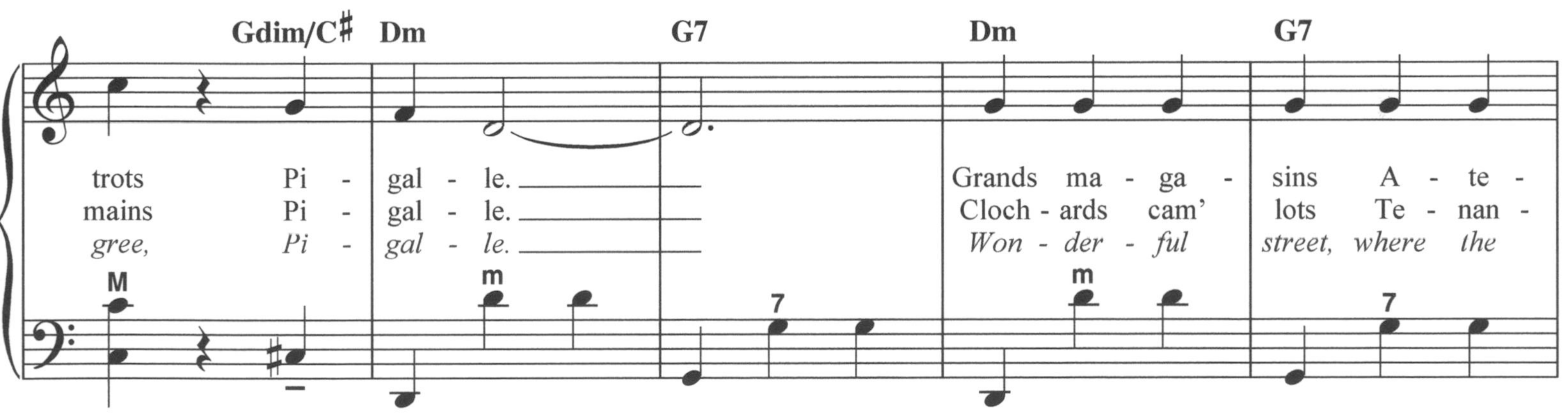

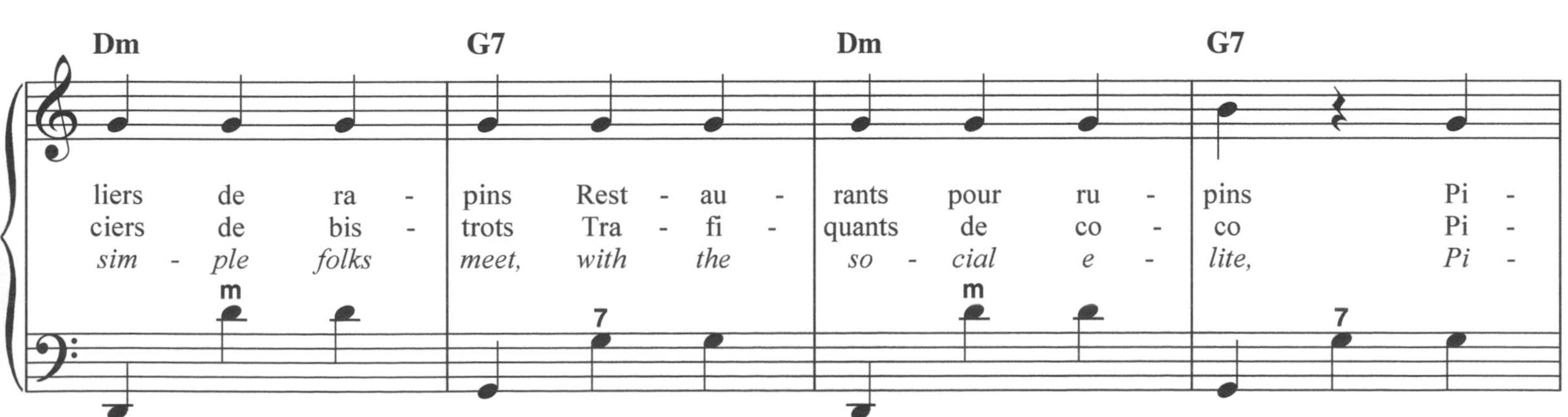

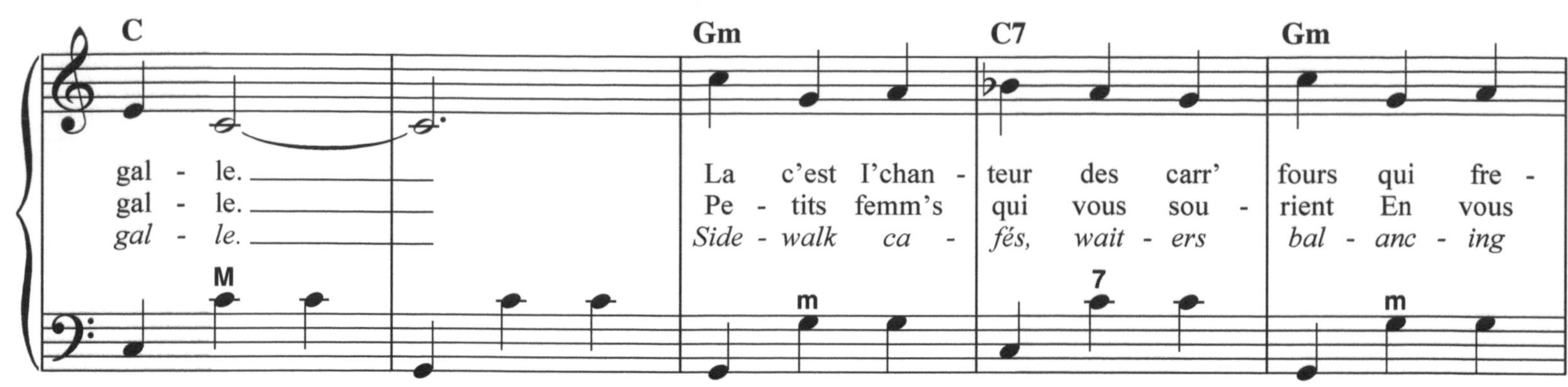
C
Gm
C7
Gm
gal - le.
La c'est l'chan - teur des carr' fours qui fre -
gal - le.
Pe - tits femm's qui vous sou - rient En vous
gal - le.
Side - walk ca - fés, wait - ers bal - anc - ing
M
m
7
m

C7
F
donn' les suc - cès du jour.
dis - ant: "Tu viens, ché - ri."
trays, morn - ing, night and noon.
7
M

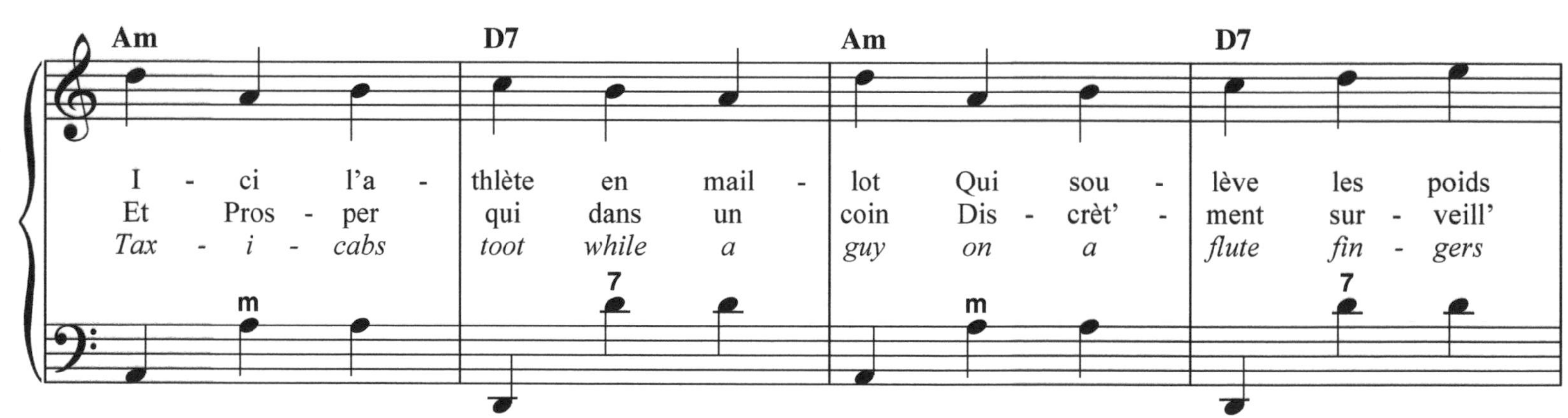
Am
D7
Am
D7
I - ci l'a - thlète en mail - lot Qui sou - lève les poids
Et Pros - per qui dans un coin Dis - crèt' - ment sur - veill'
Tax - i - cabs toot while a guy on a flute fin - gers
m
7
m
7

G7
Dm
G7
C
d'cent ki - los.
Hô - tels meu -
son gagn' - pain.
Un p'tit jet
"Clair de lune."
Ma - de - moi -
7
m
7
M

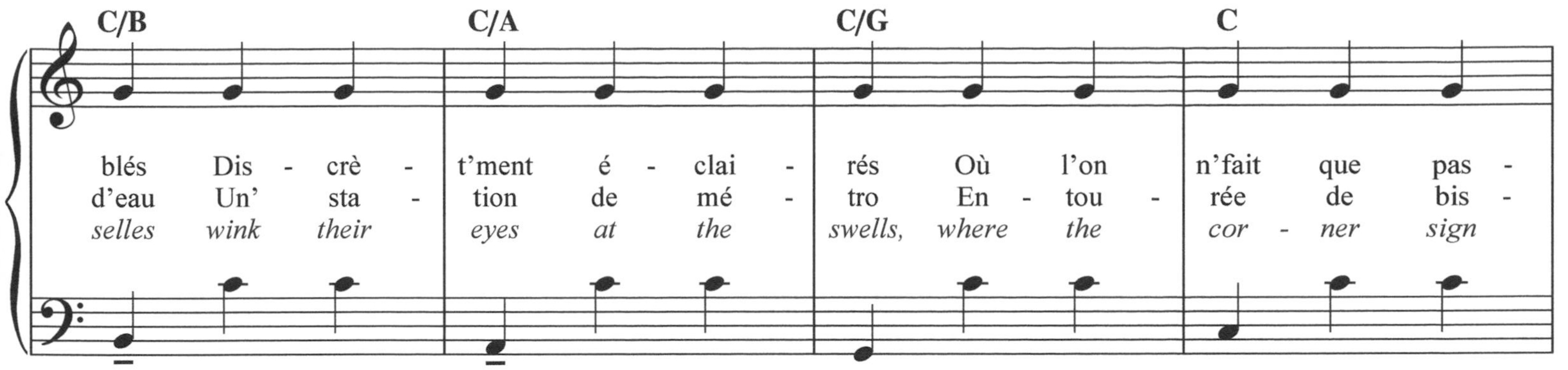
C/B
C/A
C/G
C
blés Dis - crè - t'ment é - clai - rés Où l'on n'fait que pas -
d'eau Un' sta - tion de mé - tro En - tou - rée de bis -
selles wink their eyes at the swells, where the cor - ner sign

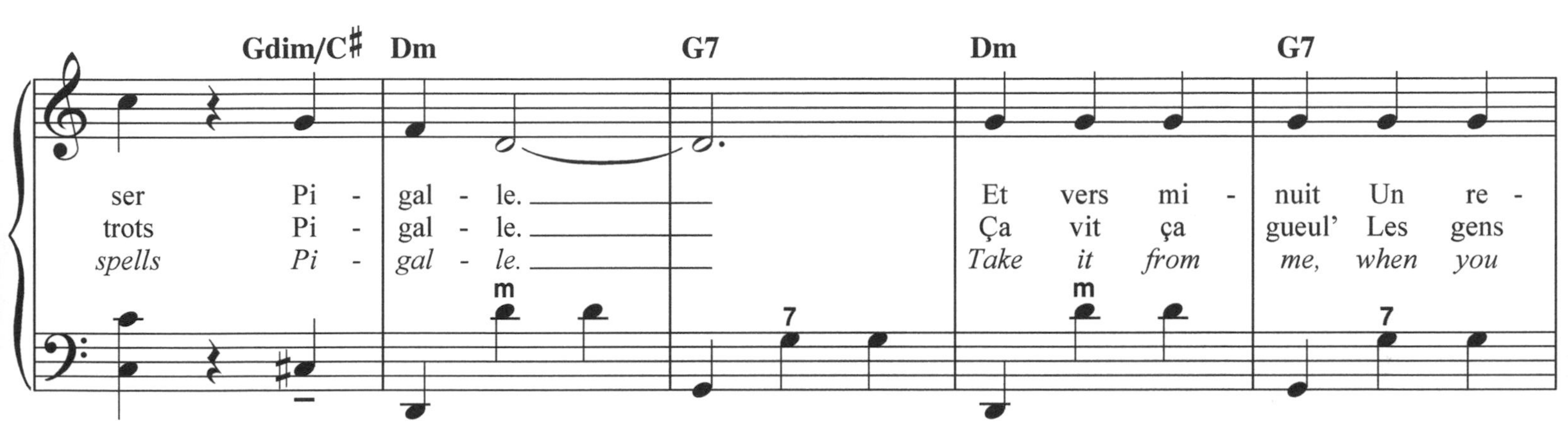
Gdim/C♯
Dm
G7
Dm
G7
ser Pi - gal - le. Et vers mi - nuit Un re -
trots Pi - gal - le. Ça vit ça gueul' Les gens
spells Pi - gal - le. Take it from me, when you
m
7
m
7

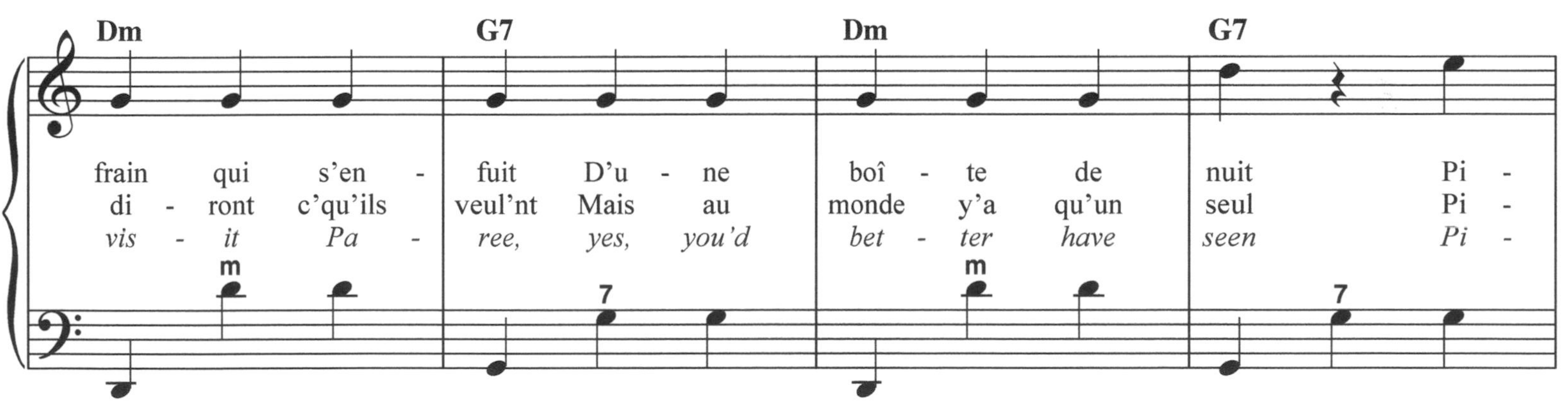
Dm
G7
Dm
G7
frain qui s'en - fuit D'u - ne boî - te de nuit Pi -
di - ront c'qu'ils veul'nt Mais au monde y'a qu'un seul Pi -
vis - it Pa - ree, yes, you'd bet - ter have seen Pi -
m
7
m
7

1.
2.
C
G7
C
gal - le.
gal - le.
gal - le.
gal - le.
gal - le.
gal - le.
M
7
M

OH MARIE

Words and Music by
EDUARDO DI CAPUA

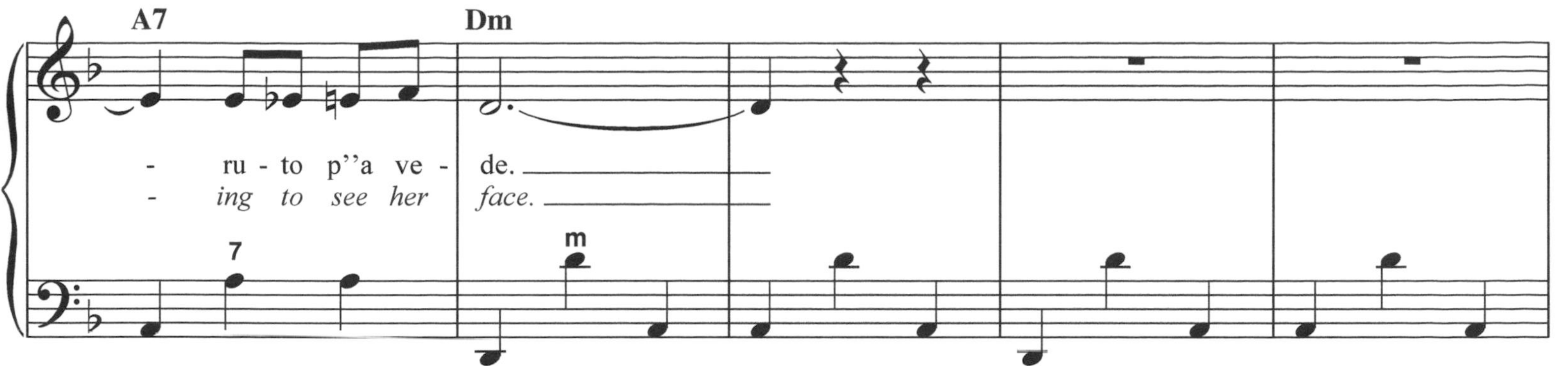
A7
Dm
- ru - to p''a ve - de.
- ing to see her face.
7
m

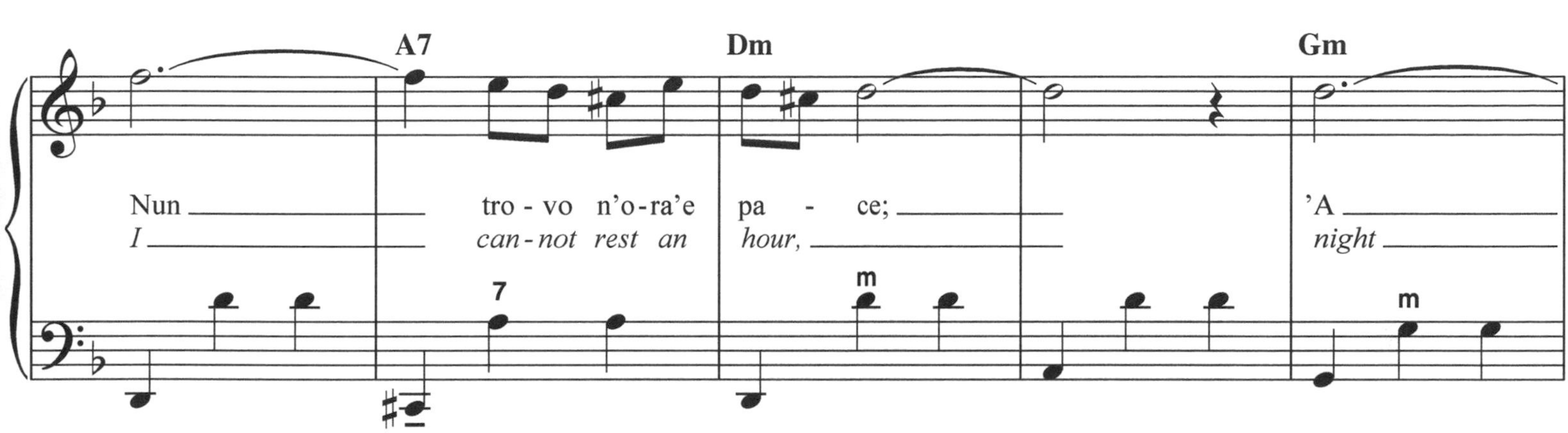
A7
Dm
Gm
Nun tro - vo n'o-ra'e pa - ce; 'A
I can-not rest an hour, night
7
m
m

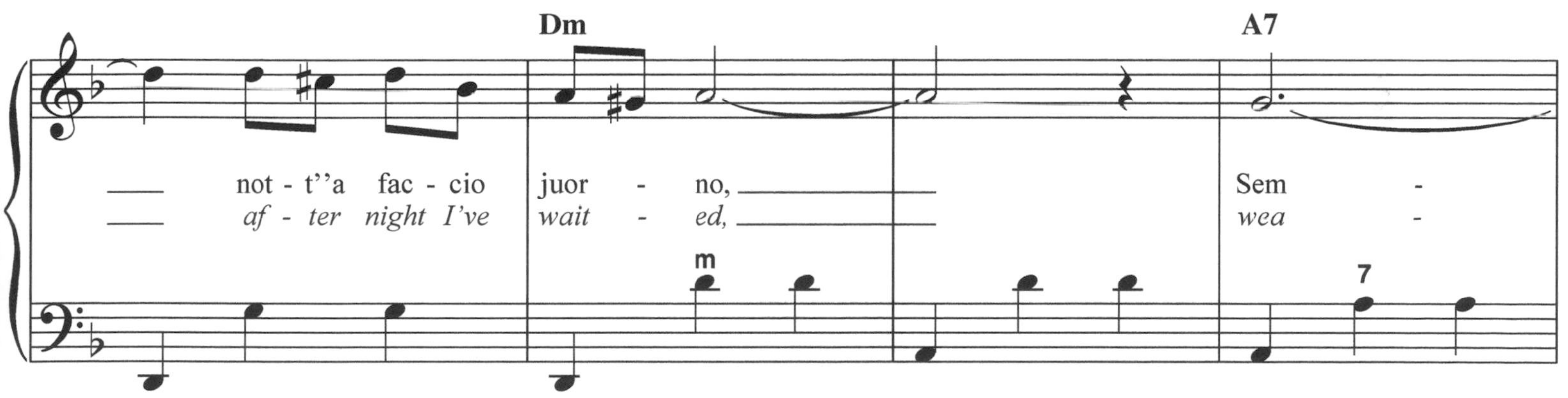
Dm
A7
not - t''a fac - cio juor - no, Sem -
af - ter night I've wait - ed, wea -
m
7

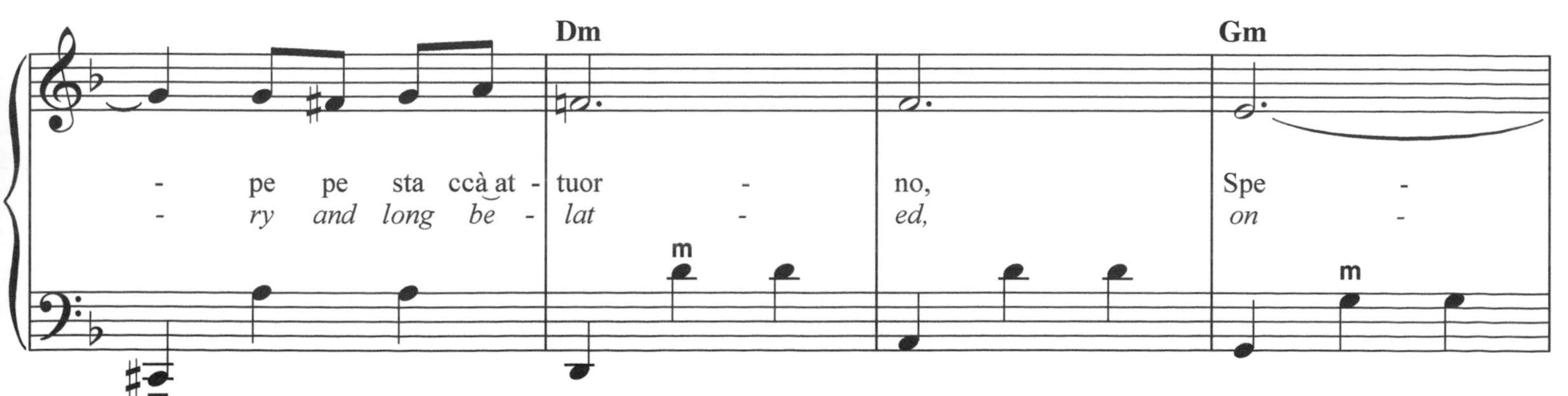
Dm
Gm
- pe pe sta ccà at - tuor - no, Spe -
- ry and long be - lat - ed, on -
m
m

A7
D
- ran-no'e ce par - là.
Ah, Ma -
- ly to hear her voice.
Oh, Ma -
7
M

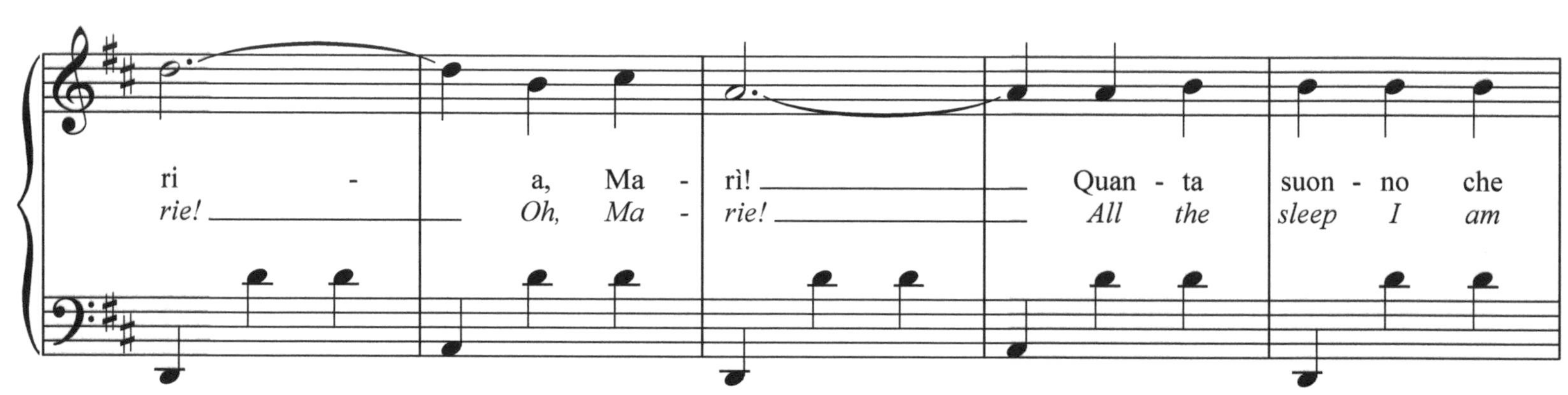
ri - a, Ma - rì! Quan - ta suon - no che
rie! Oh, Ma - rie! All the sleep I am

A7
per - do pe te; Fam - m'ad - dur -
los - ing for thee! Now let me
7

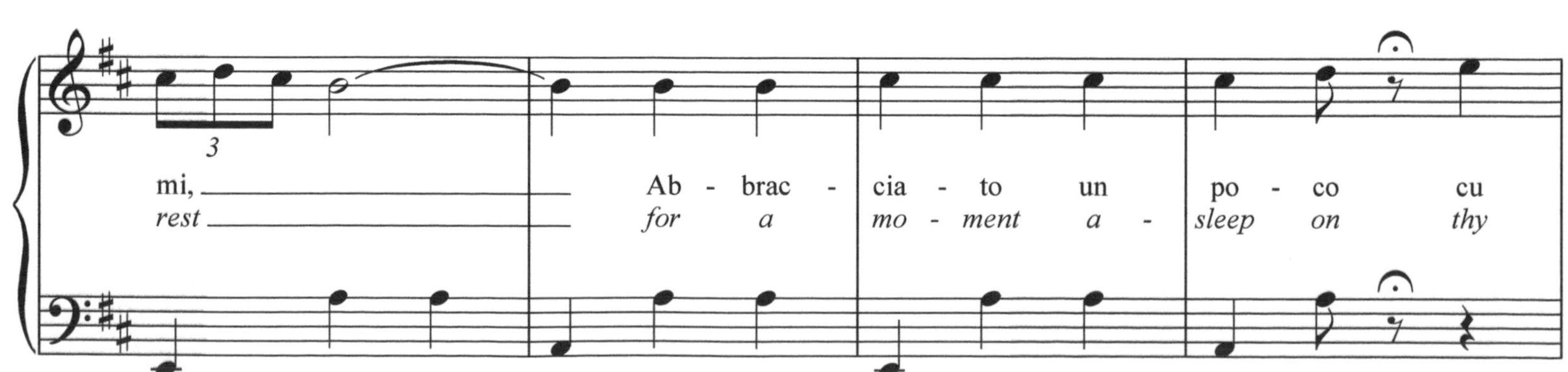
3
mi, Ab - brac - cia - to un po - co cu
rest for a mo - ment a - sleep on thy

D
3
te!
Ah, Ma - rì - a, Ma - rì!
breast!
Oh, Ma - rie! Oh, Ma - rie!
M

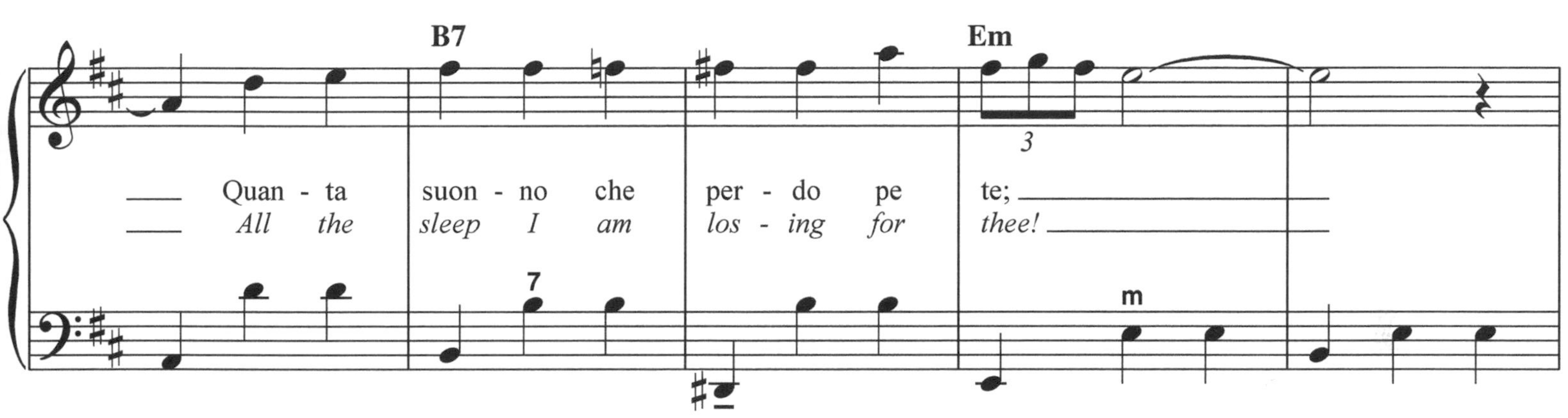
B7
Em
3
Quan - ta suon - no che per - do pe te;
All the sleep I am los - ing for thee!
7
m

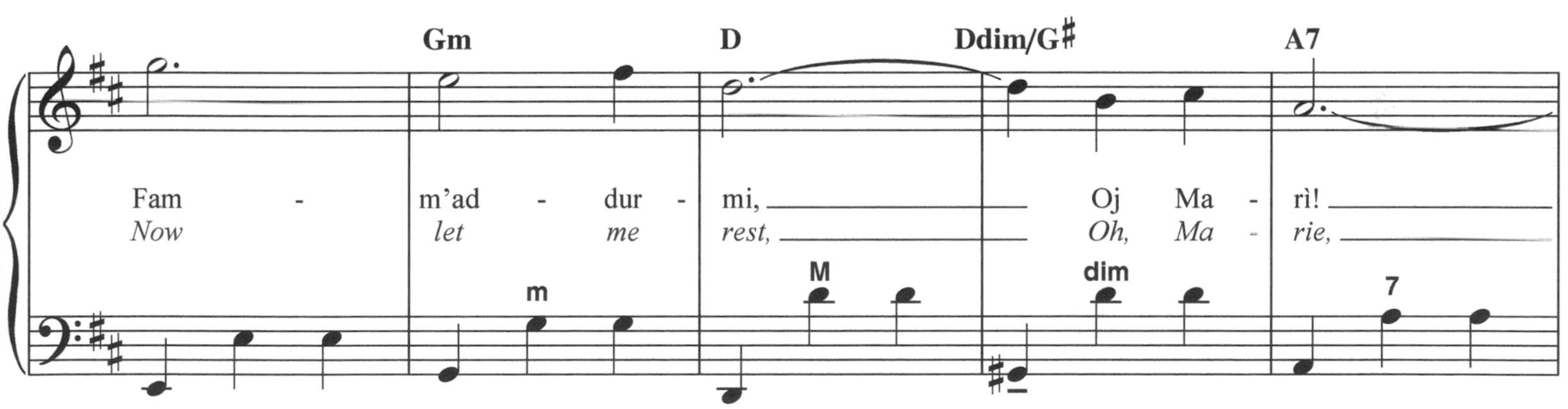
Gm
D
Ddim/G♯
A7
Fam - m'ad - dur - mi, Oj Ma - rì!
Now let me rest, Oh, Ma - rie,
m
M
dim
7

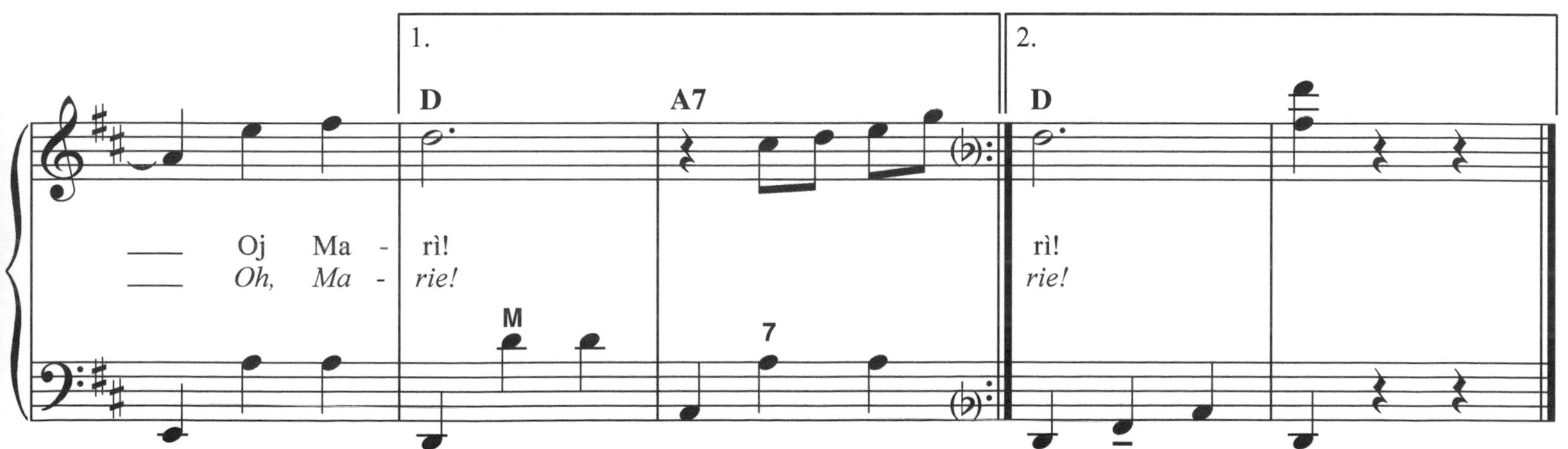
1.
2.
D
A7
D
Oj Ma - rì!
rì!
Oh, Ma - rie!
rie!
M
7

THE PHOENIX LOVE THEME

(Senza fine)

from the Motion Picture THE FLIGHT OF THE PHOENIX

English Lyrics by ALEC WILDER
Original Italian Text and Music by GINO PAOLI

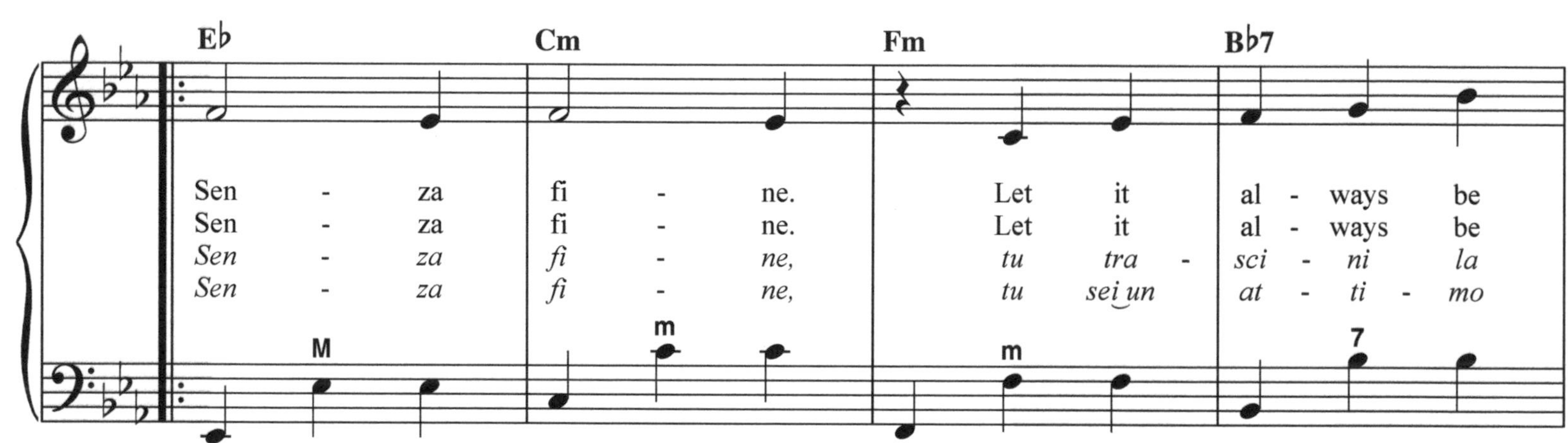

F♯7 B G♯m
love, our hopes, our dreams, our sighs, no
sun - lit days, the moon - lit nights, the
di re - spi - ro per so - gna - re,
hai do - ma - ni, tut - to é or - mai nel -
7 M m

F♯7 B
end at all no sad good - byes, no
sea, the sand, the star - ry heights are
per po - te - re ri - cor - da - re
le tue ma - ni, ma - ni gran - di,
7 M

1.
F7 B♭7
fears, no tears, no love that dies. It's
yours and mine for -
ciò che ab - bia - mo già vis - su - to.
ma - ni sen - za
7 7 7

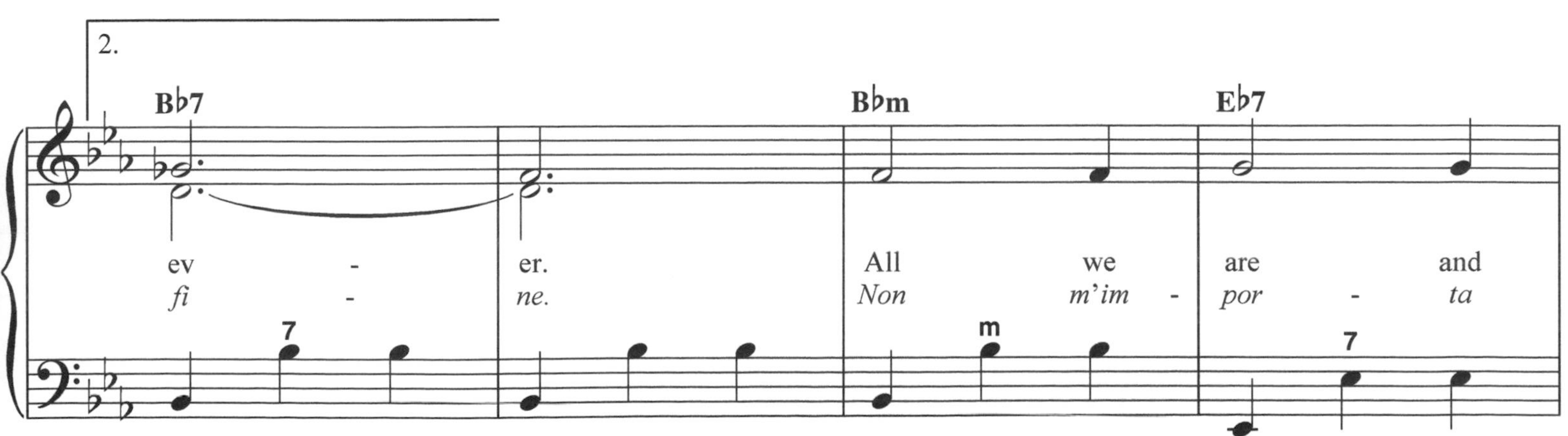
2.
B♭7 B♭m E♭7
ev - er. All we are and
fi - ne. Non m'im - por - ta
7 m 7

A♭
B♭m
E♭7
all we know is love and love a -
del - la lu - na, non m'im - por - ta
M
m
7

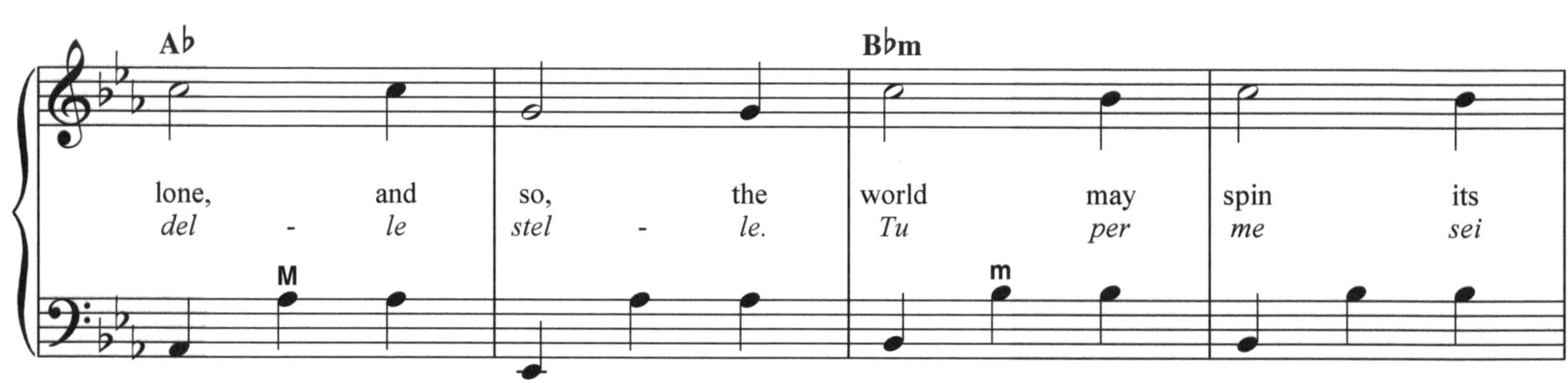
A♭
B♭m
lone, and so, the world may spin its
del - le stel - le. Tu per me sei
M
m

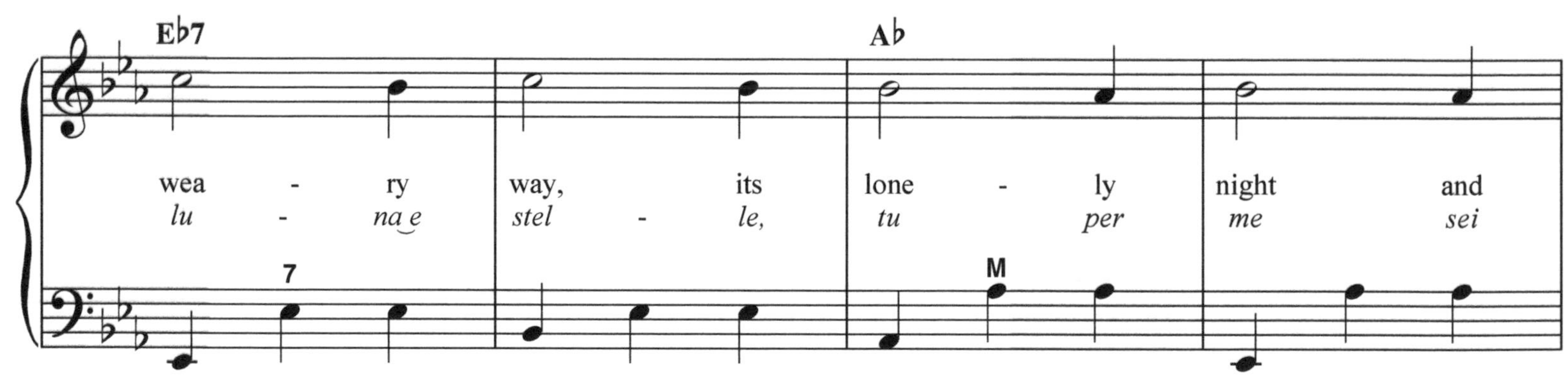
E♭7
A♭
wea - ry way, its lone - ly night and
lu - na e stel - le, tu per me sei
7
M

Fm
G7
lone - ly day, while we go float - ing
so - le e cie - lo, tu per me sei
m
7

C7
F7
far a - bove in nev - er end - ing
tut - to quan - to, tut - to quan - to io
7
7

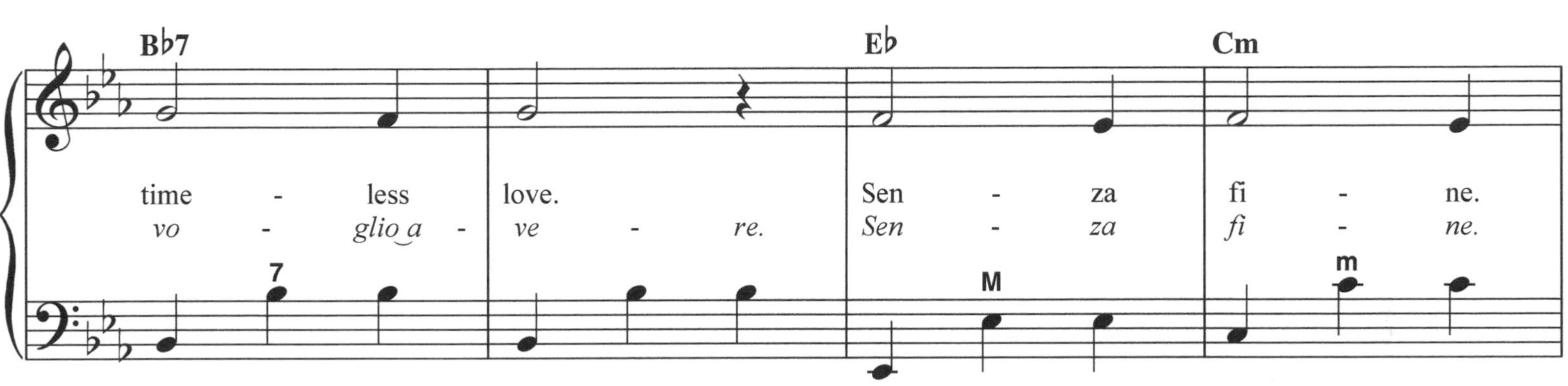
B♭7
E♭
Cm
time - less love. Sen - za fi - ne.
vo - glio a - ve - re. Sen - za fi - ne.
7
M
m

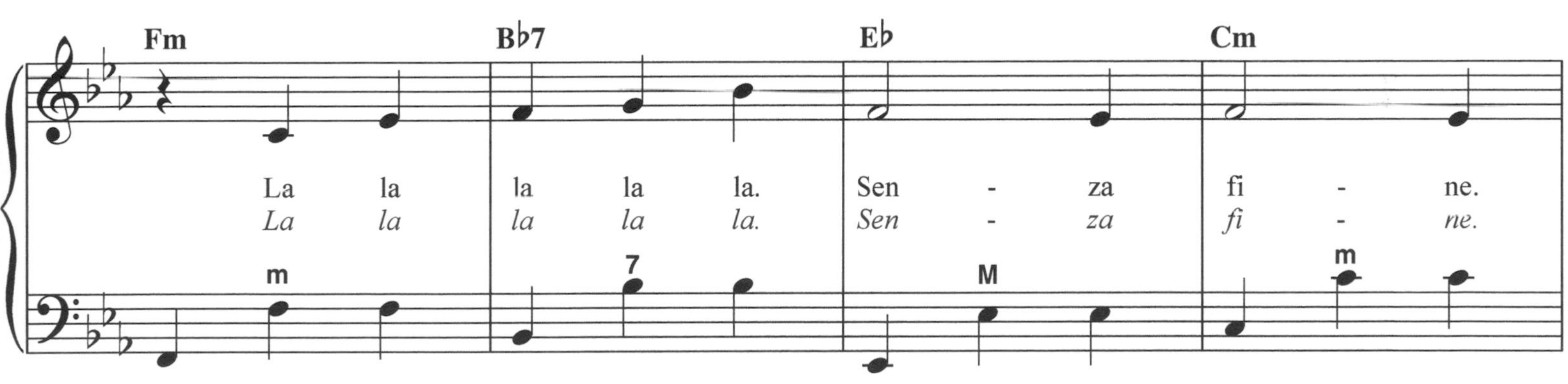
Fm
B♭7
E♭
Cm
La la la la la. Sen - za fi - ne.
La la la la la. Sen - za fi - ne.
m
7
M
m

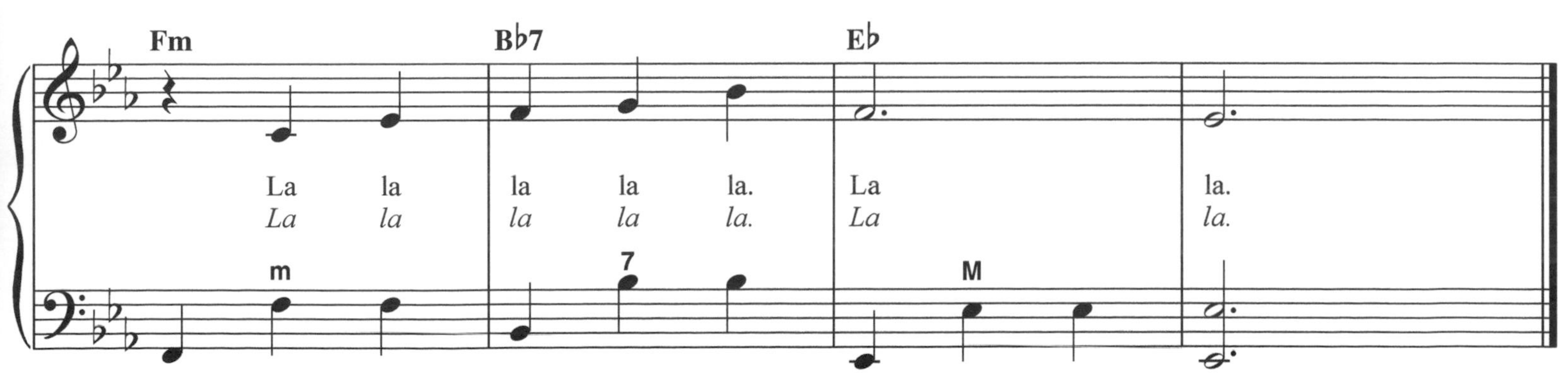
Fm
B♭7
E♭
La la la la la. La la.
La la la la la. La la.
m
7
M

POINCIANA
(Song of the Tree)

Words by BUDDY BERNIER
Music by NAT SIMON

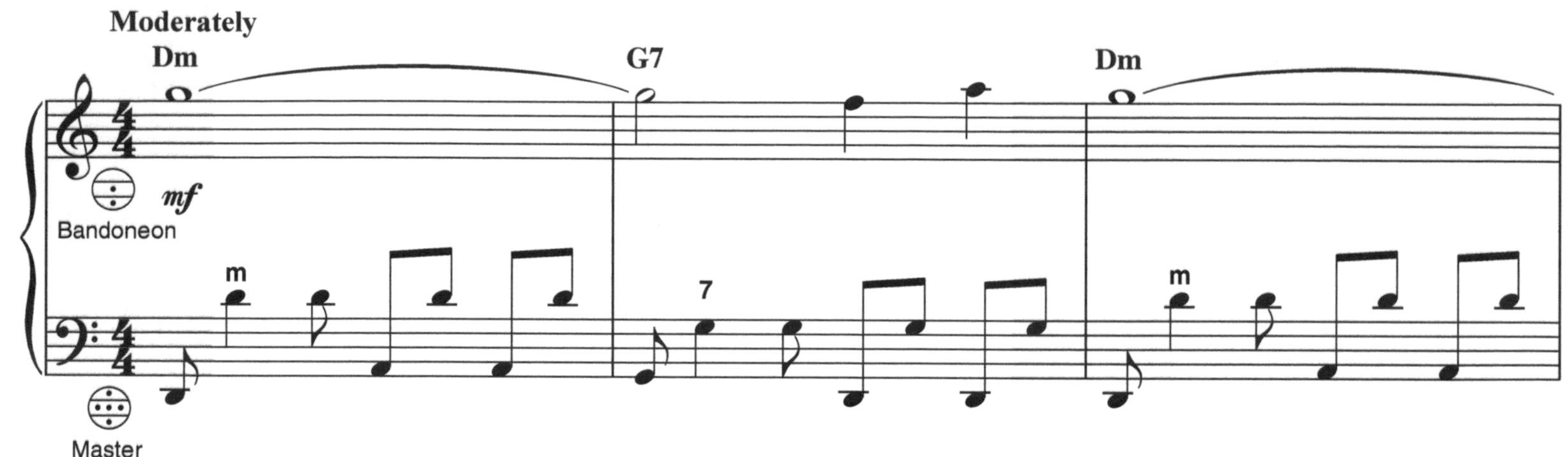

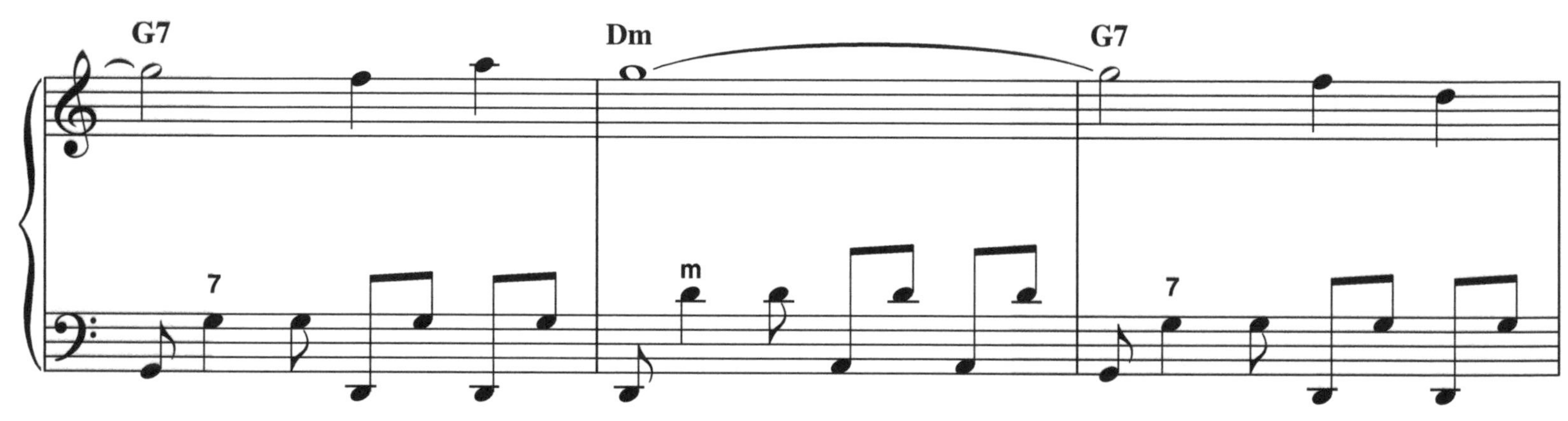

G7
C
Poin - ci an - a, your branch-es speak to me of
an - a, some-how I feel the jun-gle
M
7
Gm
C7
Fm
love.
heat.
With - in me
Pale moon
m
is cast-ing shad-ows from a - bove.
there grows a rhyth-mic sav-age
1.
C
Gdim/C♯
Dm
G7
Poin - ci -
dim
2.
beat.
Love is ev - 'ry-where, its

G
mag - ic per-fume fills the air,
M

Fm
Dm
to and fro you sway, my heart's in time, I've learned to care.
m
m

G7
C
Poin - ci - an - a, though skies may turn from blue to
7
M

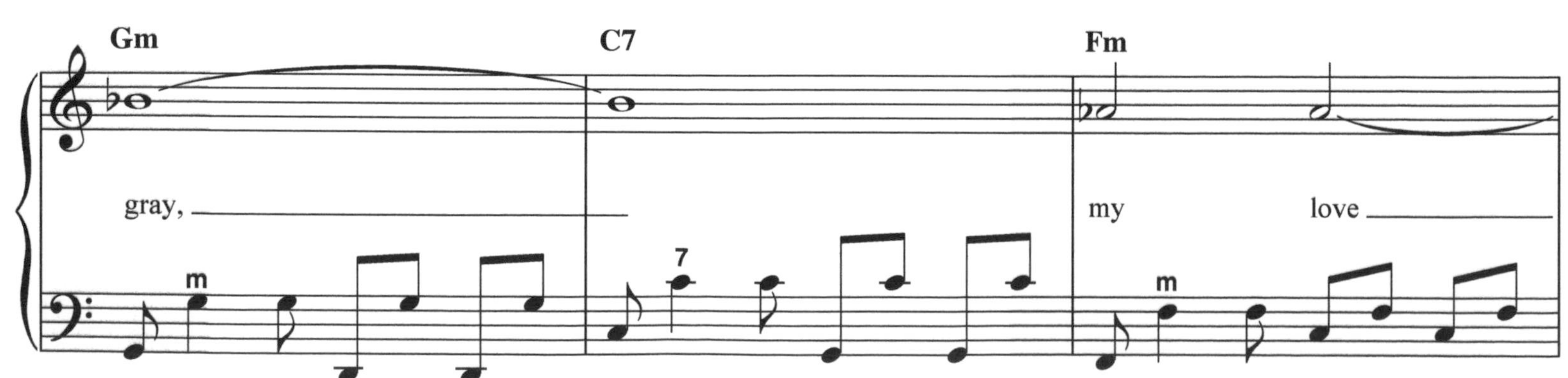
Gm
C7
Fm
gray, my love
m
7
m

C
will live for - ev - er and a
day.
M
Dm
G7
m
7
1.
2.
Db
C G7 C

RETURN TO ME

Words and Music by DANNY DI MINNO
and CARMEN LOMBARDO

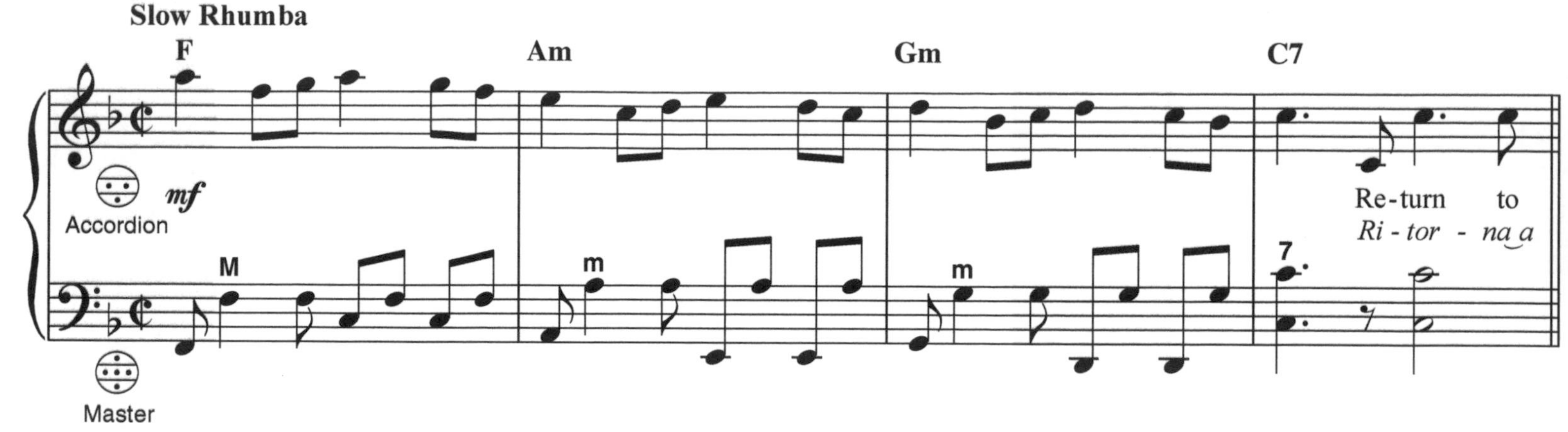

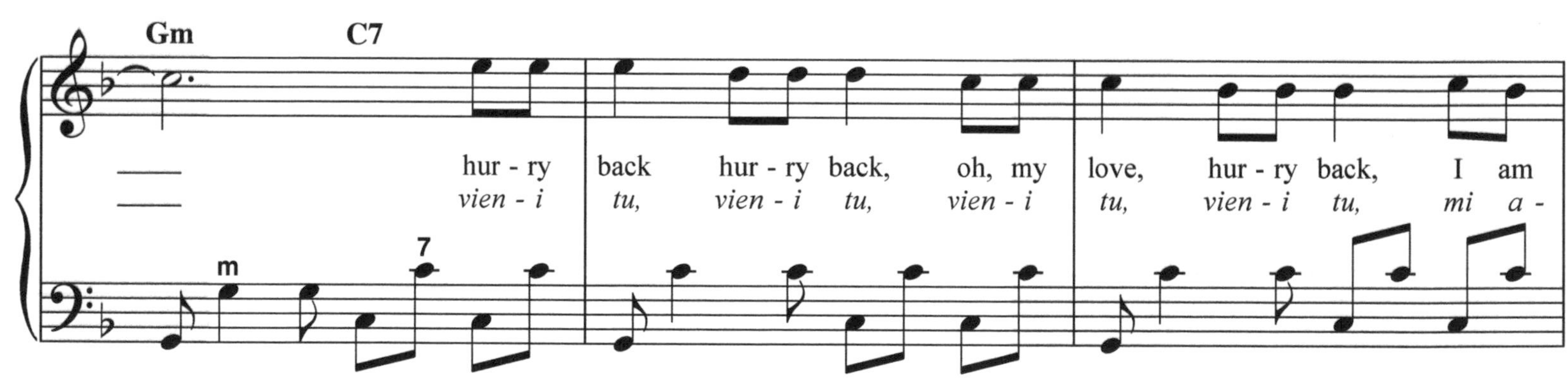

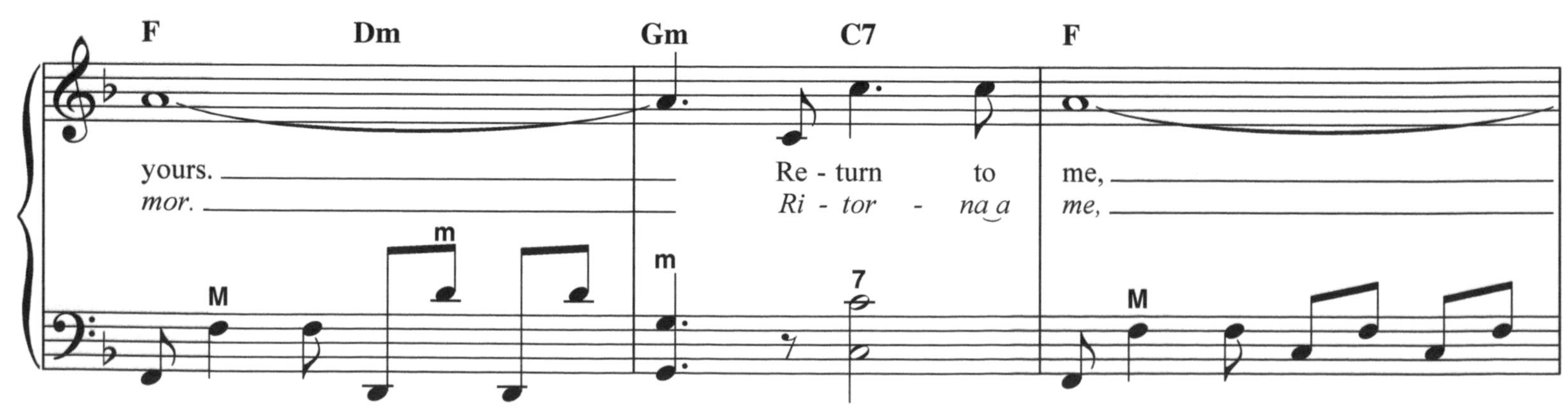

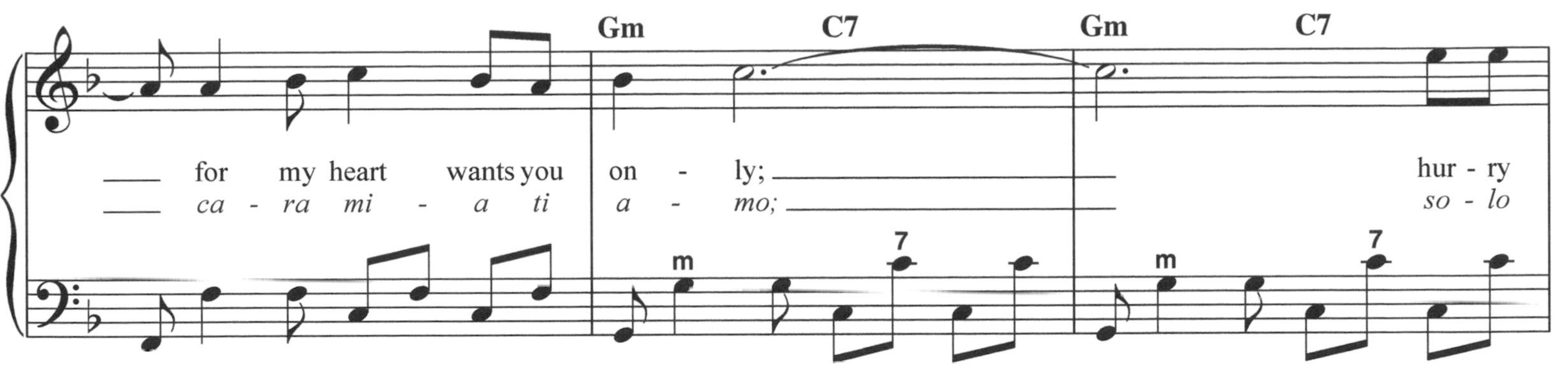
Gm C7 Gm C7
for my heart wants you on - ly; hur - ry
ca - ra mi - a ti a - mo; so - lo
m 7 m 7

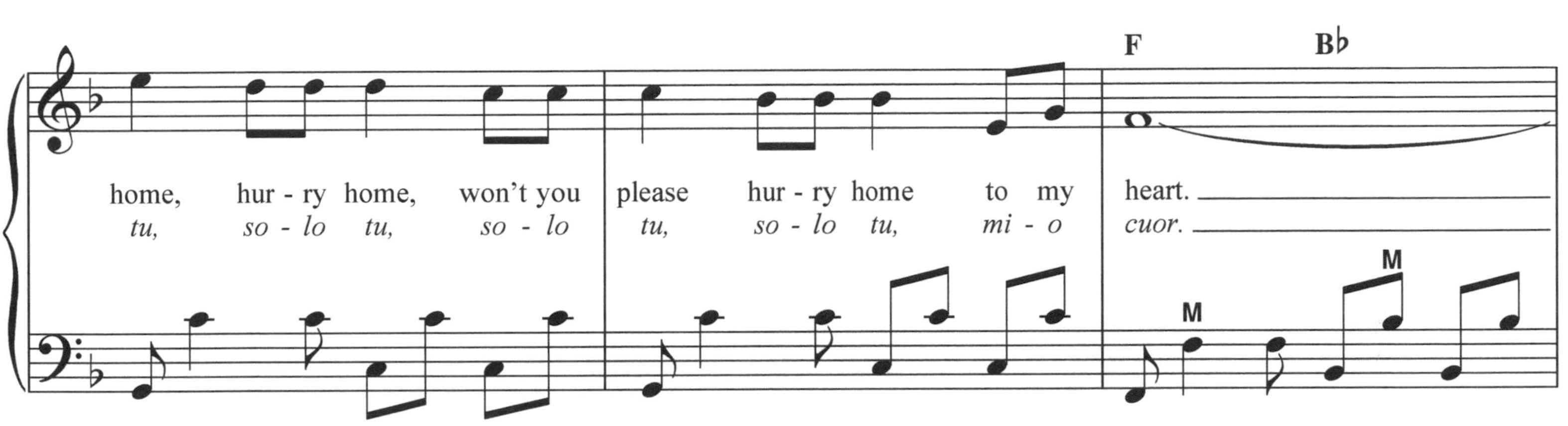
F B♭
home, hur - ry home, won't you please hur - ry home to my heart.
tu, so - lo tu, so - lo tu, so - lo tu, mi - o cuor.
M M

F F7 B♭ Gm C7
My dar - ling, if I hurt you, I'm
Bam - bi - na, dar il cour - a - nes
M 7 M m 7

F E7
sor - ry; for - give me,
su - no; man - tie - ni,
M 7

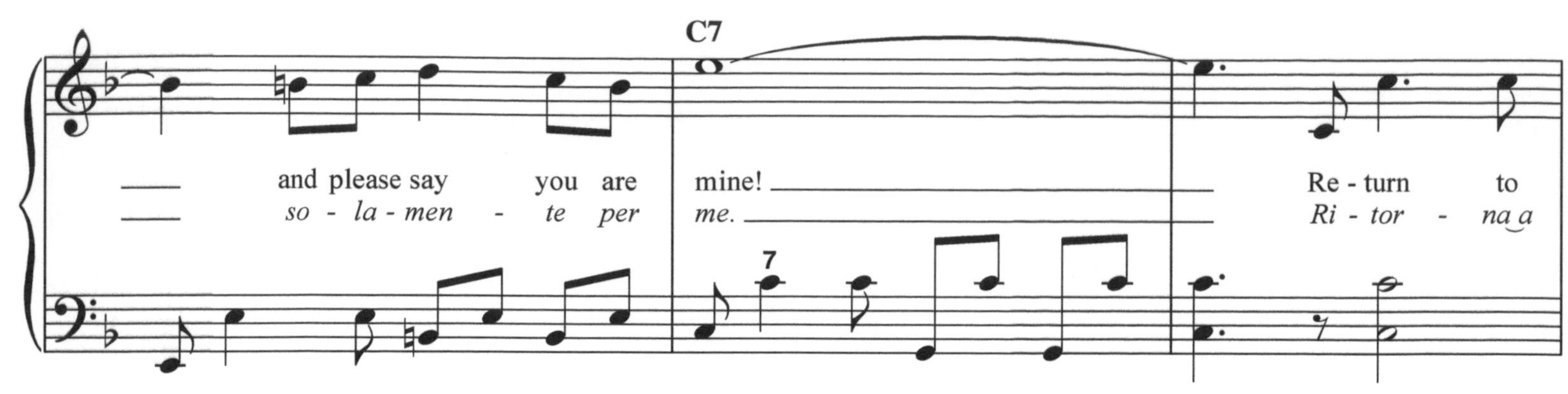
C7
and please say you are mine! Re - turn to
so - la - men - te per me. Ri - tor - na a
7

F
Gm
C7
me, please come back, bel - la mi - a;
me, e la san - ta ve - mu - ta;
M
m
7

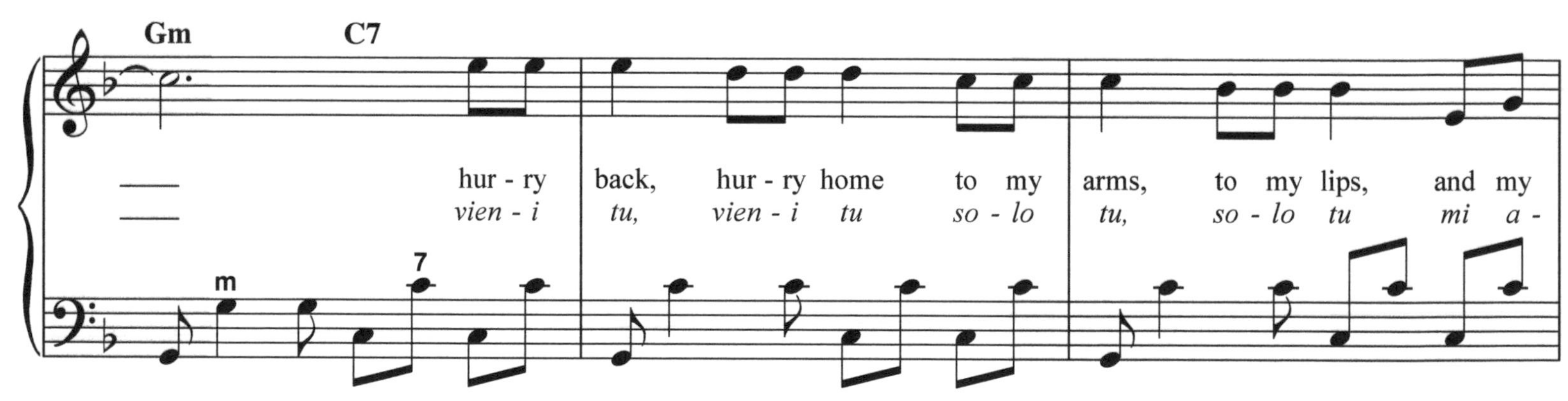
Gm
C7
hur - ry back, hur - ry home to my arms, to my lips, and my
vien - i tu, vien - i tu so - lo tu, so - lo tu mi a -
m
7

1.
2.
F
Dm
Gm
C7
F
B♭m
F
heart. Re - turn to heart.
mor! Ri - tor - na a mor!
M
m
m
7
M
m
M

SLOW POKE

Words and Music by PEE WEE KING,
CHILTON PRICE and REDD STEWART

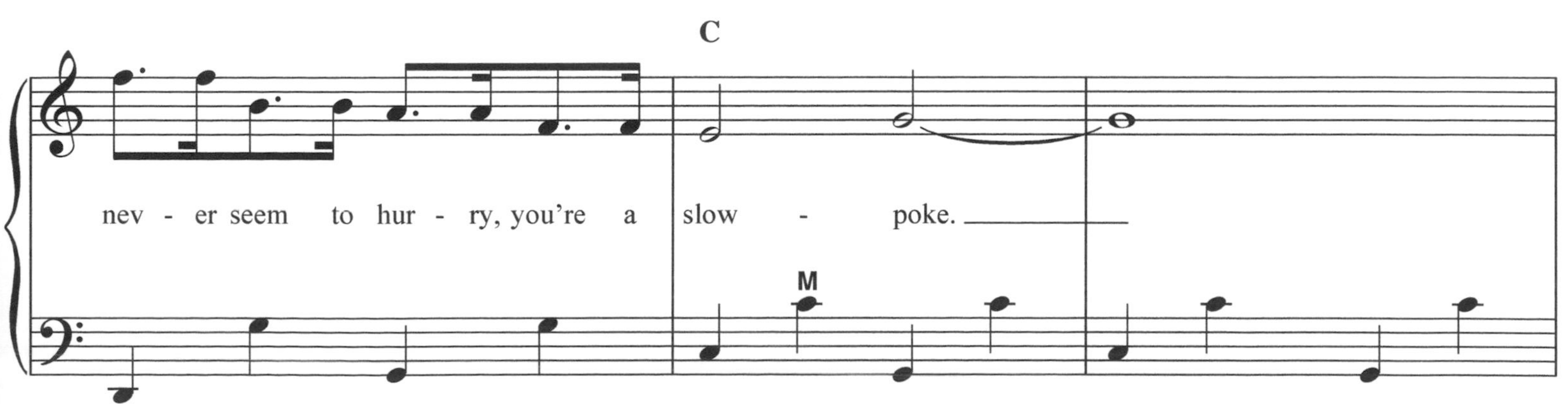

C7
F
Time means noth - in' to you I wait and
7
M

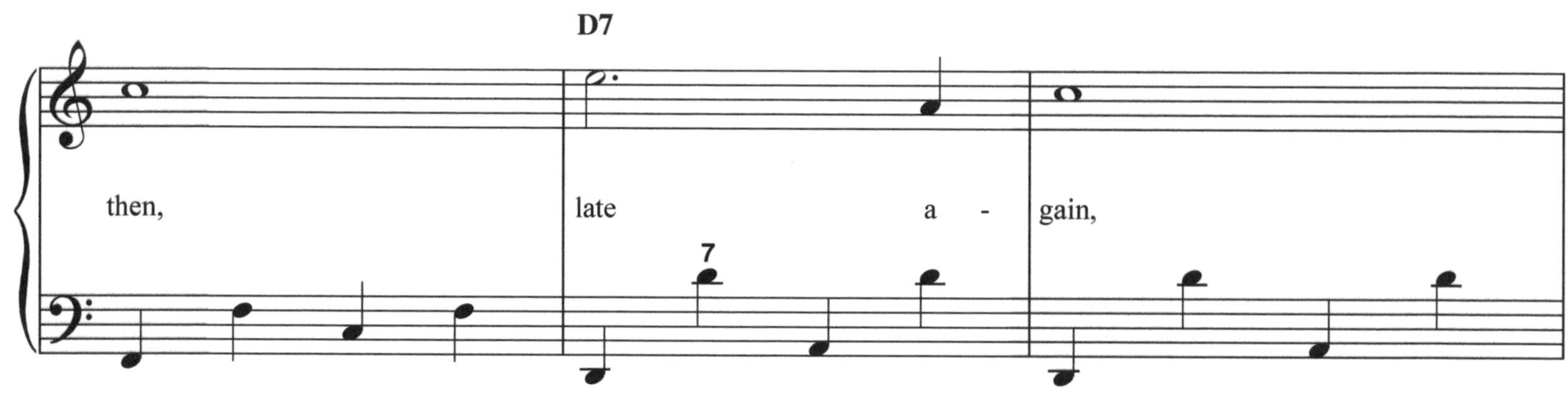
D7
then, late a - gain,
7

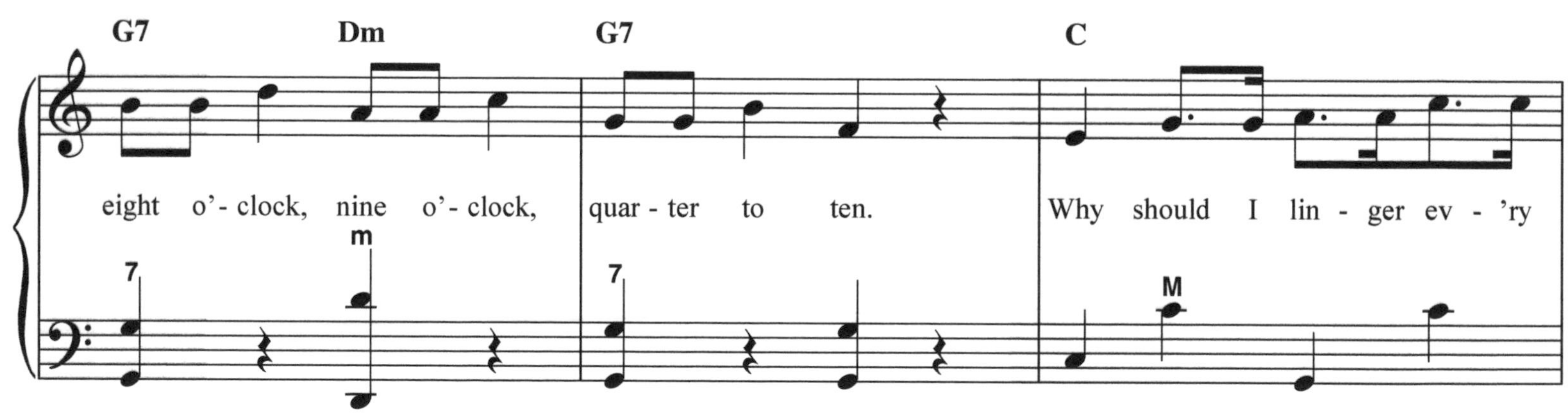
G7 Dm G7 C
eight o'- clock, nine o'- clock, quar - ter to ten. Why should I lin - ger ev - 'ry
7 m 7 M

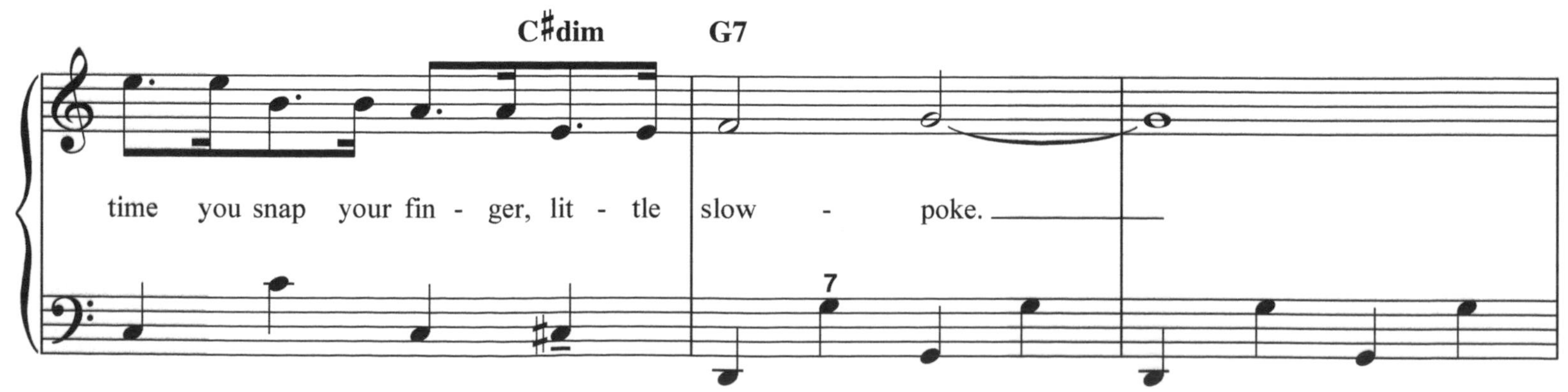
C♯dim G7
time you snap your fin - ger, lit - tle slow - poke.
7

C
Why can't you has - ten when you see the time's a - wast - in', you're a slow - poke,
M

C7
F
Fm
dear. Why should I keep try - in' to change you,
M
m

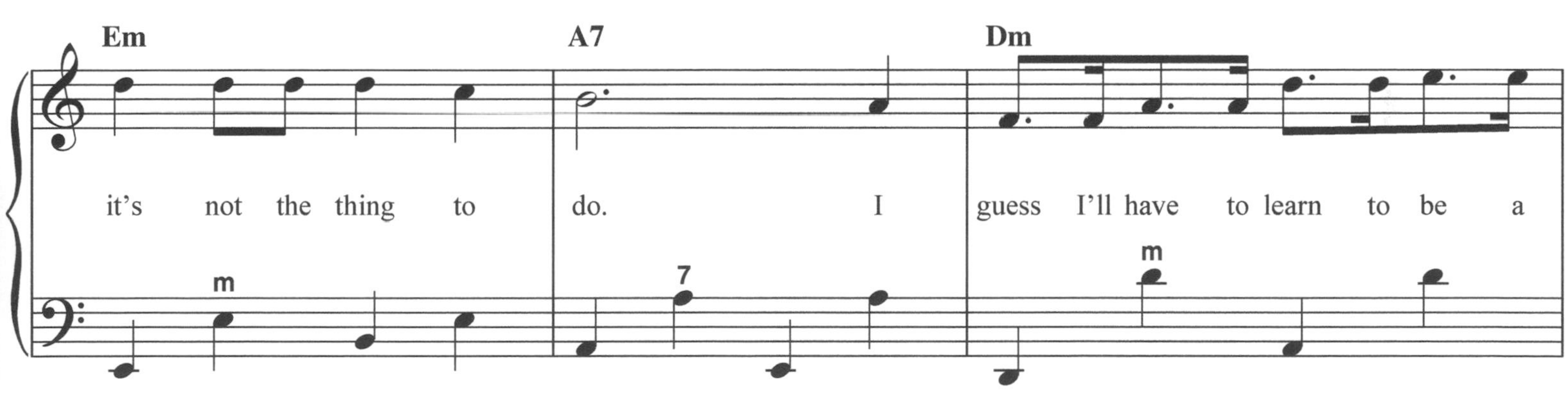
Em
A7
Dm
it's not the thing to do. I guess I'll have to learn to be a
m
7
m

G7
C
slow - poke too!
7
M

SANTA LUCIA

By TEODORO COTTRAU

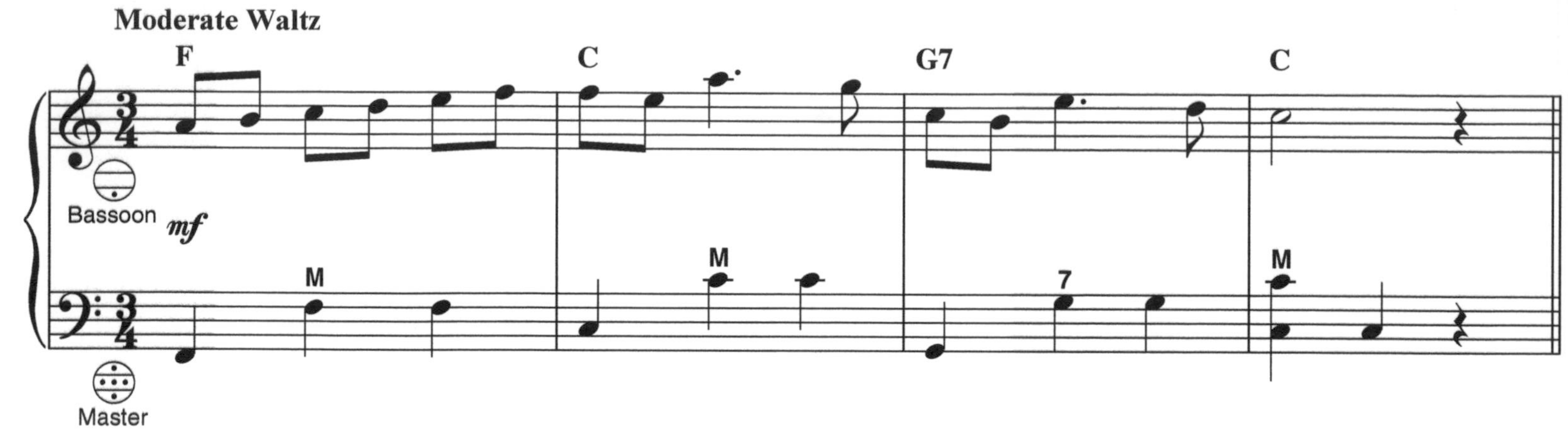

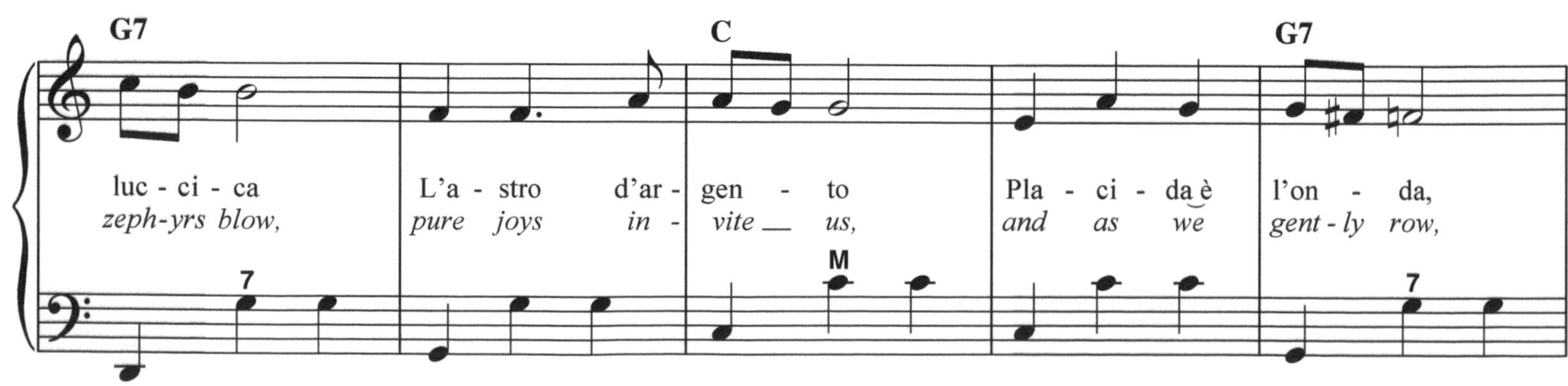

C
Dm/F
Pro - spe - ro è il ven - tò; Ve - ni - te al - l'a - gi - le Bar - chet - ta
all things de - light us. Hark, how the sail - or's cry joy - ous - ly
M
m

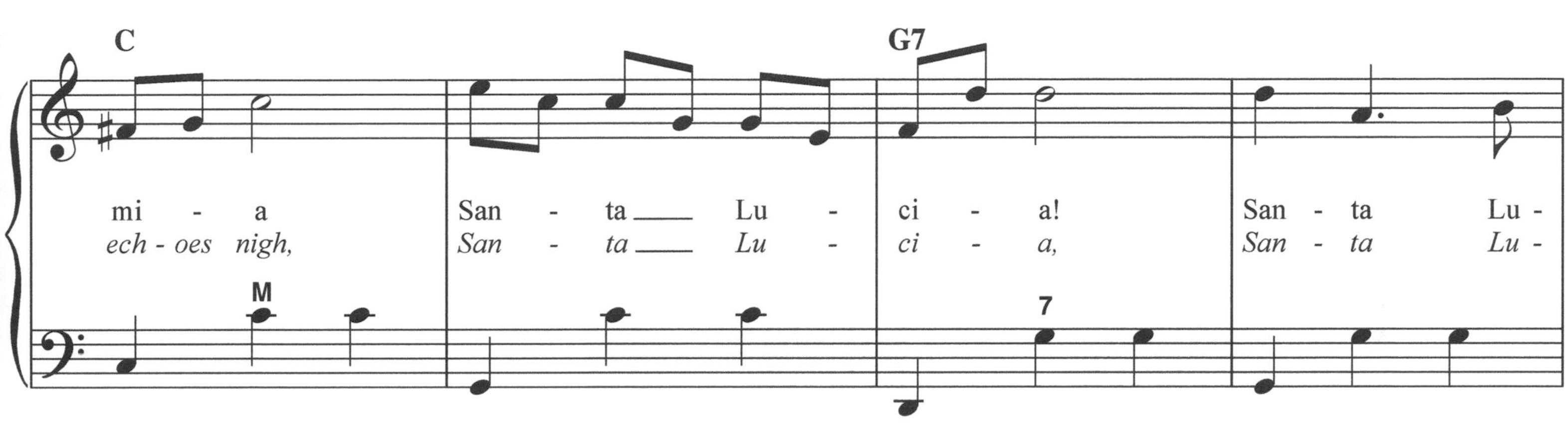

C
G7
mi - a San - ta Lu - ci - a! San - ta Lu -
ech - oes nigh, San - ta Lu - ci - a, San - ta Lu -
M
7

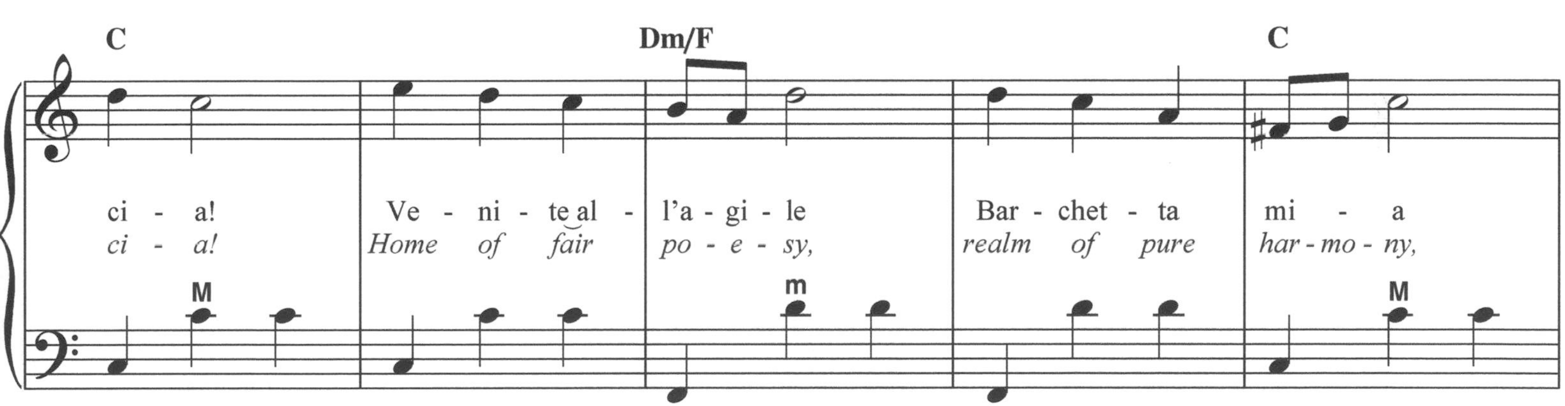

C
Dm/F
C
ci - a! Ve - ni - te al - l'a - gi - le Bar - chet - ta mi - a
ci - a! Home of fair po - e - sy, realm of pure har - mo - ny,
M
m
M

G7
C
San - ta Lu - ci - a! San - ta Lu - ci - a!
San - ta Lu - ci - a! San - ta Lu - ci - a!
7
M

SENTIMENTAL JOURNEY

Words and Music by BUD GREEN,
LES BROWN and BEN HOMER

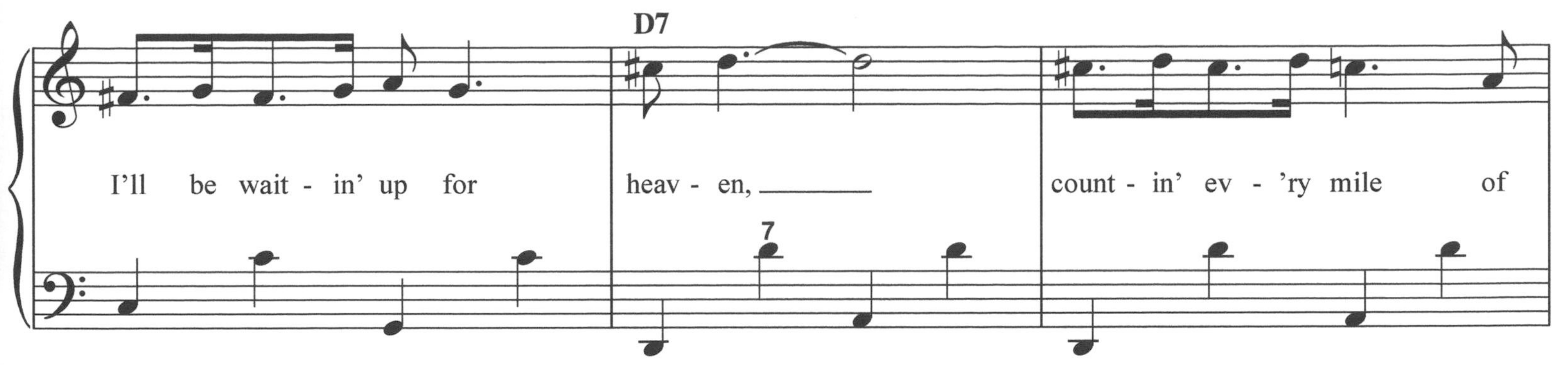
D7
I'll be wait - in' up for
heav - en,
count - in' ev - 'ry mile of
7

G7
C
rail- road track that
takes me back.
Nev - er thought my
heart could be so "yearn - y."
M

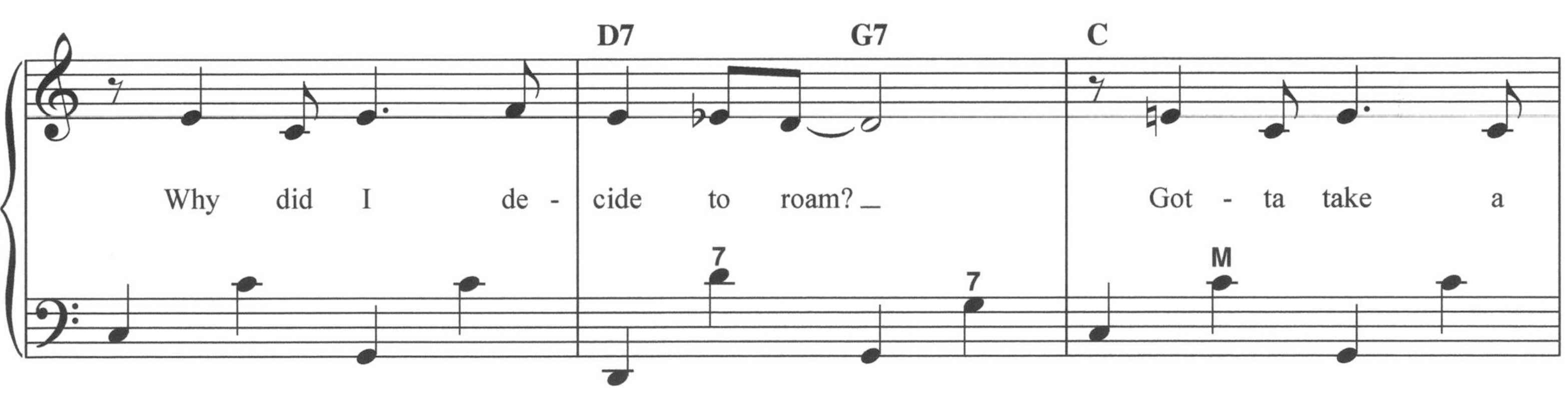
D7
G7
C
Why did I de -
cide to roam?
Got - ta take a
7
7
M

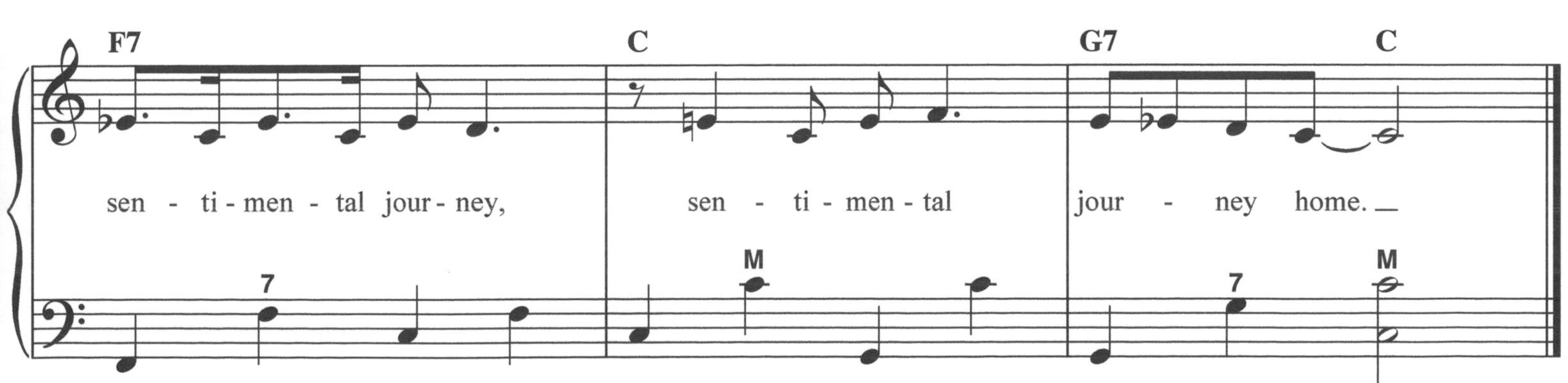
F7
C
G7
C
sen - ti - men - tal jour - ney,
sen - ti - men - tal
jour - ney home.
7
M
7
M

SOMEWHERE, MY LOVE

Lara's Theme from DOCTOR ZHIVAGO

Lyrics by PAUL FRANCIS WEBSTER
Music by MAURICE JARRE

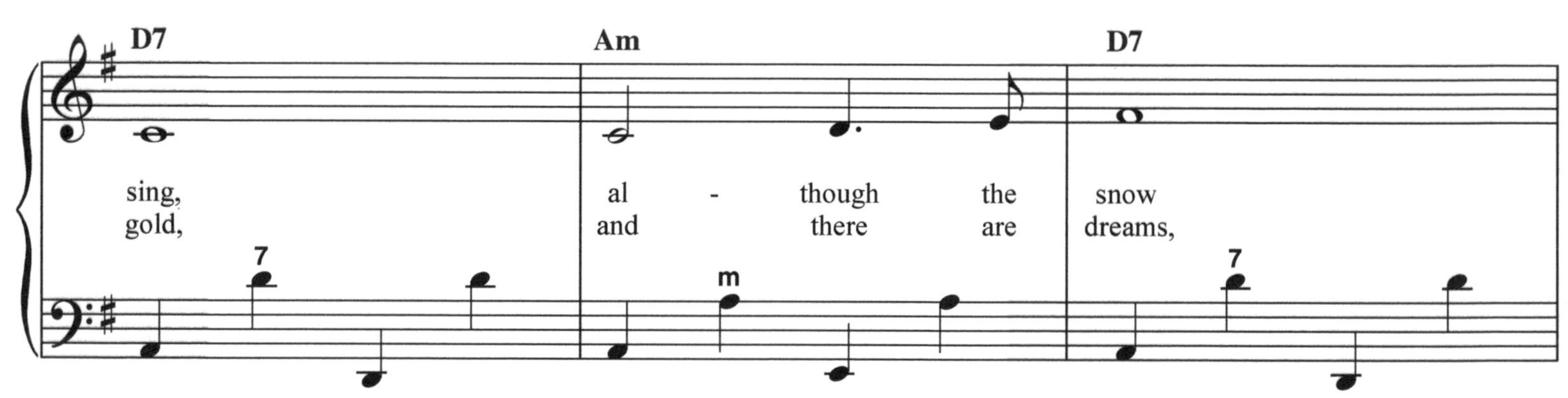

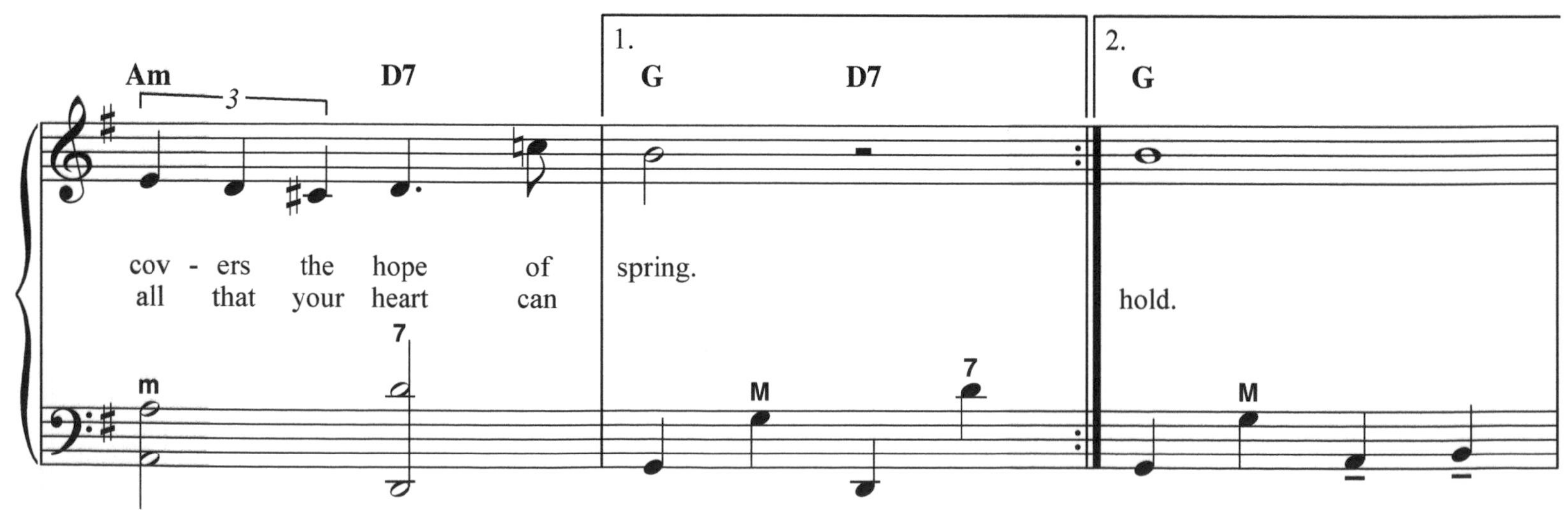

C
3
Some - day we'll meet a - gain, my
M

G
B♭
3
love.
Some - day when - ev - er the
M
M

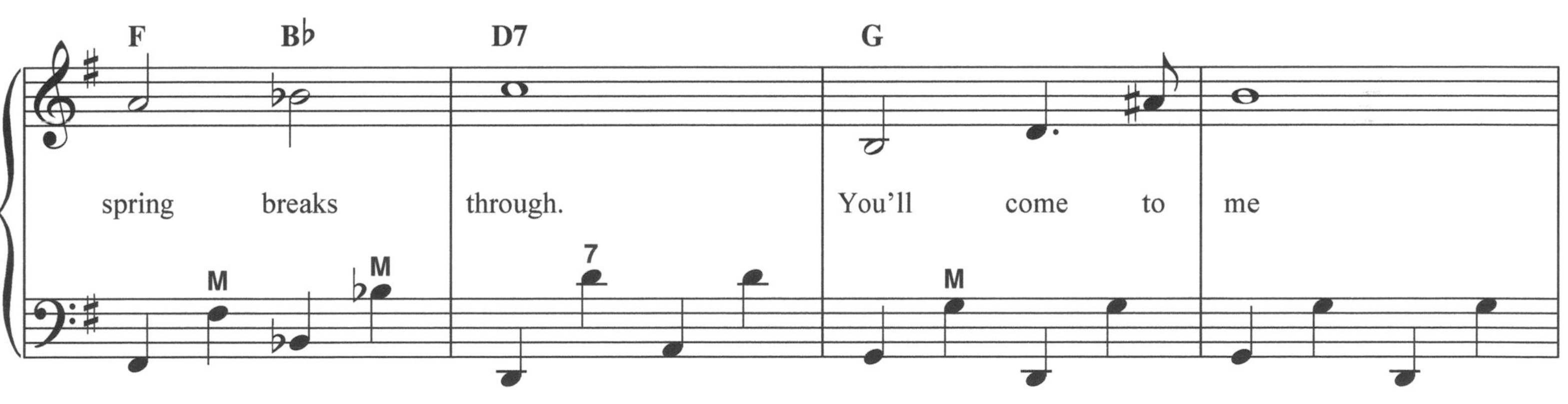
F
B♭
D7
G
spring breaks through.
You'll come to me
M
M
7
M

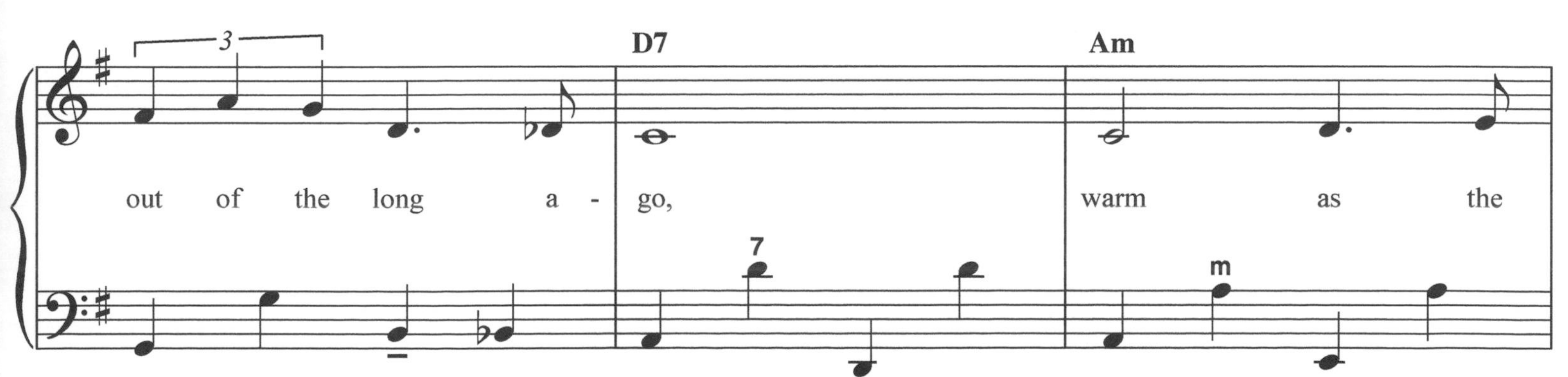
3
D7
Am
out of the long a - go,
warm as the
7
m

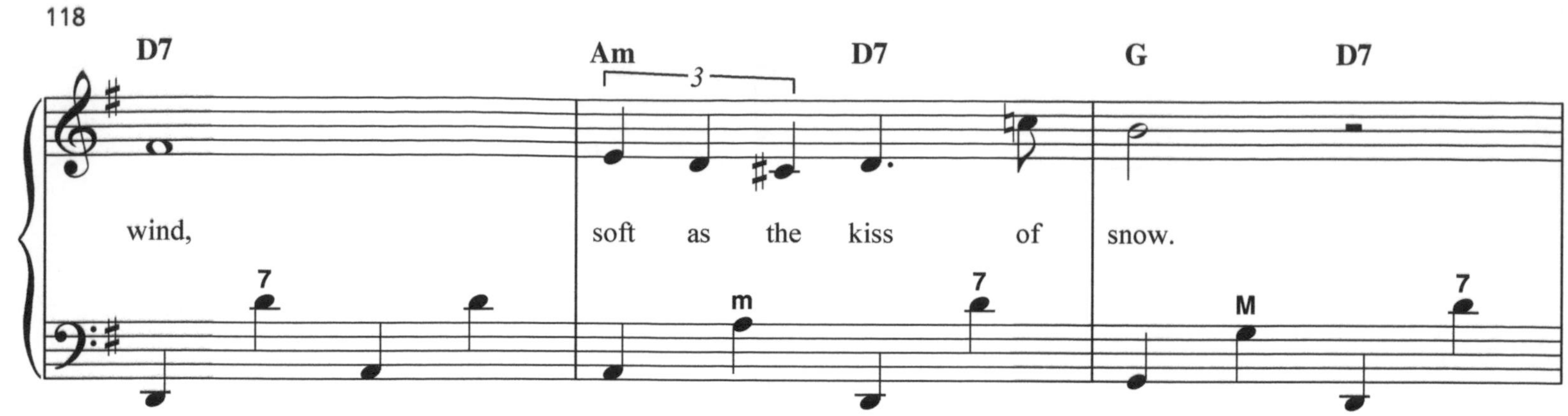
D7
Am
3
D7
G
D7
wind,
soft as the kiss of
snow.
7
7
m
7
M
7

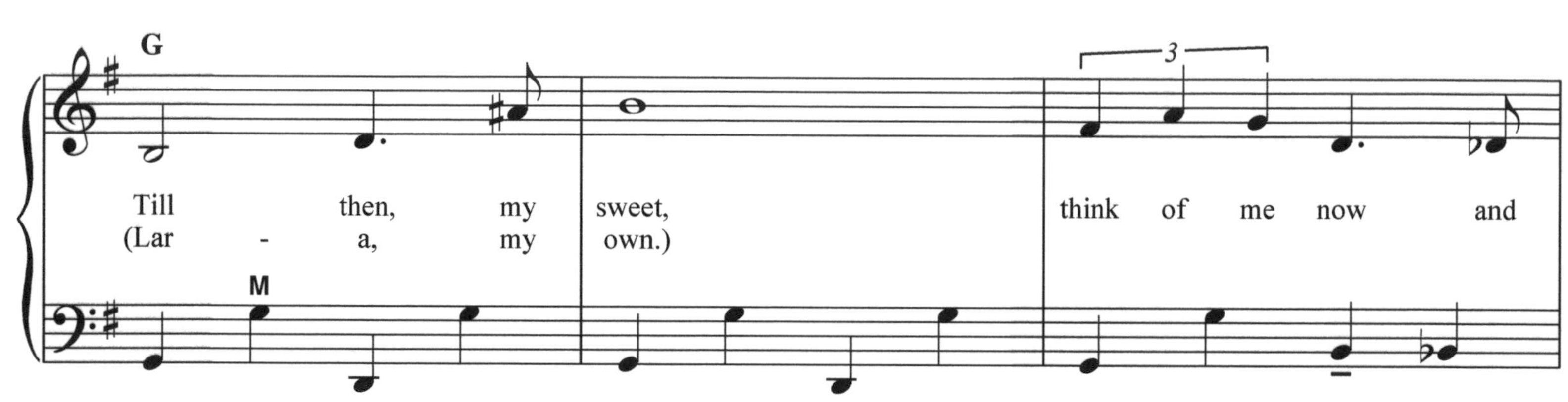
G
3
Till then, my
(Lar - a, my
sweet,
own.)
think of me now and
M

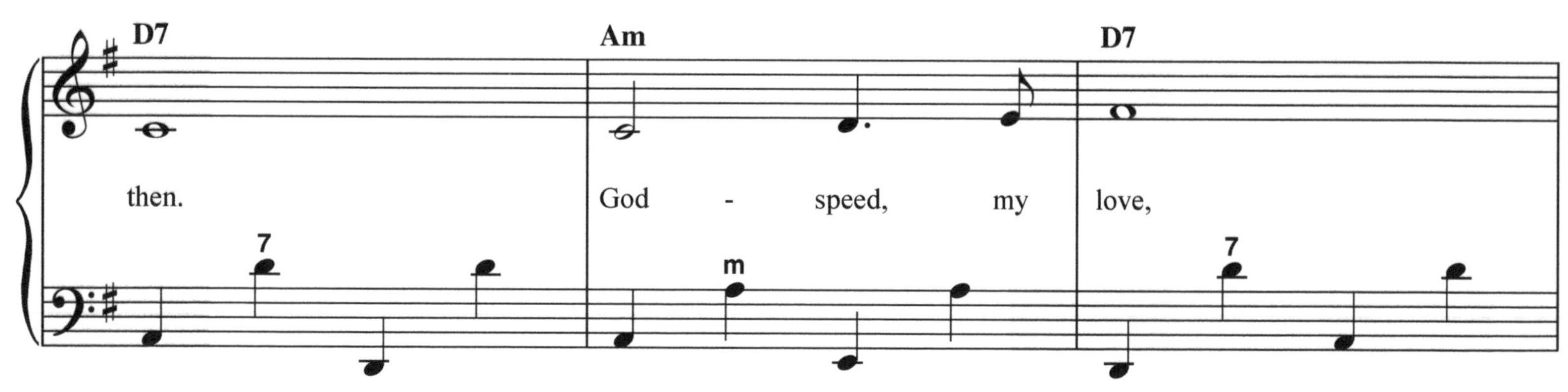
D7
Am
D7
then.
God - speed, my
love,
7
m
7

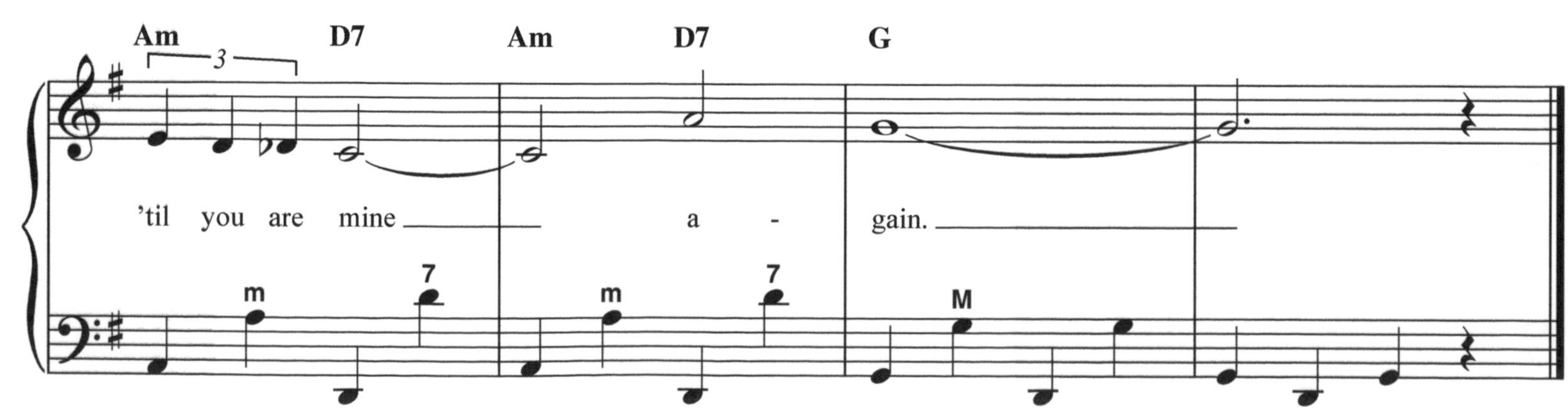
Am
3
D7
Am
D7
G
'til you are mine
a - gain.
m
7
m
7
M

SPANISH EYES

Words by CHARLES SINGLETON and EDDIE SNYDER
Music by BERT KAEMPFERT

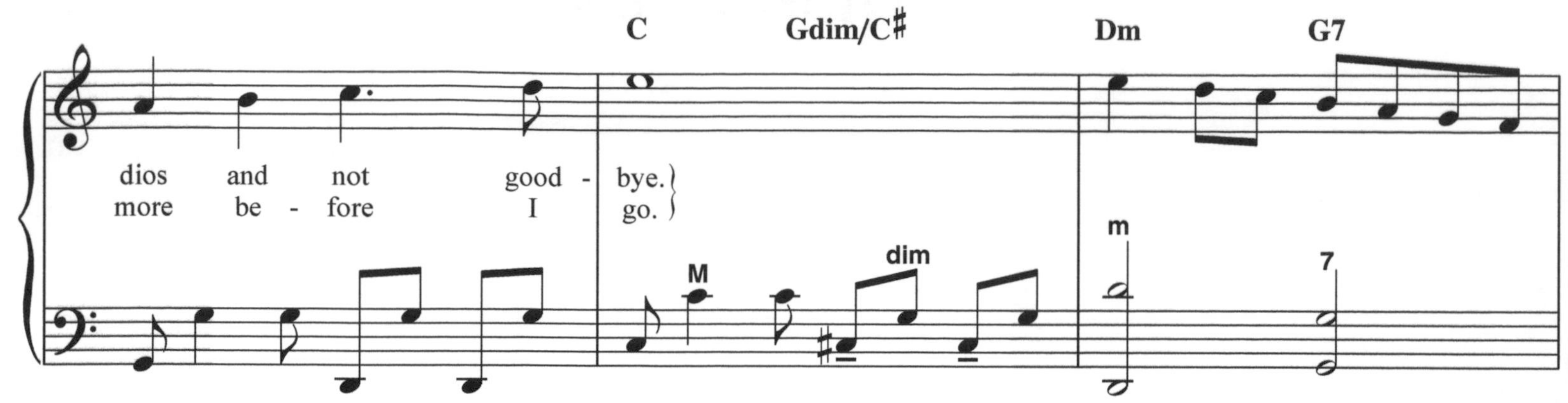
C
Gdim/C♯
Dm
G7
dios and not good - bye.
more be - fore I go.
M
dim
m
7

C
Soon I'll re - turn,
M

C7
F
bring - ing you all the love your heart can hold.
7
M

Fm
Please say Sí
m

C
A7
Dm
Sí.
Say
you and your Span - ish
M
7
m
G7
1.
C
Am
Dm
G7
eyes will wait for
me.
M
m
m
7
7
2.
C
D♭
me.
M
C
G7
C
G7
C
M
7
M

SPEAK SOFTLY, LOVE

(Love Theme)

from the Paramount Picture THE GODFATHER

Words by LARRY KUSIK
Music by NINO ROTA

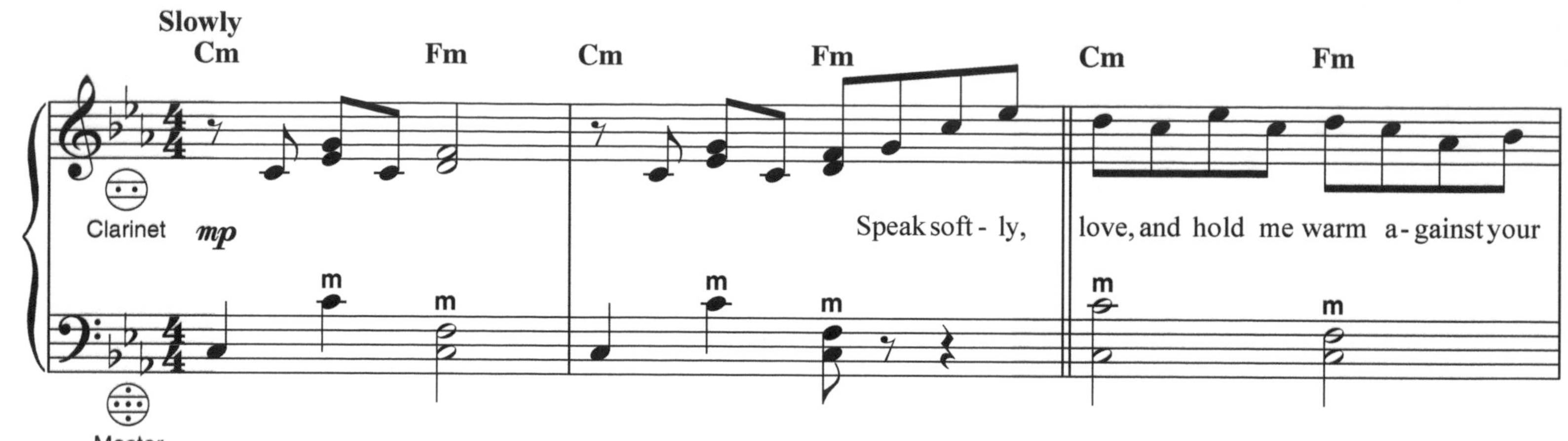

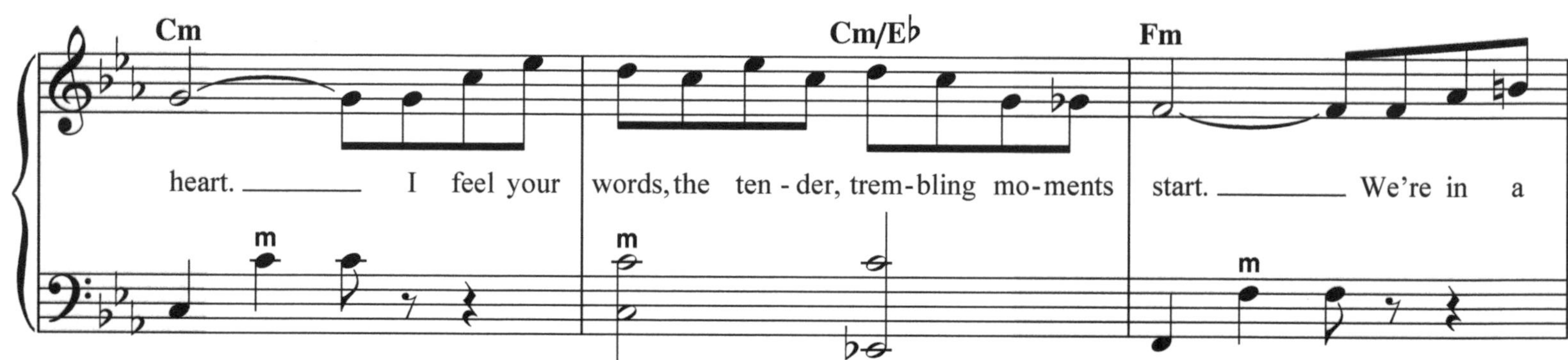

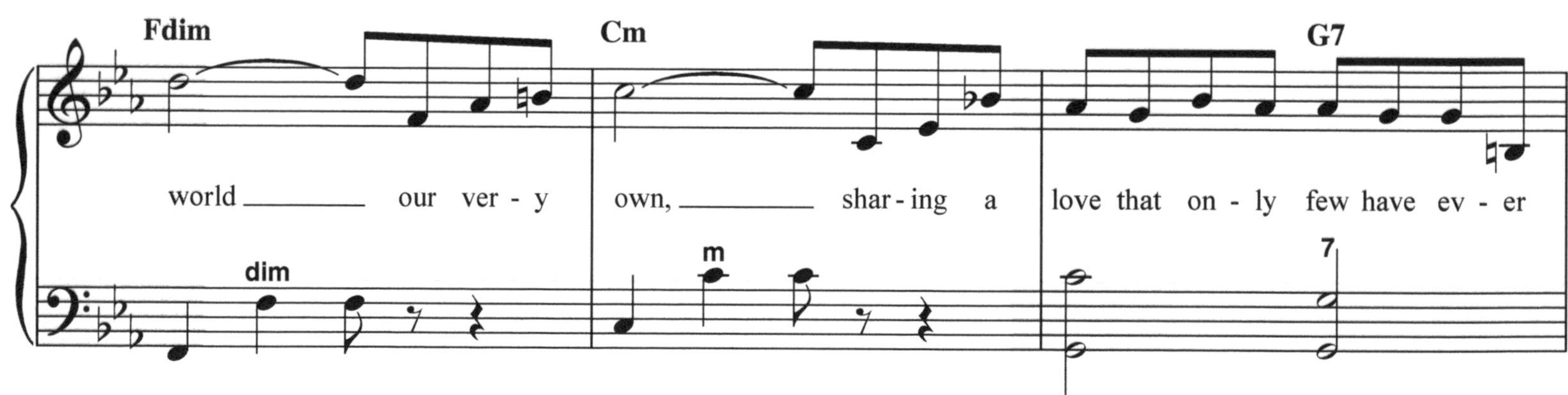

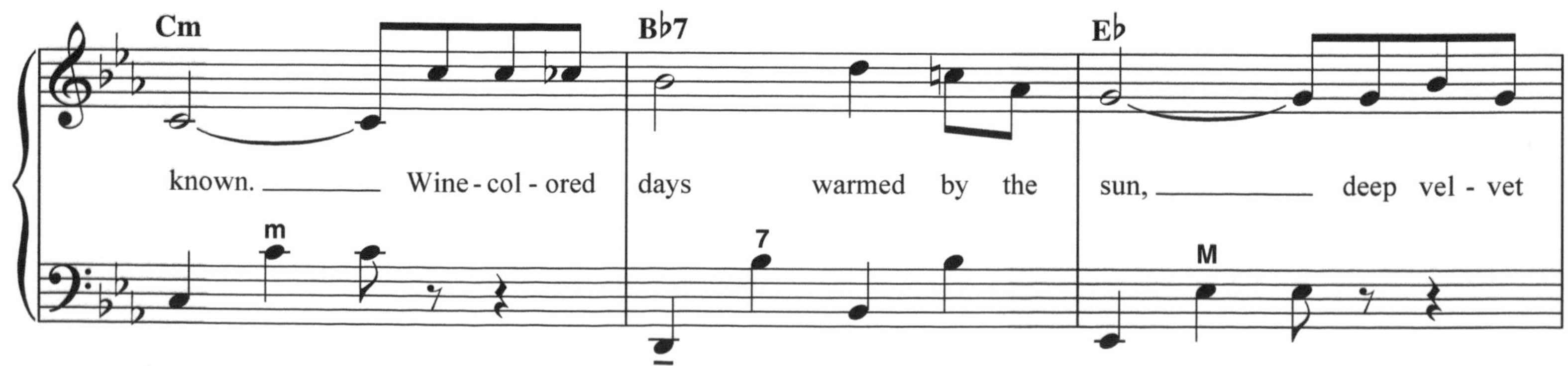

D♭
G
Cm
Fm
nights when we are one. Speak soft - ly, love, so no one hears us but the
M
M
m
m

Cm
Cm/E♭
Fm
sky. The vows of love we make will live un - til we die. My life is
m
m

Fdim
Cm
G7
yours and all be - cause you came in - to my world with love so soft - ly,
dim
m
7

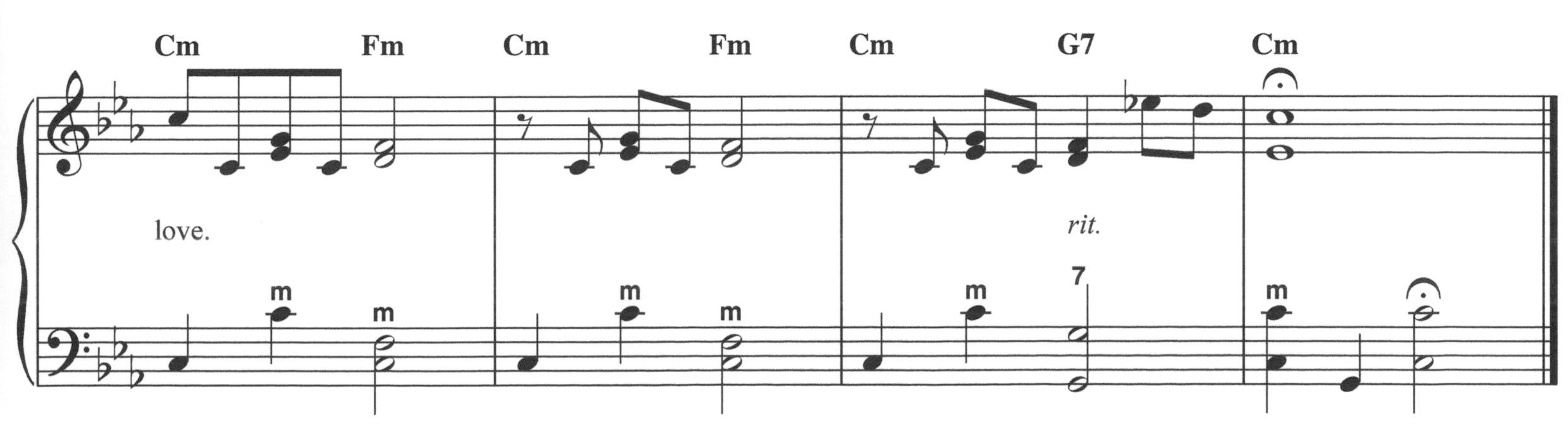

Cm
Fm
Cm
Fm
Cm
G7
Cm
love.
rit.
m
m
m
m
m
7
m

SWAY
(Quien será)

English Words by NORMAN GIMBEL
Spanish Words and Music by PABLO BELTRÁN RUIZ
and LUIS DEMETRIO TRACONIS MOLINA

E♭7
D7
E♭7
D7
When we dance you have a way with me, stay with me,
Yo no sé si vol - ve - ré a que - rer Yo no sé
7
7

Gm
F7
sway with me. Oth - er danc - ers may be on the floor,
Yo no sé. He que - ri - do vol - ver a vi - vir
m
7

B♭
dear, but my eyes will see on - ly you. On - ly you have that
la pa - sión y el ca - lor de o - tro a - mor de o - tro a - mor que me hi -
M

D7
Gm
E♭7
mag - ic tech - nique, when we sway I grow weak.
cie - ra sen - tir que me hi - cie - ra fe - liz co - mo a - yer lo
7
m
7

D7
I can hear the sound of vi - o - lins, long be - fore
fui quien se - rá la que me quie - ra a mí Quien se - rá
7

Gm
Eb7
D7
it be - gins. Make me thrill as on - ly you know how,
Quien se - rá. Quien se - rá la que me dé su a - mor
m
7

Eb7
D7
1.
Gm
sway me smooth, sway me now. When ma - rim - ba rhy - thms
Quien se - rá Quien se - rá. Quien se - rá la que me
7
m

2.
Gm
D7
Gm
sway me now. Sway me smooth, sway me now.
Quien se - rá. Quien se - rá, quien se - rá.
m
7

SWEET GEORGIA BROWN

Words and Music by BEN BERNIE,
MACEO PINKARD and KENNETH CASEY

D7
They all sigh and wan - na die for Sweet Geor - gia Brown.
7

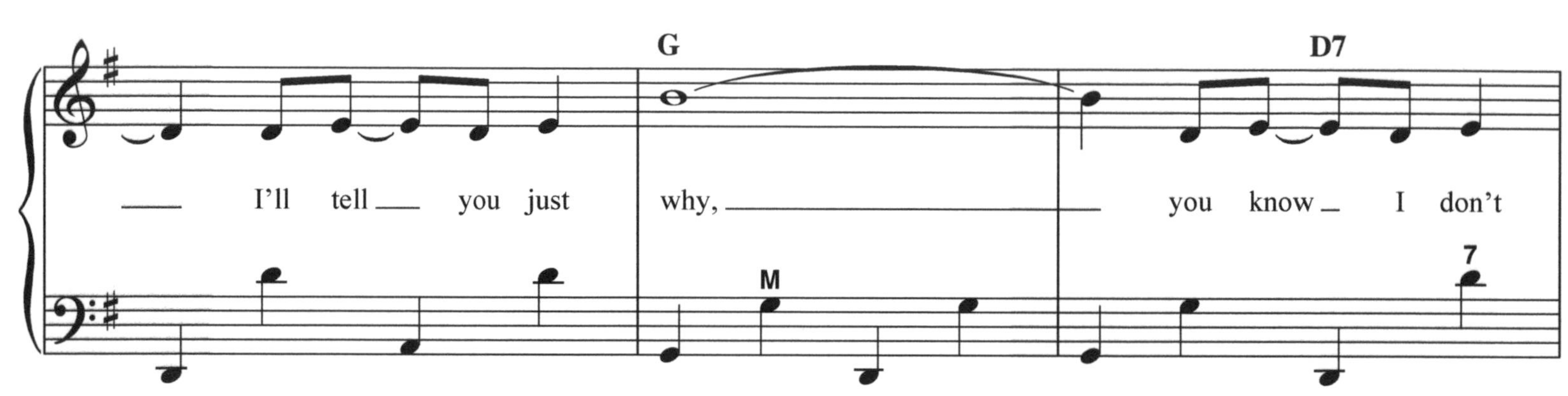
G
D7
I'll tell you just why, you know I don't
M
7

G
B7
E7
lie, not much!
It's been said she
All those tips the
M
7
7

knocks 'em dead when she lands in town.
por - ter slips to Sweet Geor - gia Brown.

A7
Since she came, why it's a shame how she cool's 'em down.
They buy clothes at fash - ion shows with one dol - lar down.
7

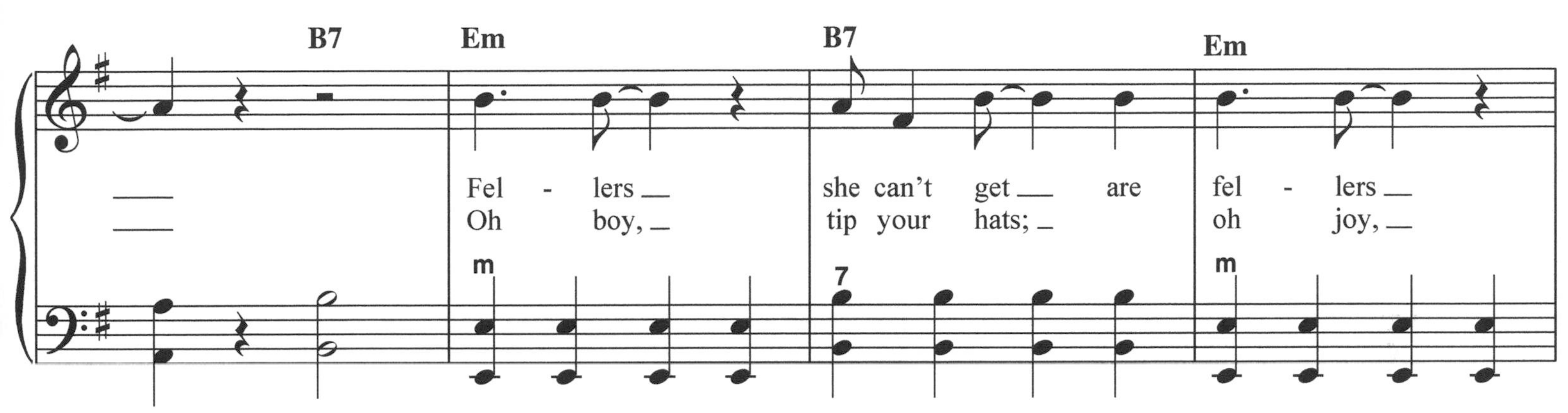
B7 Em B7 Em
Fel - lers she can't get are fel - lers
Oh boy, tip your hats; oh joy,
m 7 m

B7 G E7
she ain't met. Geor - gia claimed her, Geor - gia named her
she's the "cat's." Who's that, mis - ter? 'Tain't her sis - ter,
7 M 7

1. 2.
A7 D7 G G
Sweet Geor - gia Brown.
Sweet Geor - gia Brown.
7 7

TANGO OF ROSES

Words by MARJORIE HARPER
Music by VITTORIO MASCHERONI

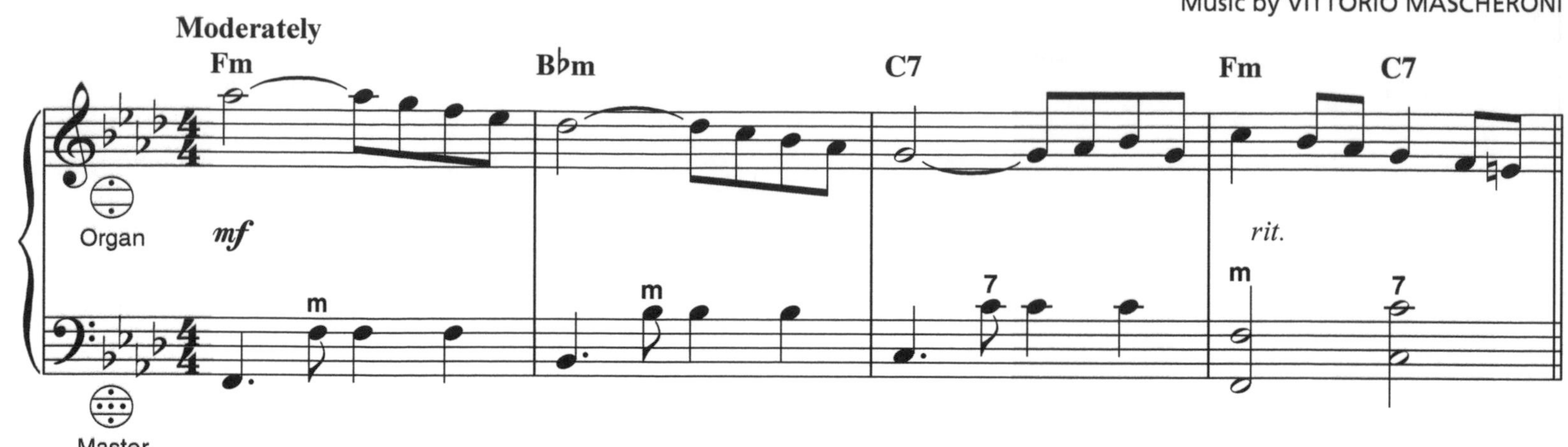

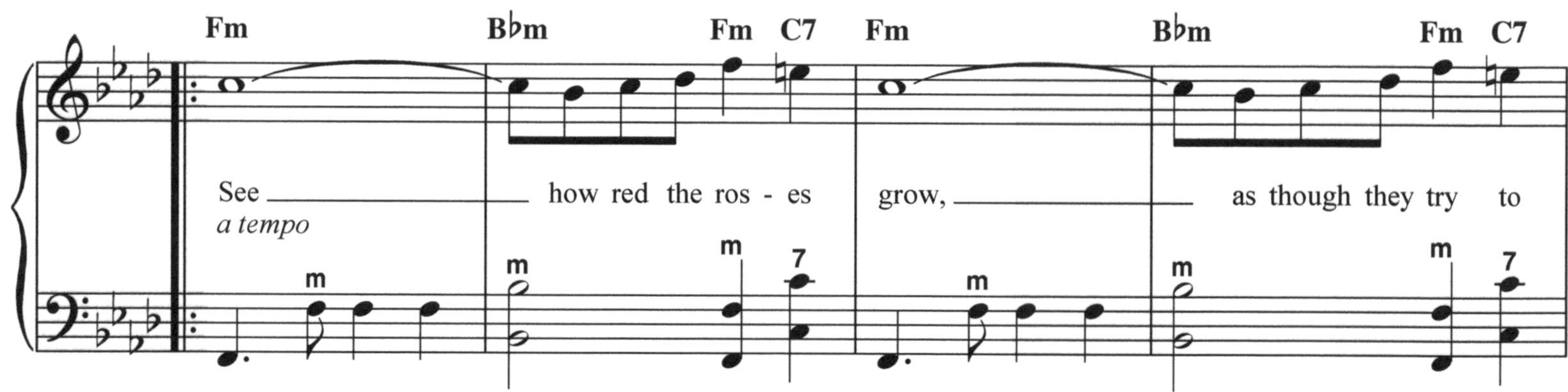

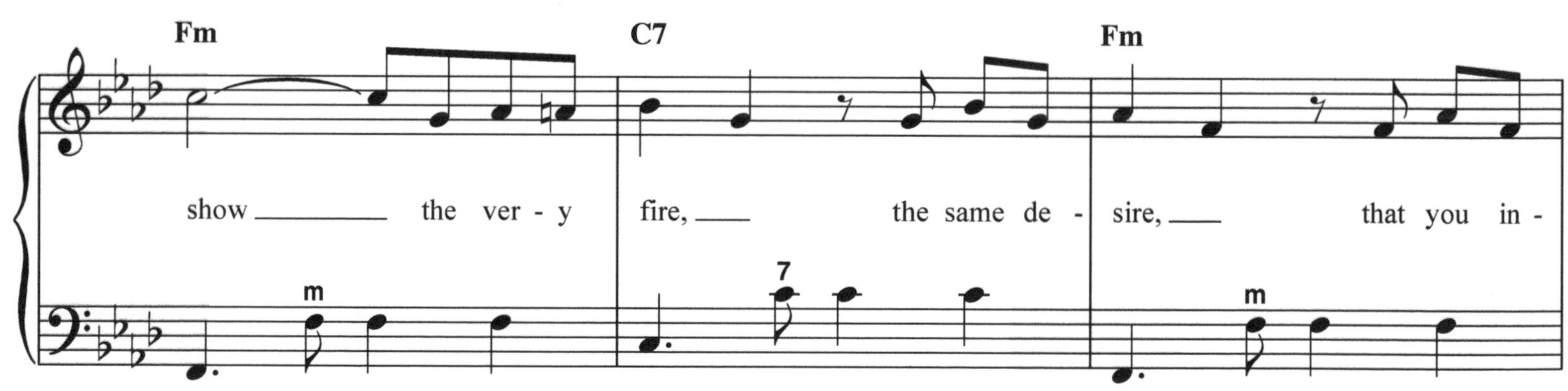

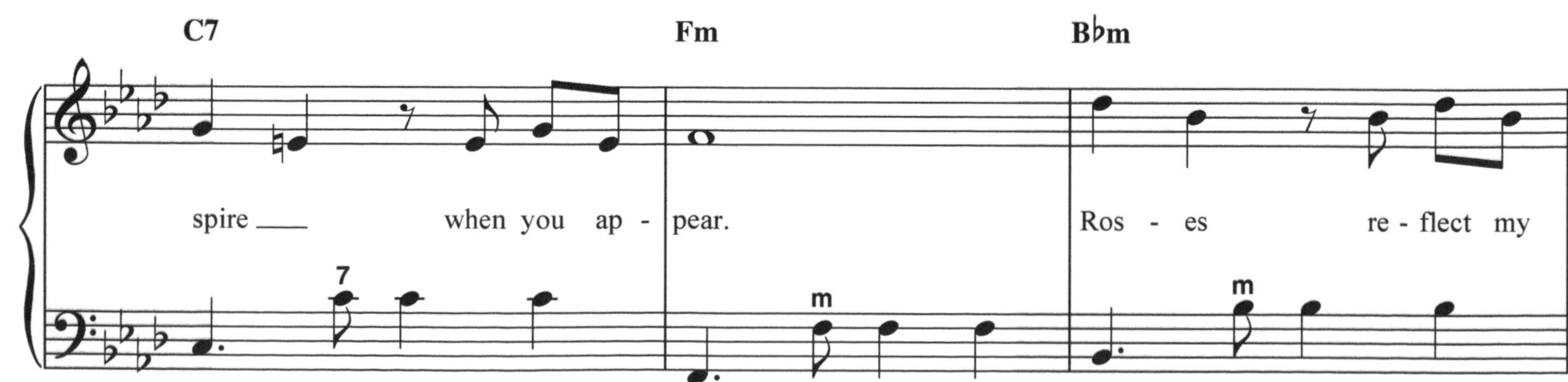

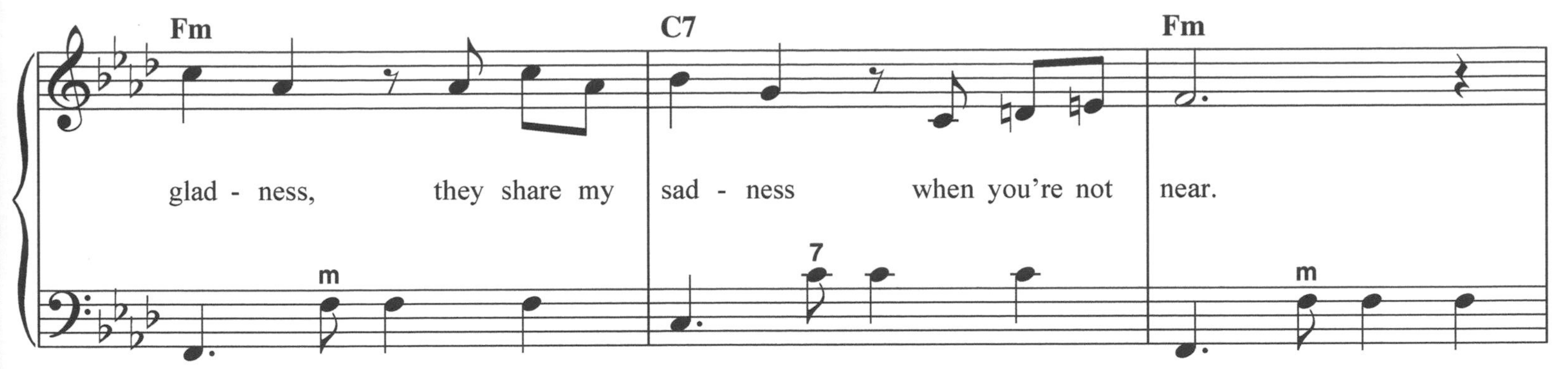
Fm
C7
Fm
glad - ness, they share my sad - ness when you're not near.
m
7
m

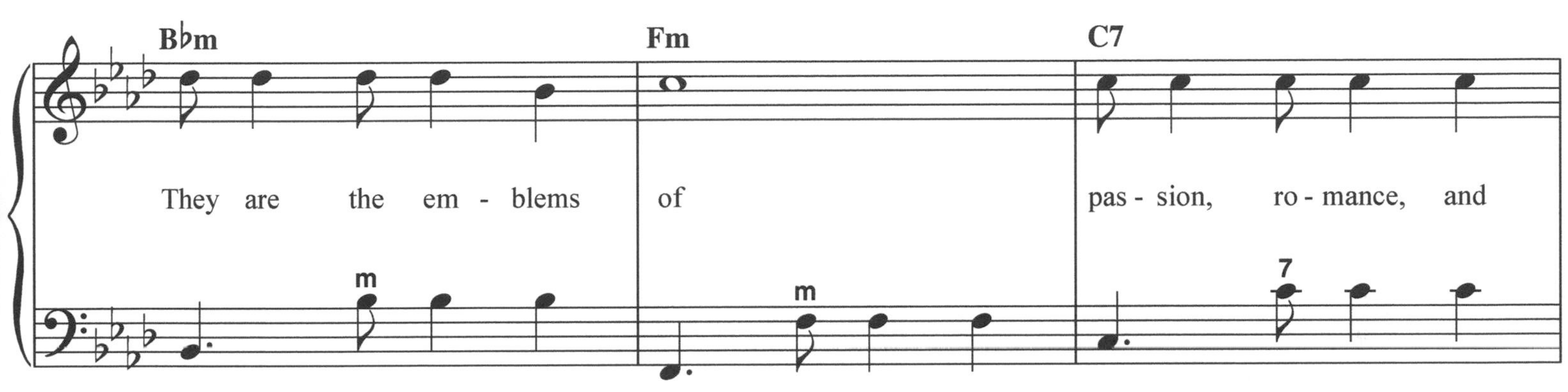
B♭m
Fm
C7
They are the em - blems of pas - sion, ro - mance, and
m
m
7

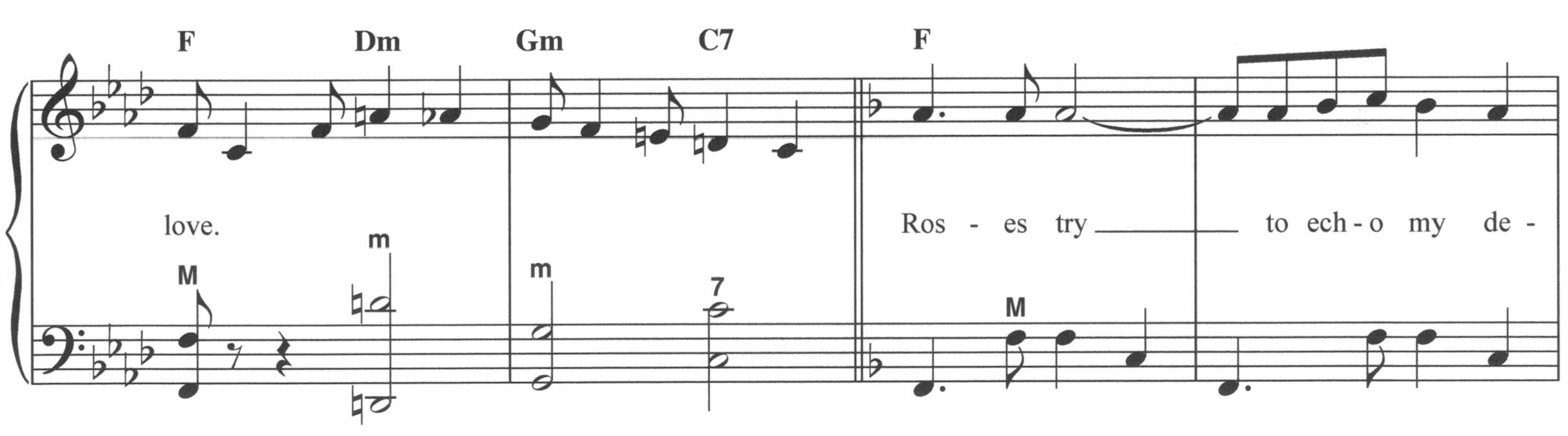
F
Dm
Gm
C7
F
love. Ros - es try to ech - o my de -
M
m
m
7
M

C7
vo - tion. Ros - es seem to mir - ror my e -
7

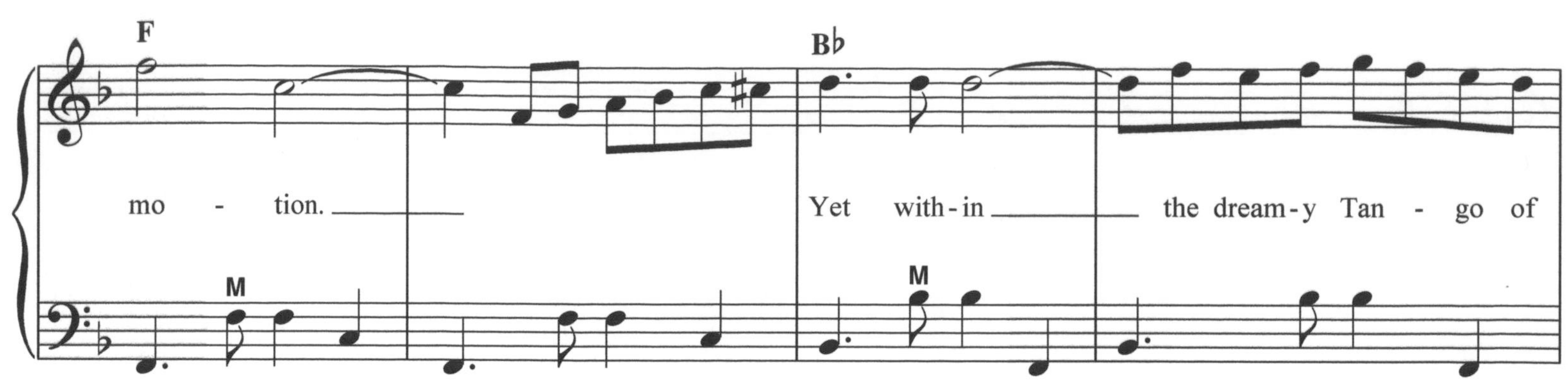
F
Bb
M
M
mo - tion.
Yet with-in
the dream-y Tan - go of

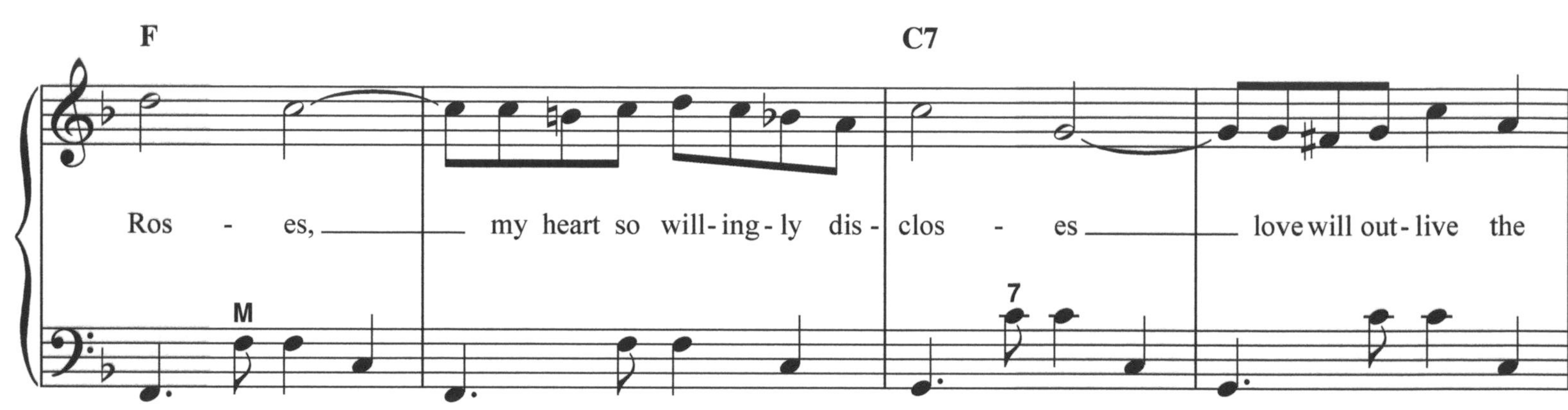
F
C7
M
7
Ros - es,
my heart so will-ing-ly dis-
clos - es
love will out-live the

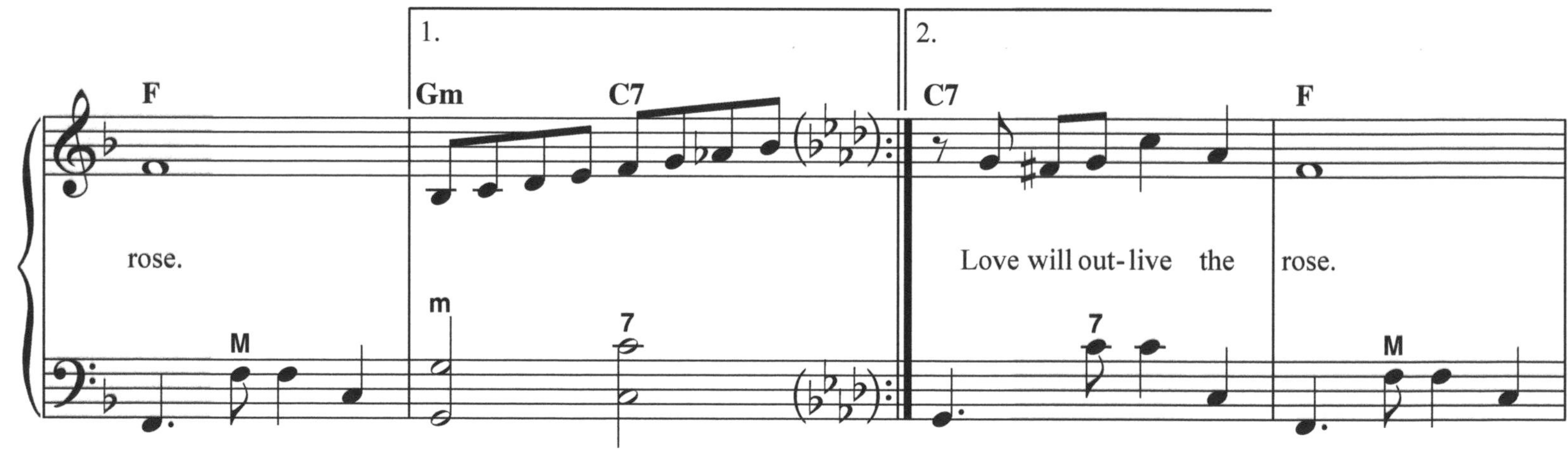
1.
2.
F
Gm
C7
C7
F
M
m
7
7
M
rose.
Love will out-live the
rose.

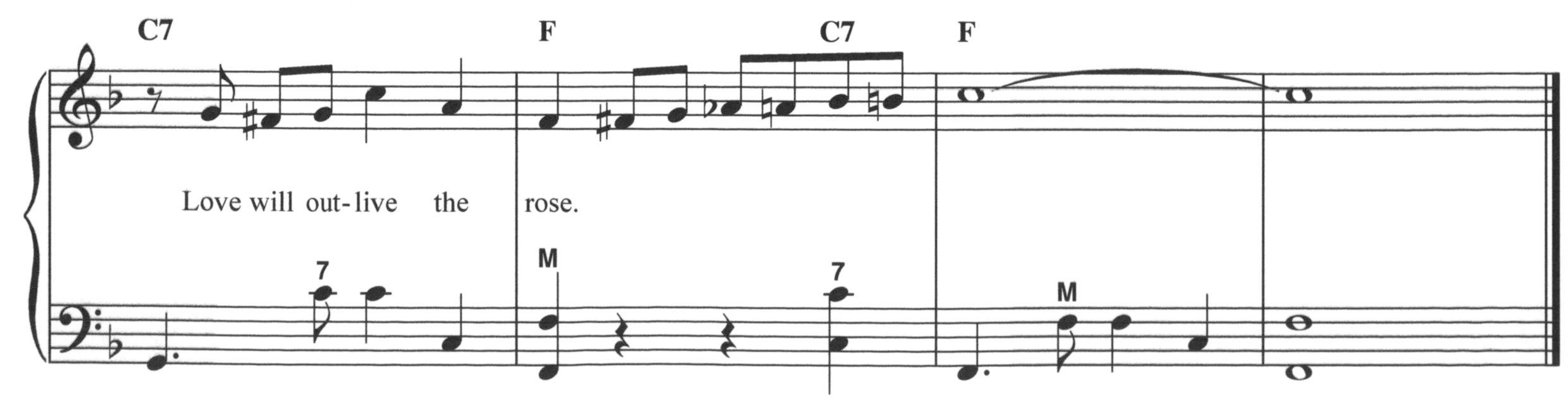
C7
F
C7
F
7
M
7
M
Love will out-live the
rose.

THAT'S AMORÉ

(That's Love)

from the Paramount Picture THE CADDY

Words by JACK BROOKS
Music by HARRY WARREN

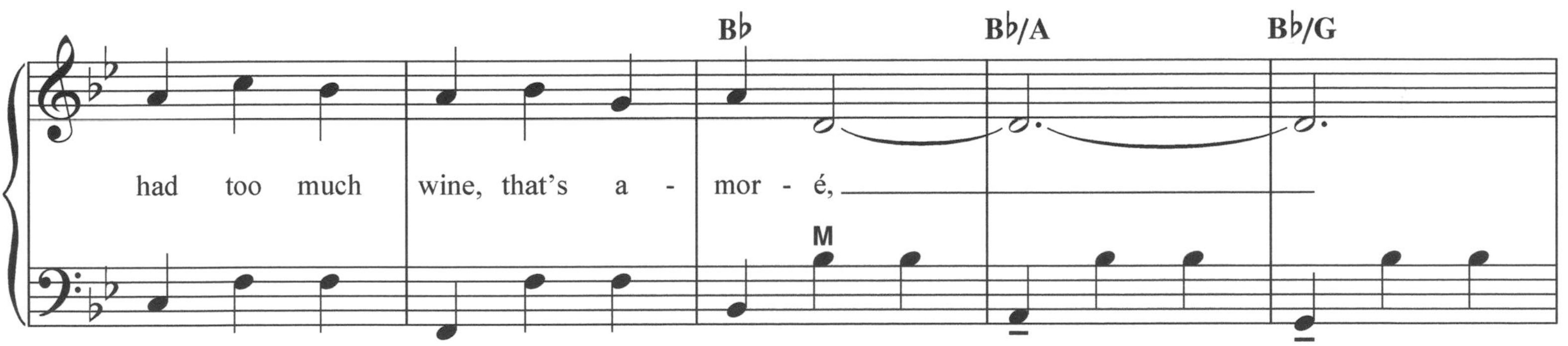

F7/C
F7
7
bel - la." ___
Hearts will
play, tip - py - tip - py
tay, tip - py - tip - py

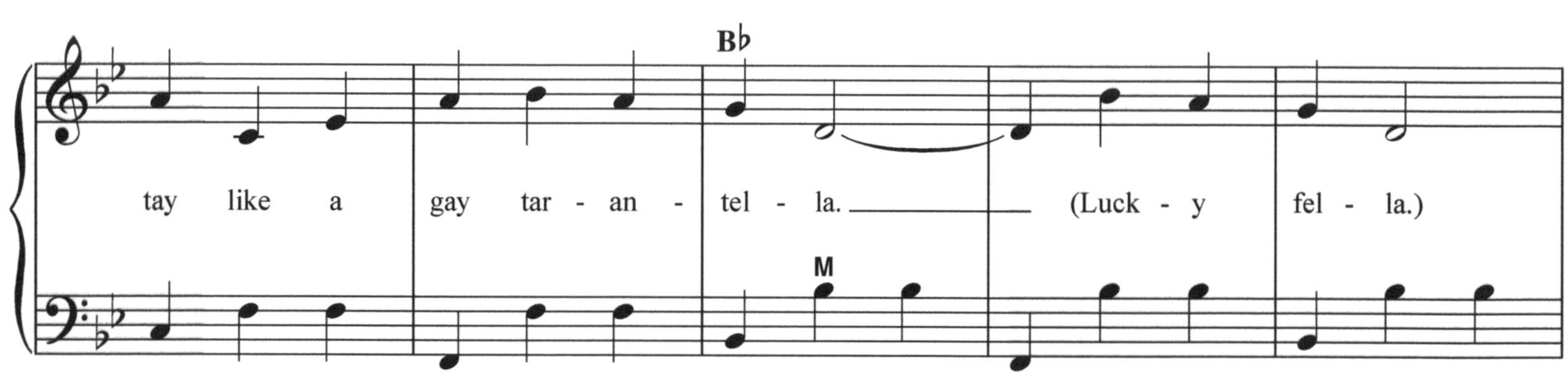
B♭
M
tay like a
gay tar - an -
tel - la. ___
(Luck - y
fel - la.)

B♭/D
D♭dim
F7
7
When the
stars make you
drool just like
pas - ta fa -
zool, that's a -
mor - é. ___

When you
dance down the
street with a
cloud at your

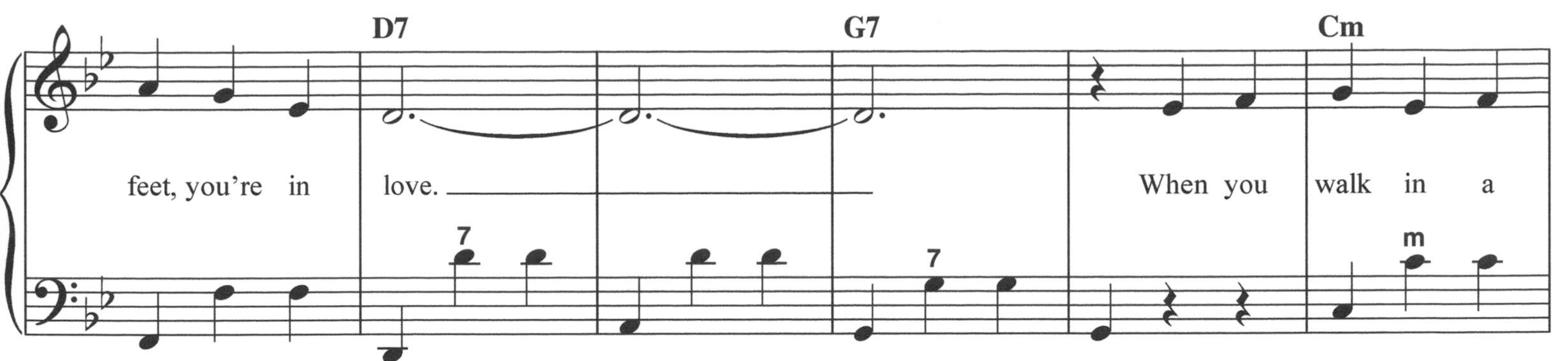
D7
G7
Cm
feet, you're in love.
When you walk in a
7
7
m

B♭
B♭/A
dream but you know you're not dream - ing, Sig - nor - é,
M

B♭/G
B♭/F
F7
scuz - za me, but you see, back in old Na - po -
7

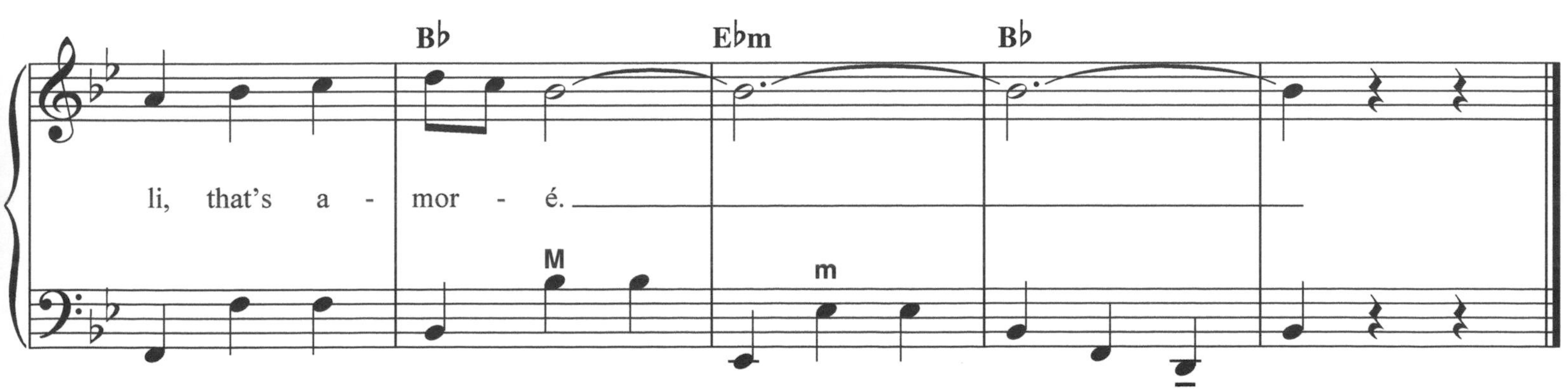
B♭
E♭m
B♭
li, that's a - mor - é.
M
m

TARANTELLA

Traditional

2.

Dm

m

F

M

C7

7

F

M

D7

7

1.

2.

Gm

m

C7

7

F

M

F

M

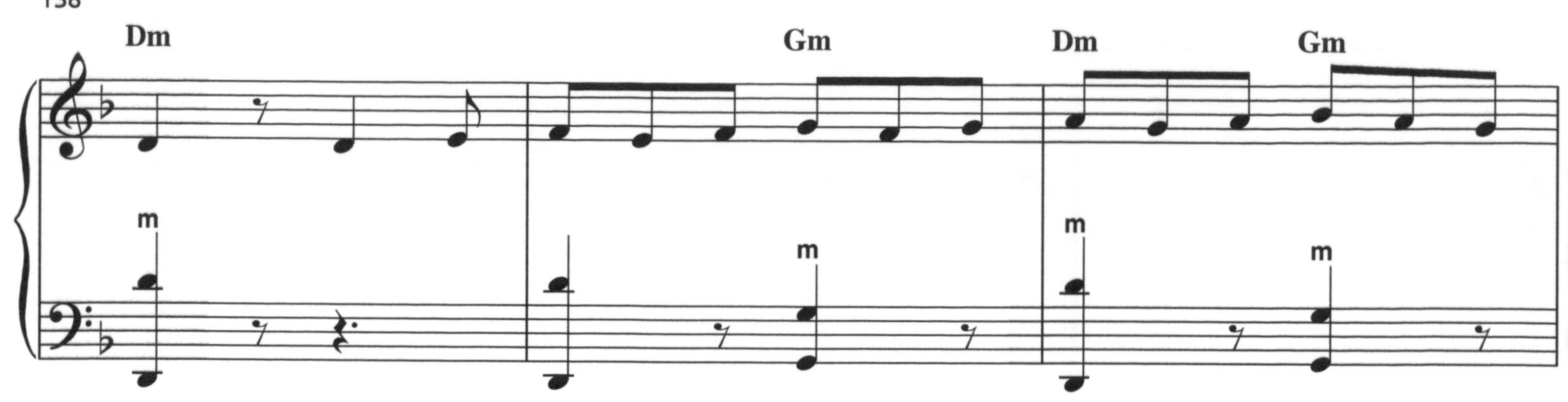
Dm
Gm
Dm
Gm
m
m
m
m

1.
2.
Dm
A7
Dm
Dm
m
7
m
m

Dm
Gm
m
m

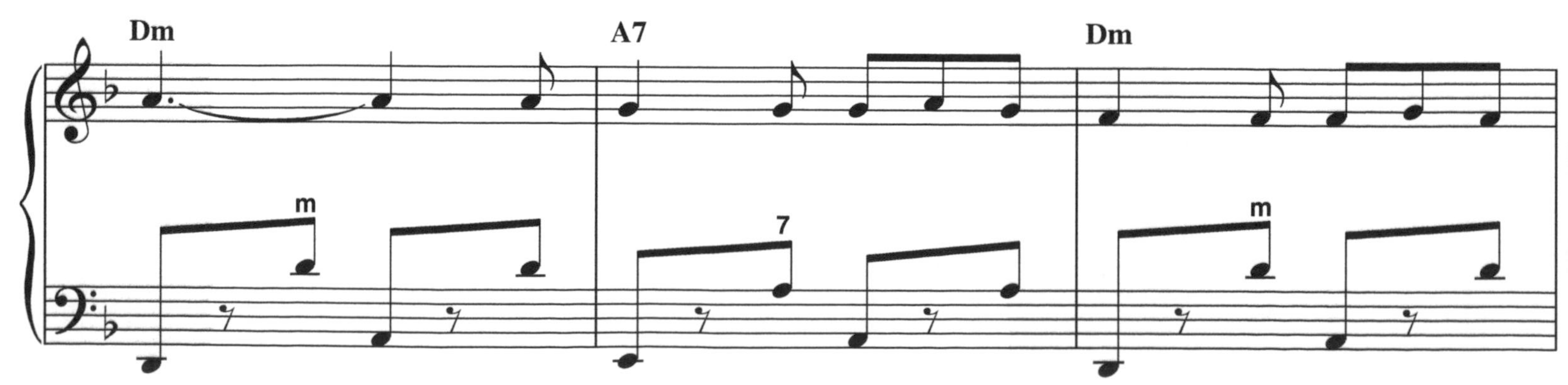
Dm
A7
Dm
m
7
m

A7
To Coda
1.
Dm
2.
Dm
C7
F
7
m
m
M
C7
F
7
M
C7
7
1.
F
C7
2.
F
D.S. al Coda
CODA
Dm
M
M
m

THE THIRD MAN THEME

from THE THIRD MAN

By ANTON KARAS

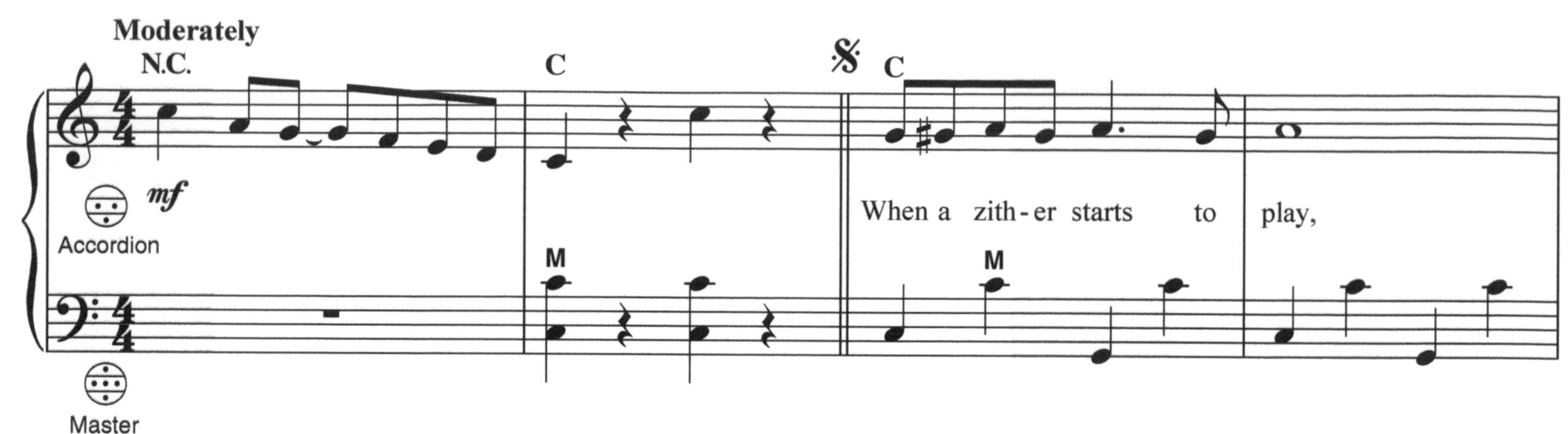

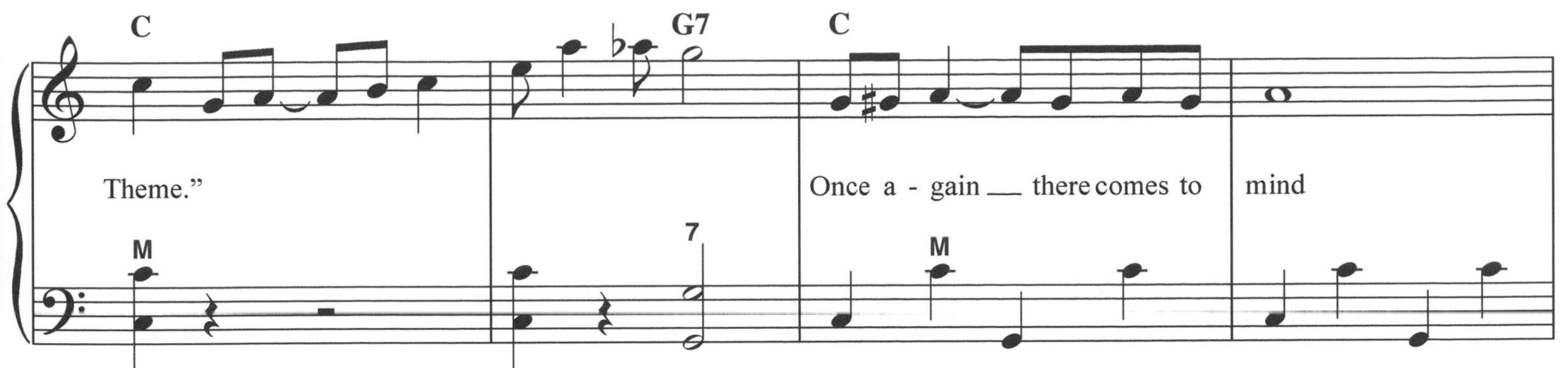
C
G7
C
Theme."
Once a - gain there comes to
mind
M
7
M

G7
some- one that you left be -
hind,
love that some - how did - n't
last
7

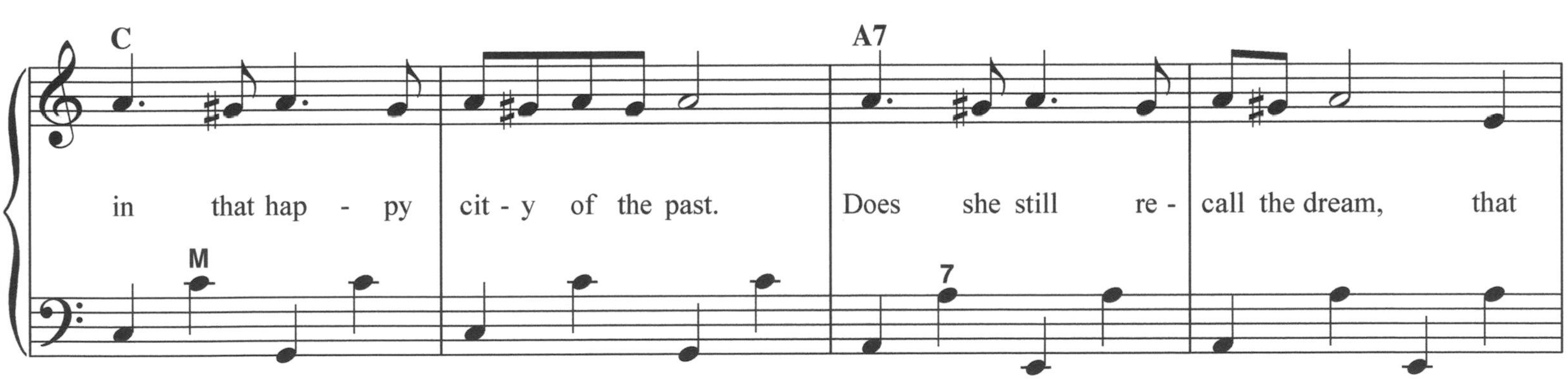
C
A7
in that hap - py
cit - y of the past.
Does she still re -
call the dream, that
M
7

Dm
G7
rap - ture so su -
preme when
first she heard the haunt- ing
"Third Man
m
7

C
G7
C
Theme"?
Car - ni - vals and car - ou - sels and
M
7
M

Fer - ris wheels and par - a - sols, the
Dan - ube nights, the danc - ing lights a -
gain will shine.

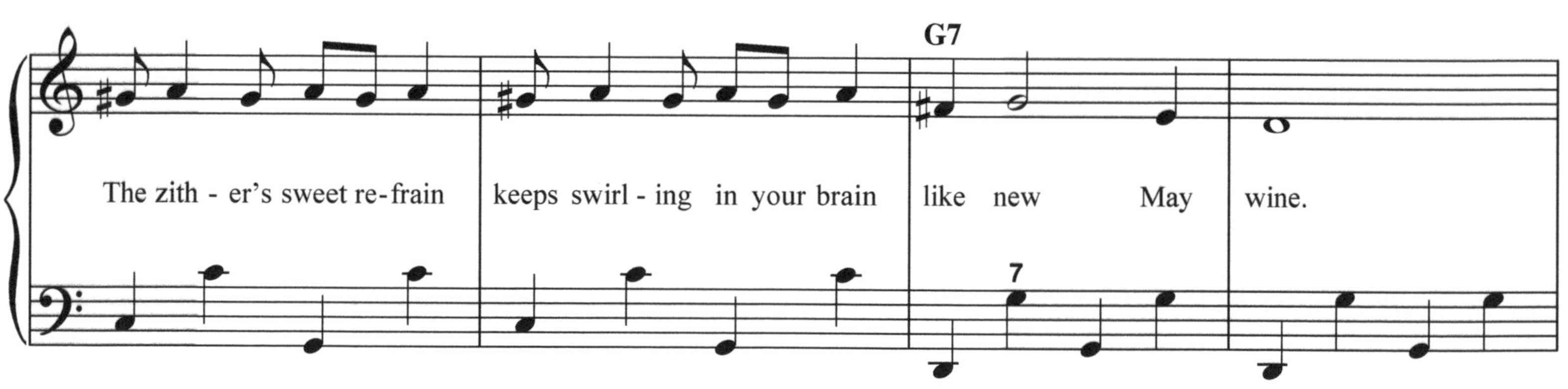
G7
The zith - er's sweet re - frain
keeps swirl - ing in your brain
like new May
wine.
7

Strauss waltz - es,
can - dle glow, and the
laugh - ter of
long a - go

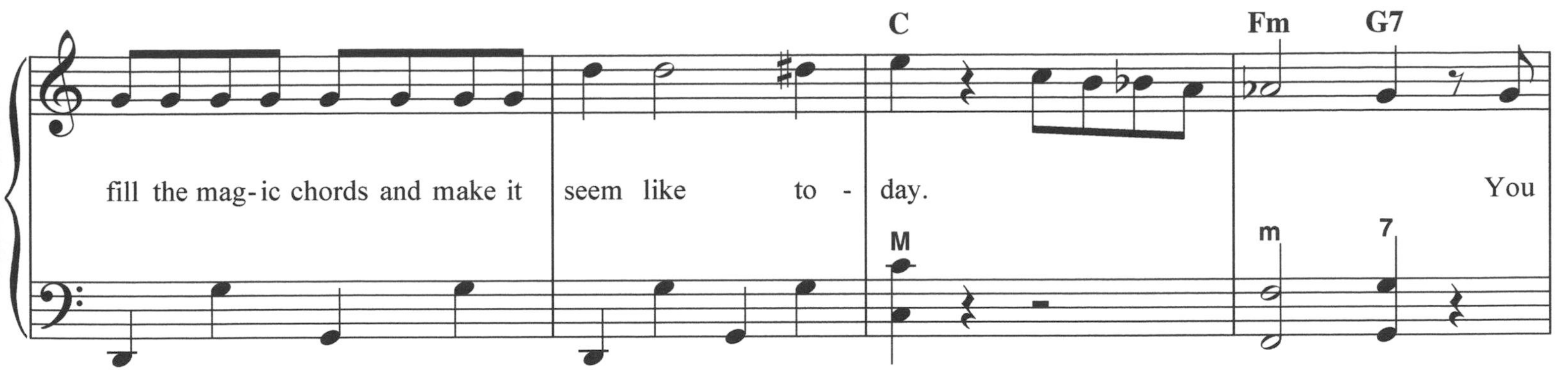
C
Fm
G7
fill the mag-ic chords and make it seem like to - day. You
M
m
7

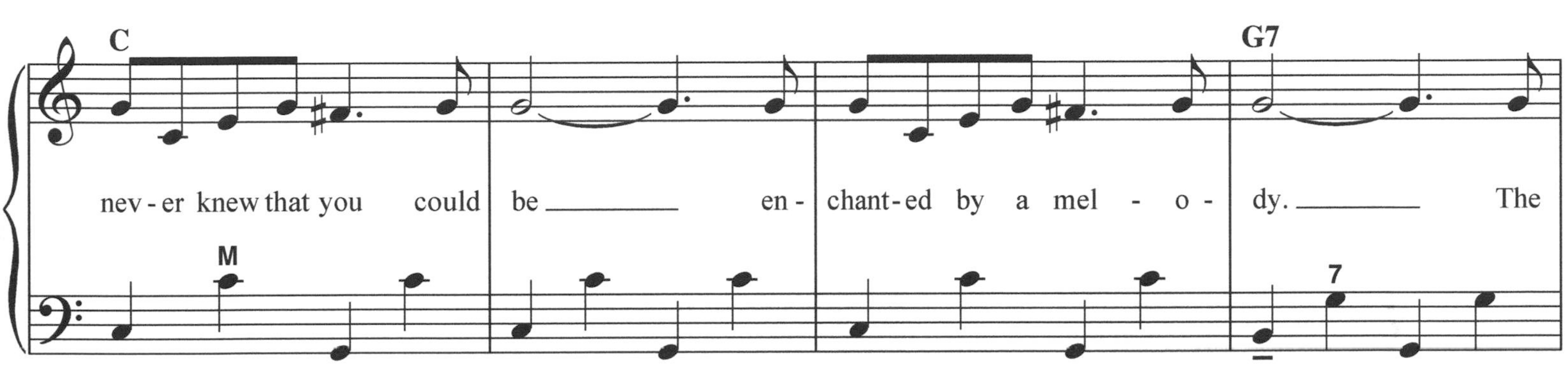
C
G7
nev - er knew that you could be en - chant - ed by a mel - o - dy. The
M
7

years will nev - er drive it out; you don't know why it's some - thing

C
you can't live with - out. You hear it in the twi - light hush and
M

G7
in the morn-ing traf - fic rush; a song that's al-ways new in
7

D.S. al Coda
C
G7
your heart, a part of you. Oh.
M
7

CODA
G7
of a well - re-mem-bered dream shines so bright-ly when you
7

C
hear "The Third Man Theme."
M

UNDER PARIS SKIES

English Words by KIM GANNON
French Words by JEAN DREJAC
Music by HUBERT GIRAUD

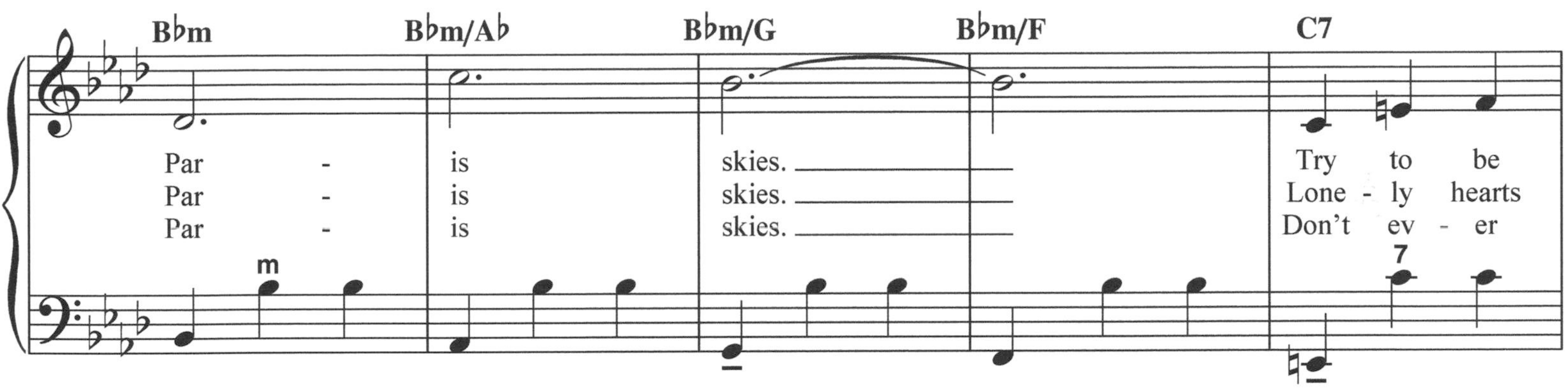

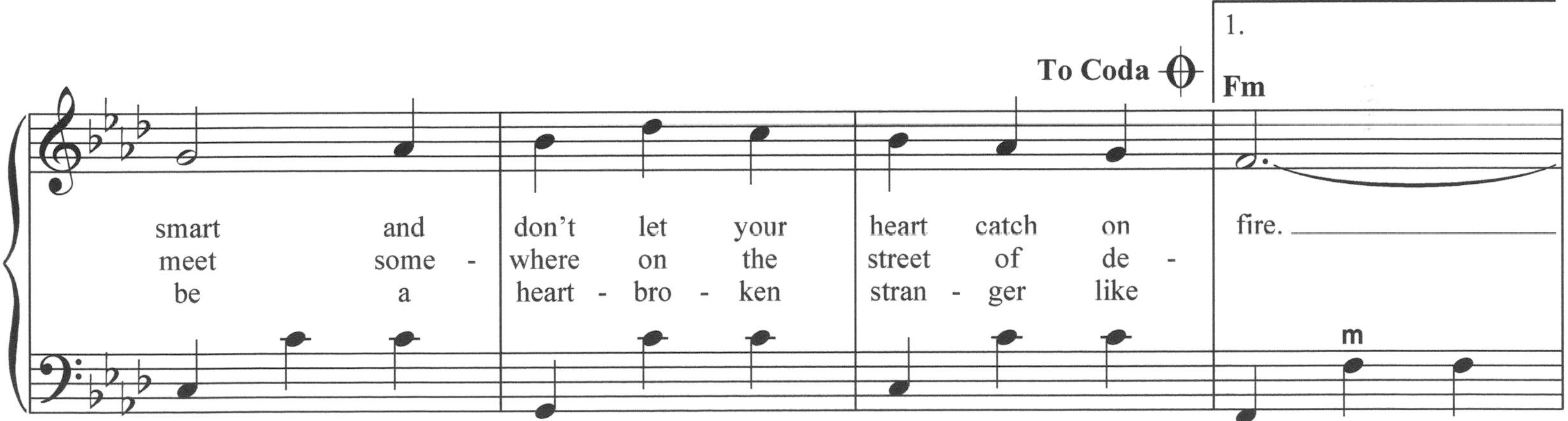

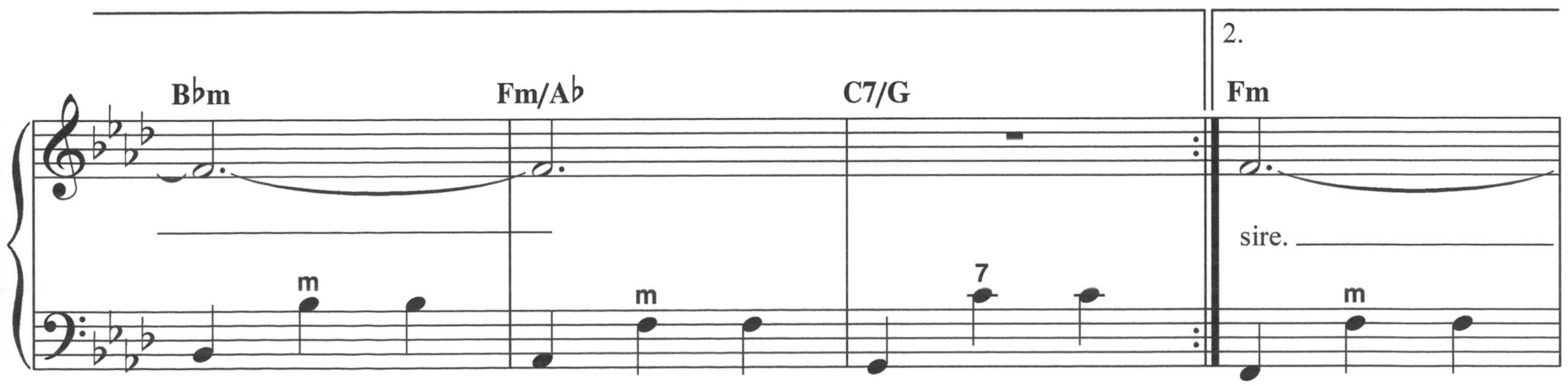

B♭m
Fm
B♭m
Pa - ri - sian
love
can
m
m
m

E♭7
A♭
bloom,
high in a
sky -
light
room,
7
M

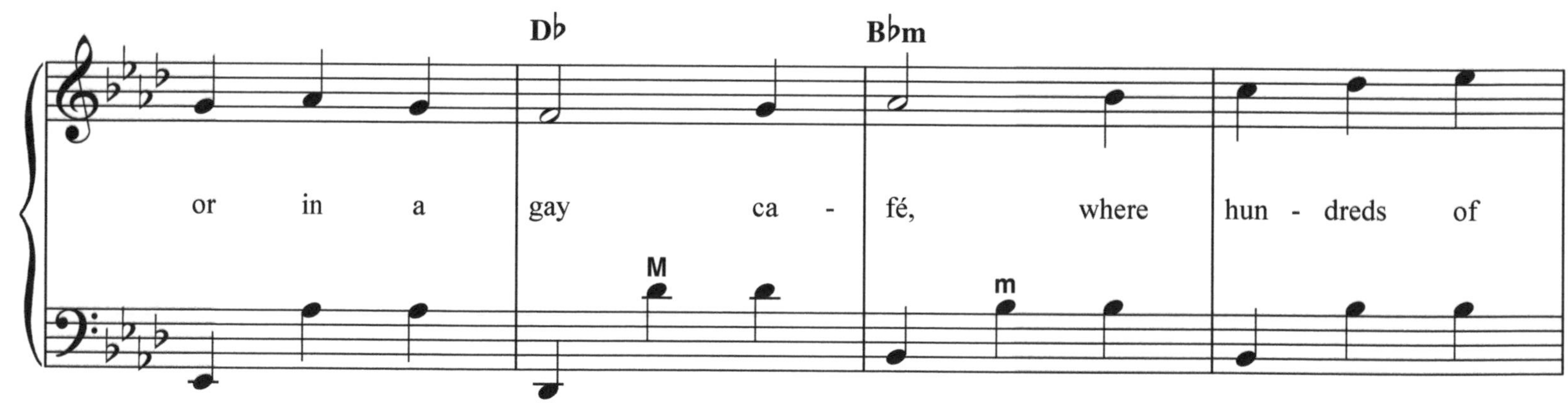

D♭
B♭m
or in a
gay
ca -
fé,
where
hun - dreds of
M
m

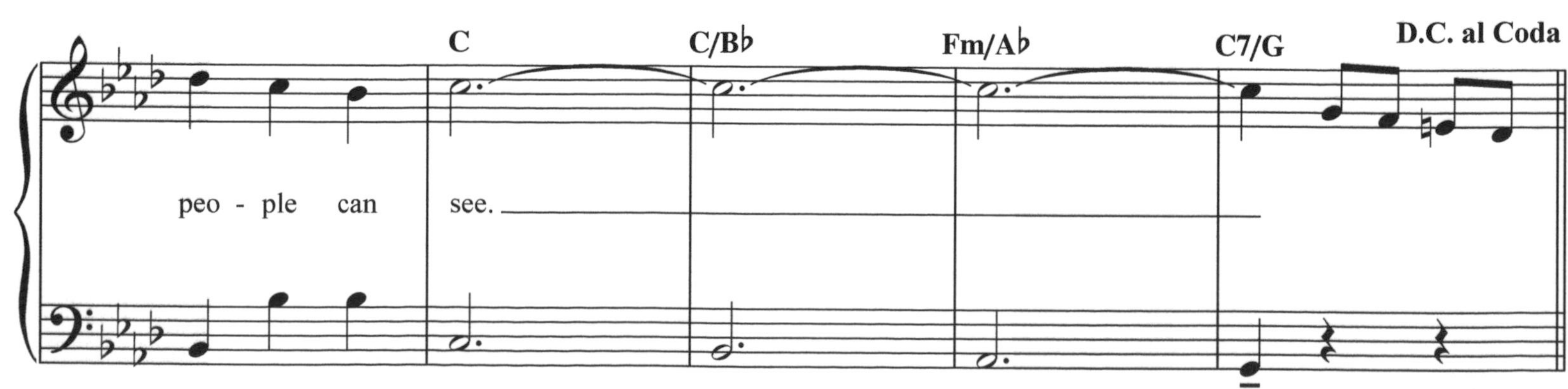

C
C/B♭
Fm/A♭
C7/G
D.C. al Coda
peo - ple can
see.

CODA

F
me.
Oh,
I
fell
in
M

F
love,
yes,
I
was
a
M

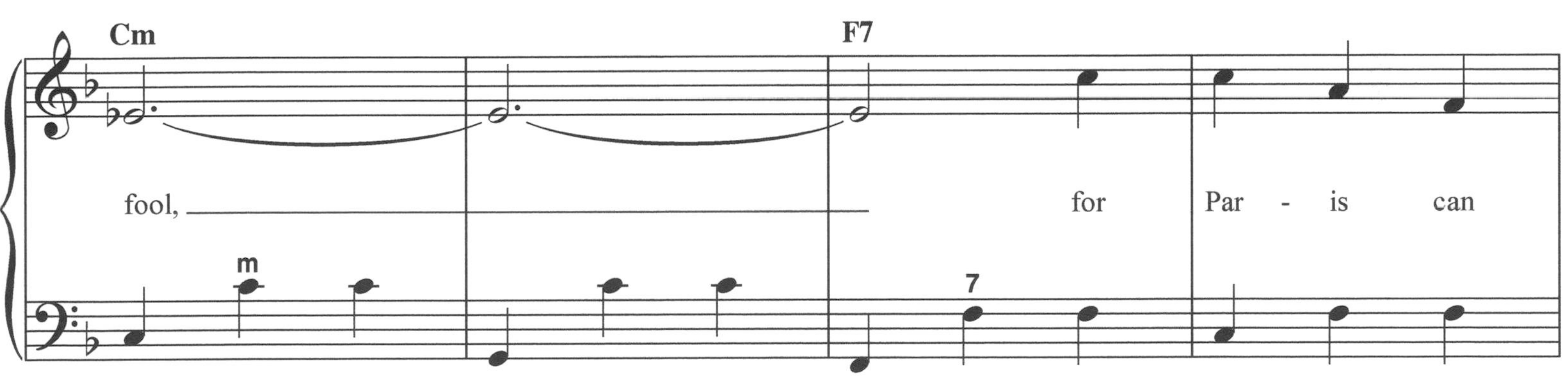
Cm
F7
fool,
for
Par - is
can
m
7

B♭
be
so
beau - ti - f'lly
M

B♭m
E♭7
F
cruel.
Par - is is just a
m
7
M

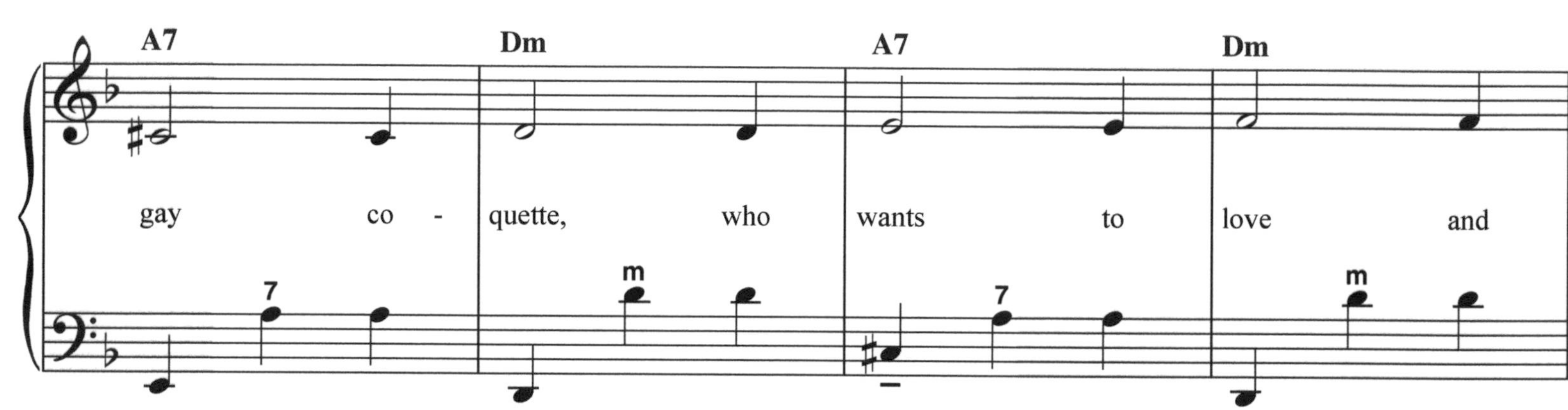
A7
Dm
A7
Dm
gay co - quette, who wants to love and
7
m
7
m

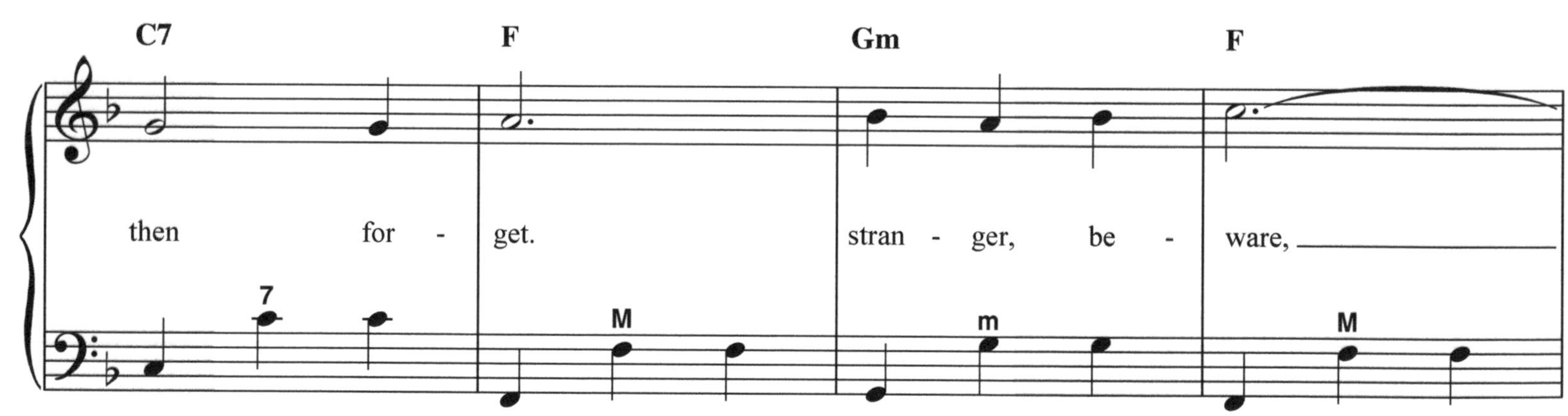
C7
F
Gm
F
then for - get. stran - ger, be - ware,
7
M
m
M

Cdim/F♯
C
there's love in the air.

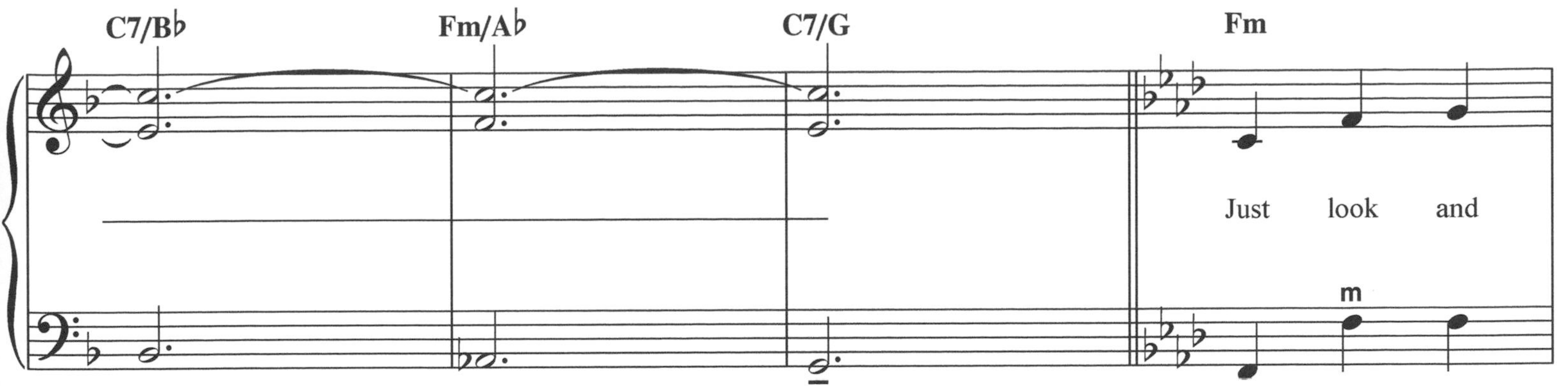
C7/B♭
Fm/A♭
C7/G
Fm
Just look and
m

B♭m
B♭m/A♭
see what hap - pened to me un - der Par - is
m

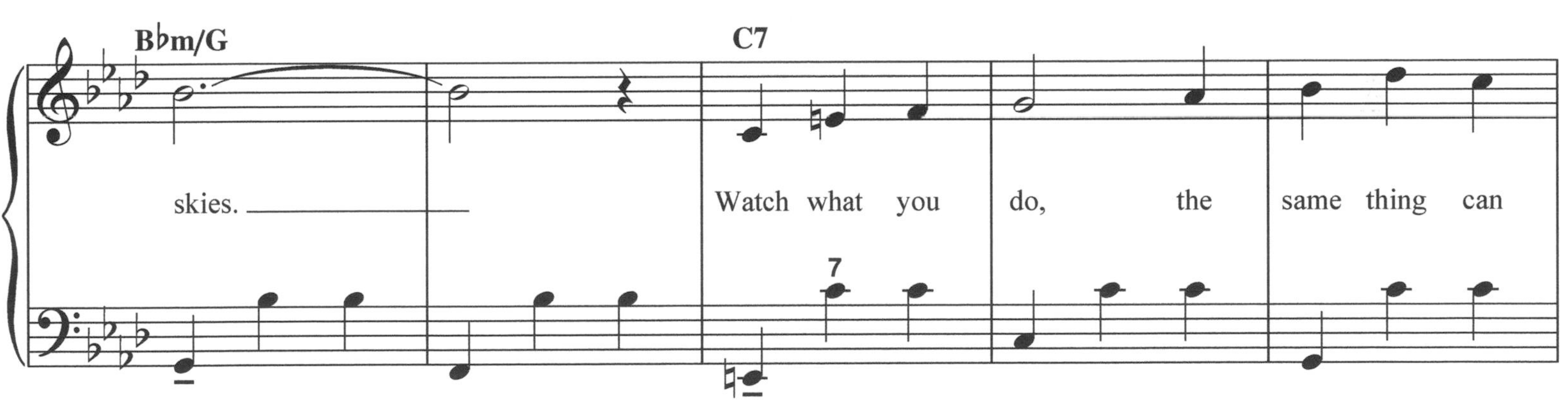
B♭m/G
C7
skies.
Watch what you do, the same thing can
7

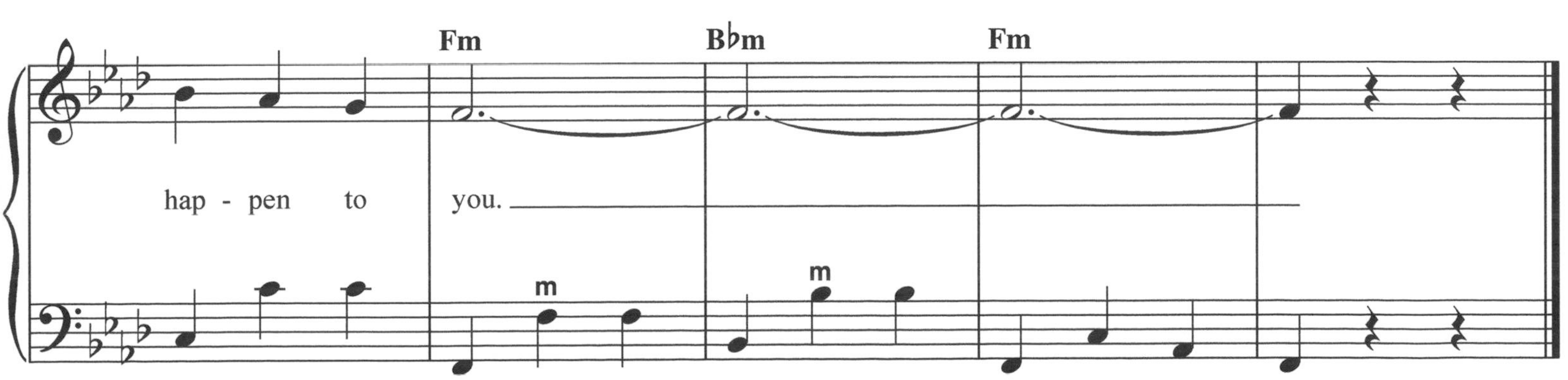
Fm
B♭m
Fm
hap - pen to you.
m
m

TRUE LOVE
from HIGH SOCIETY

Words and Music by
COLE PORTER

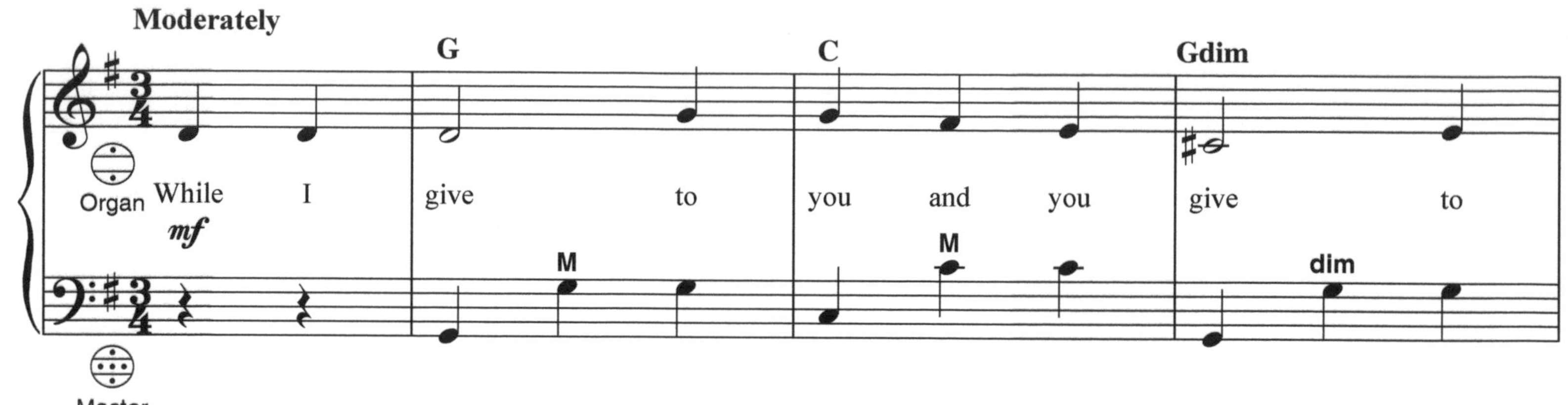

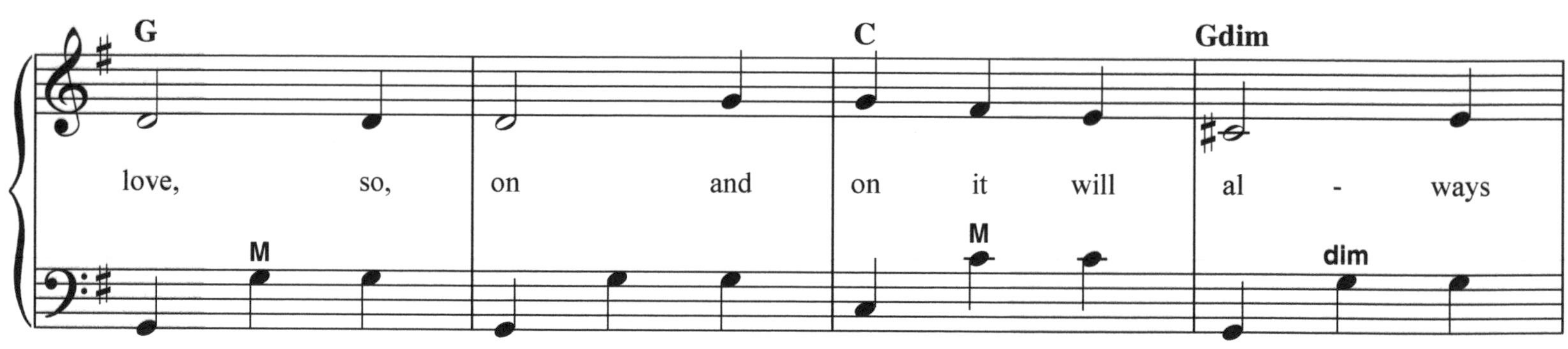

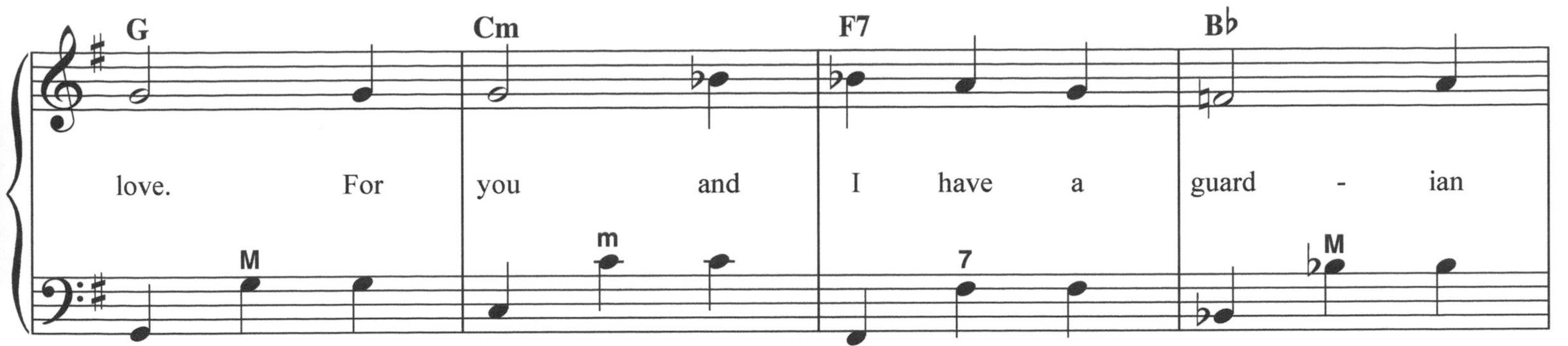
G
Cm
F7
B♭
love. For
you and
I have a
guard - ian
M
m
7
M

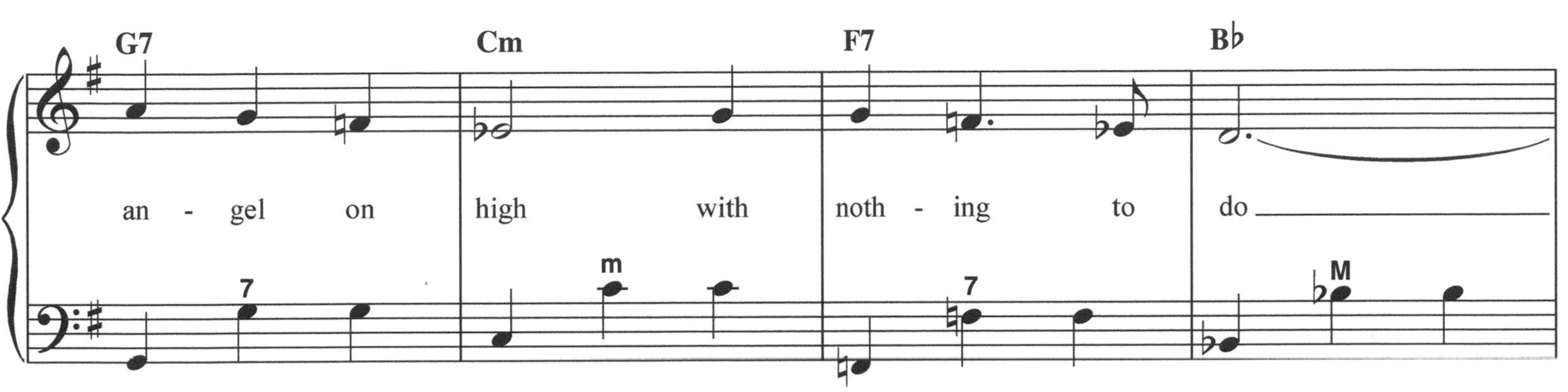
G7
Cm
F7
B♭
an - gel on
high with
noth - ing to
do
7
m
7
M

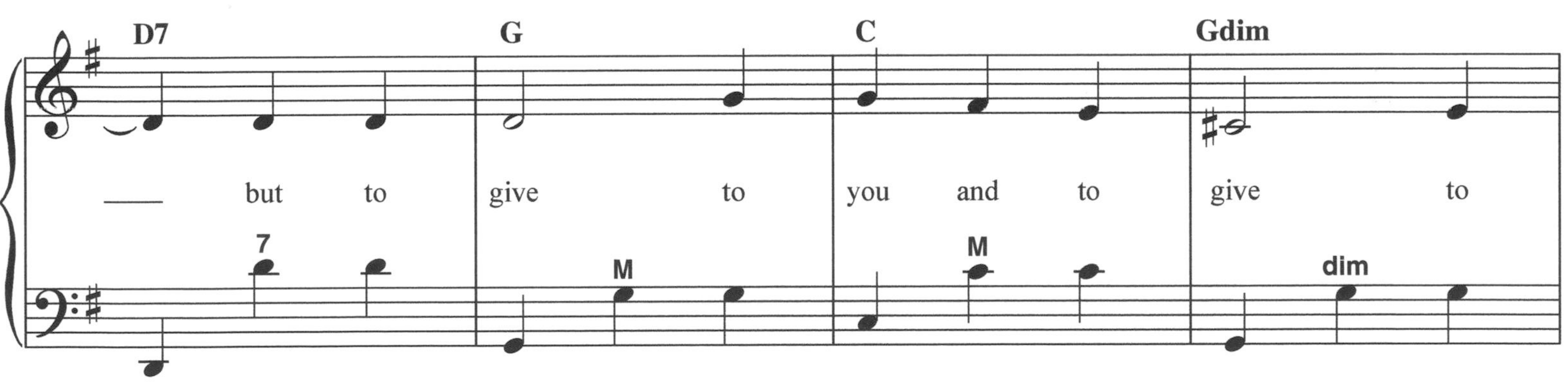
D7
G
C
Gdim
but to
give to
you and to
give to
7
M
M
dim

G
D7
G
me
love for -
ev - er
true.
M
7

WHERE IS YOUR HEART

(The Song from Moulin Rouge)

featured in MOULIN ROUGE

Words by WILLIAM ENGVICK
Music by GEORGE AURIC

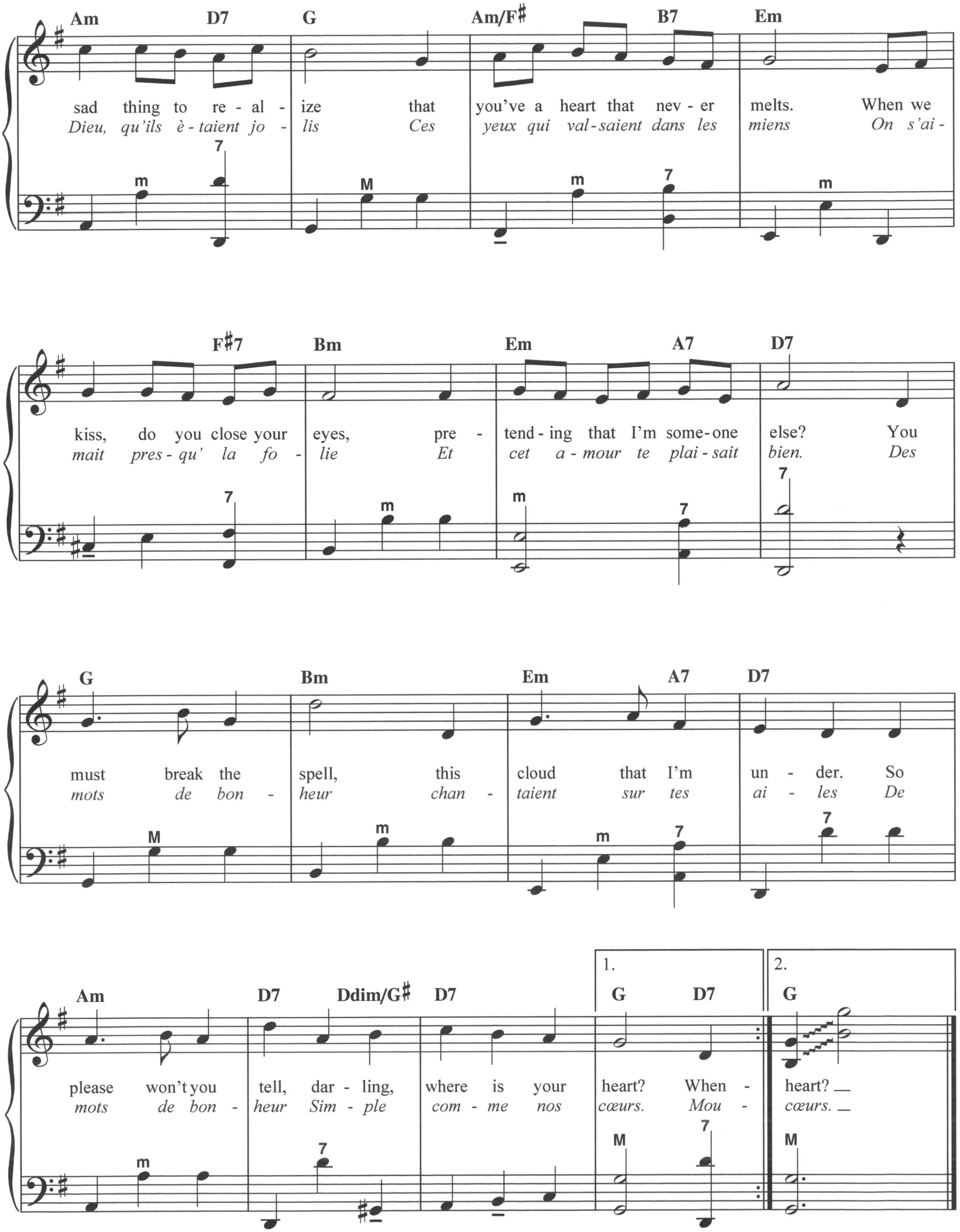

Am D7 G Am/F♯ B7 Em
sad thing to re - al - ize that you've a heart that nev - er melts. When we
Dieu, qu'ils è - taient jo - lis Ces yeux qui val - saient dans les miens On s'ai -
F♯7 Bm Em A7 D7
kiss, do you close your eyes, pre - tend - ing that I'm some - one else? You
mait pres - qu' la fo - lie Et cet a - mour te plai - sait bien. Des
G Bm Em A7 D7
must break the spell, this cloud that I'm un - der. So
mots de bon - heur chan - taient sur tes ai - les De
Am D7 Ddim/G♯ D7 1. G D7 2. G
please won't you tell, dar - ling, where is your heart? When - heart?
mots de bon - heur Sim - ple com - me nos cœurs. Mou - cœurs.

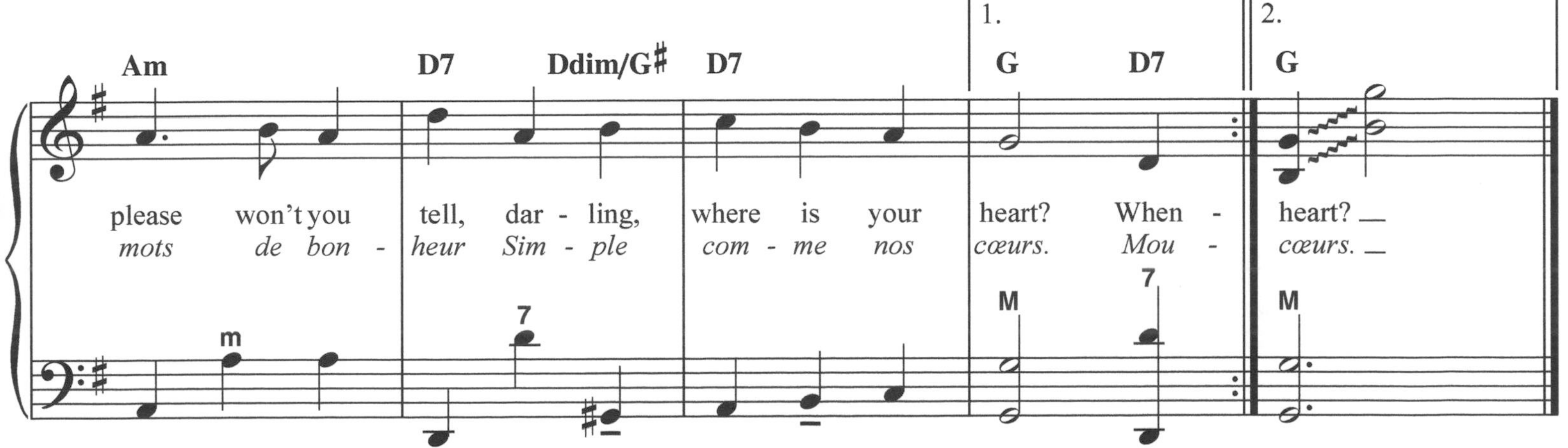

WONDERFUL COPENHAGEN

from the Motion Picture HANS CHRISTIAN ANDERSEN

By FRANK LOESSER

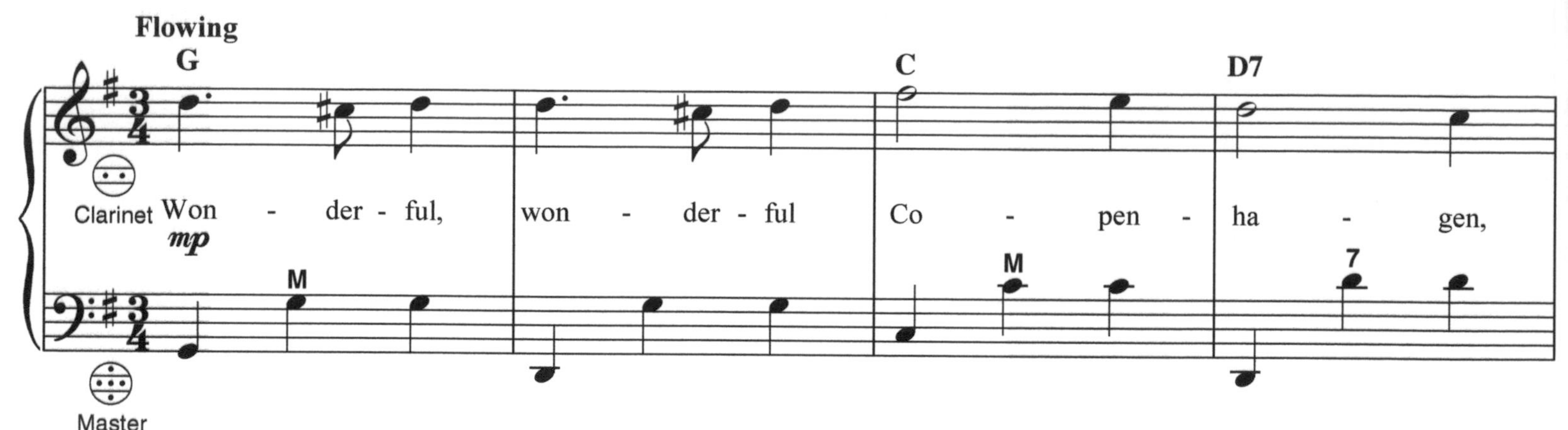

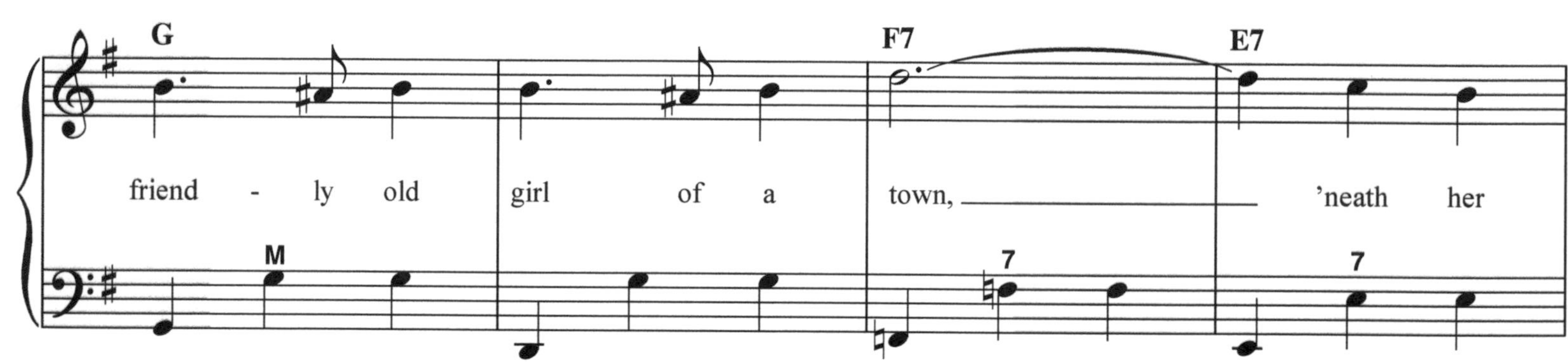

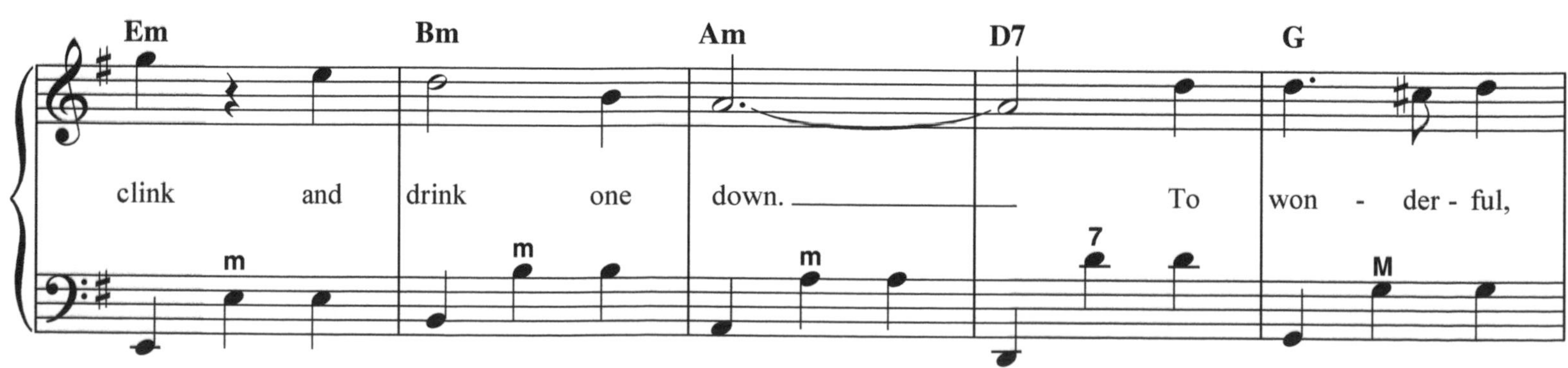

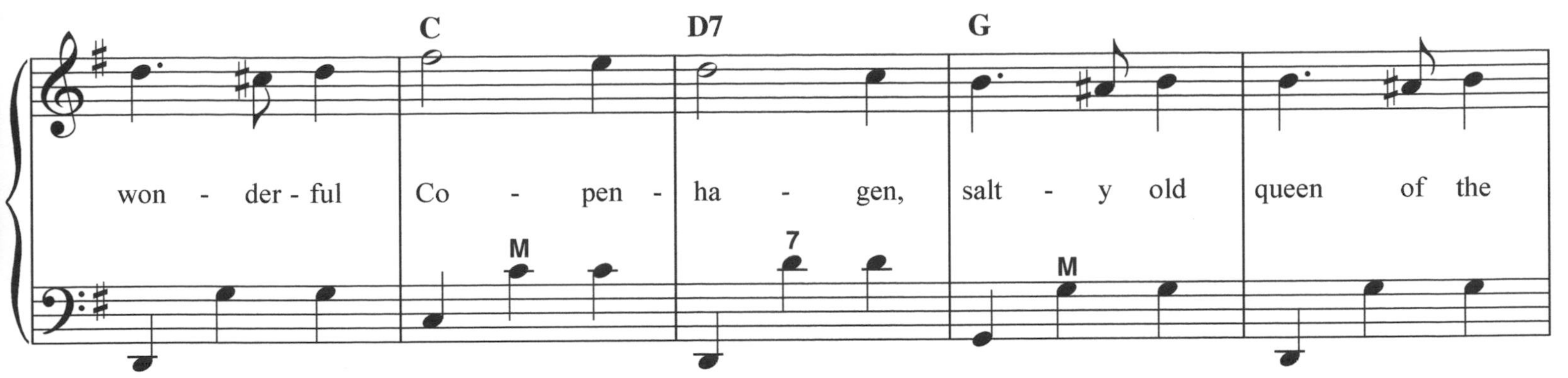
C
D7
G
won - der - ful Co - pen - ha - gen, salt - y old queen of the
M
7
M

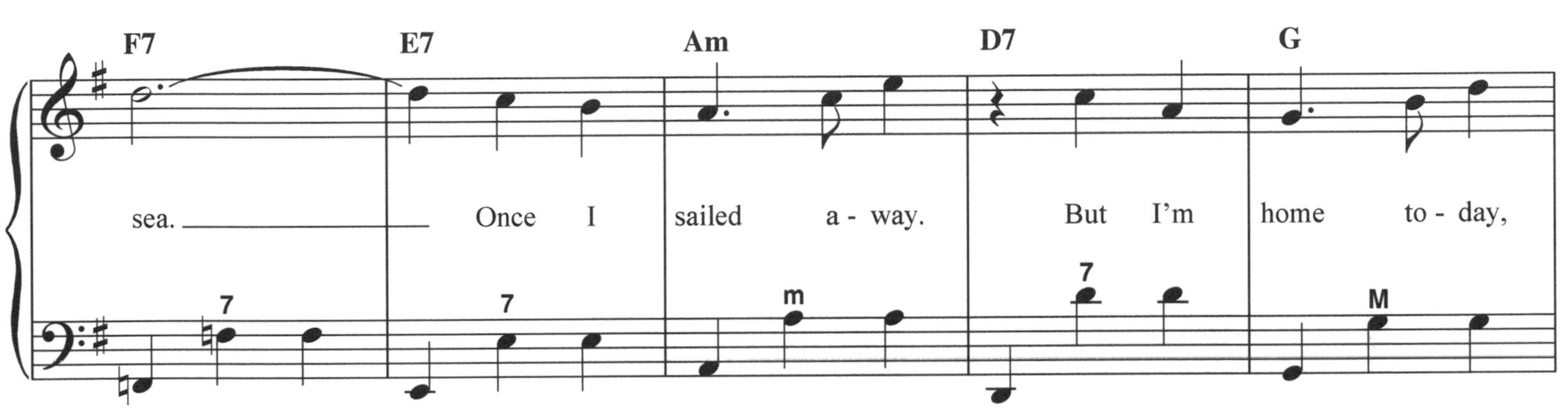
F7
E7
Am
D7
G
sea. Once I sailed a - way. But I'm home to - day,
7
7
m
7
M

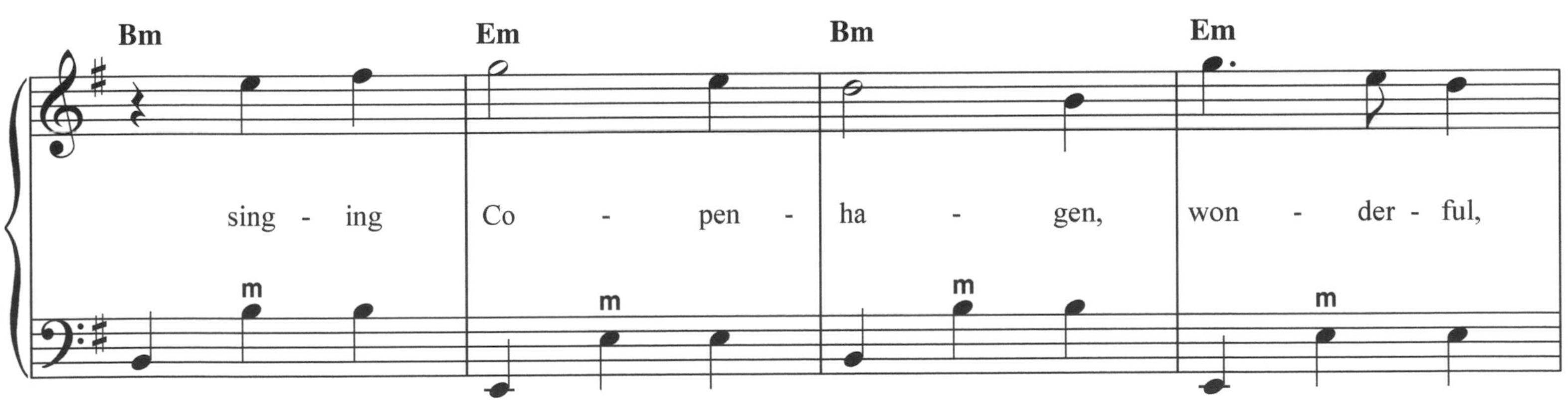
Bm
Em
Bm
Em
sing - ing Co - pen - ha - gen, won - der - ful,
m
m
m
m

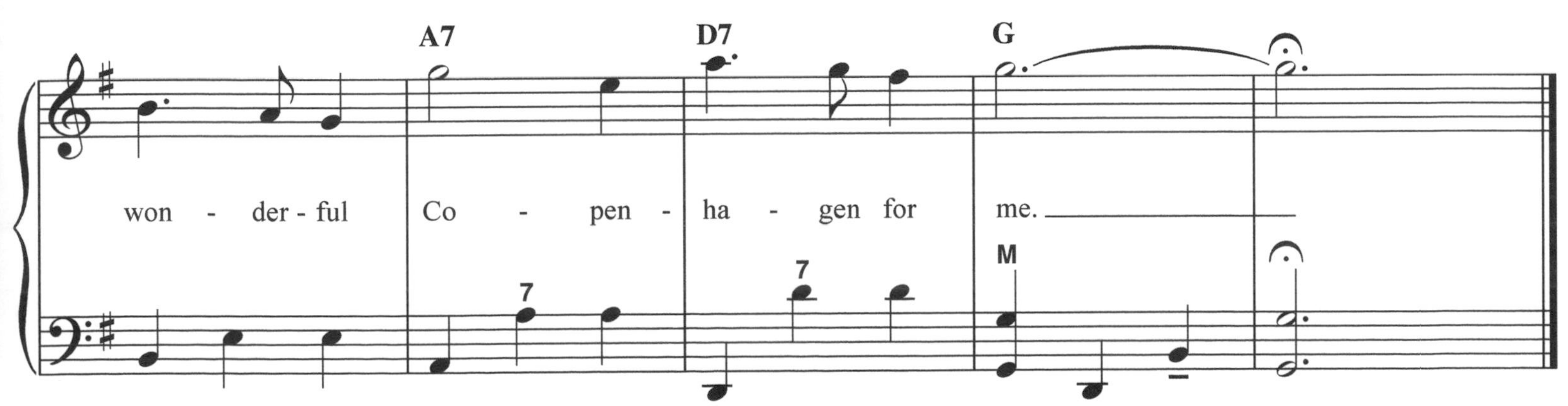
A7
D7
G
won - der - ful Co - pen - ha - gen for me.
7
7
M

ZIP-A-DEE-DOO-DAH

from SONG OF THE SOUTH

Words by RAY GILBERT
Music by ALLIE WRUBEL

Gm
C7
F
Dm
G7
Blue - bird on my shoul - der, it's the truth, it's
m
7
M
m
7

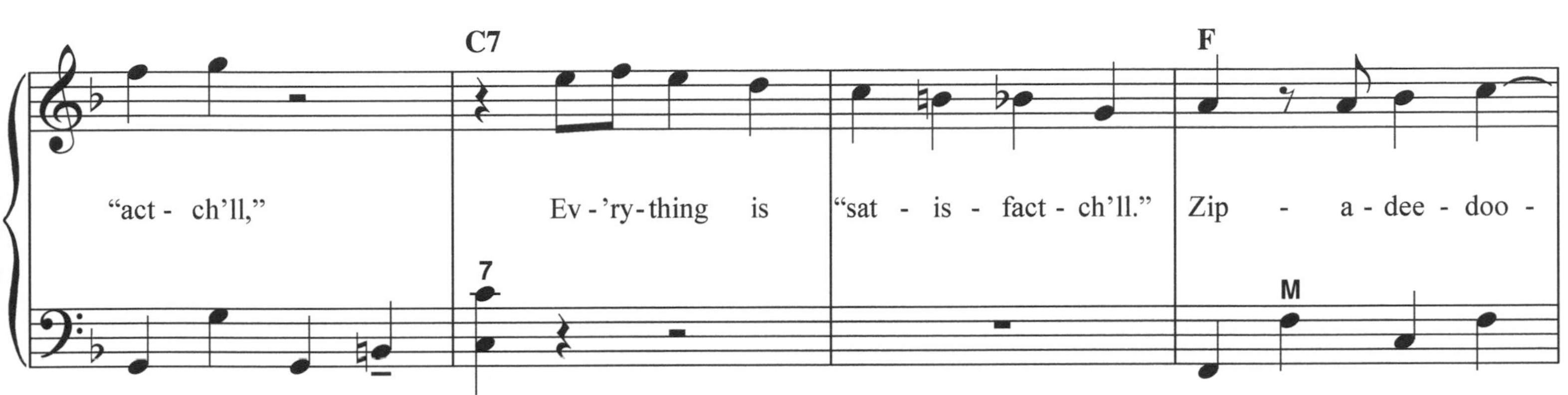
C7
F
"act - ch'll," Ev - 'ry - thing is "sat - is - fact - ch'll." Zip - a - dee - doo -
7
M

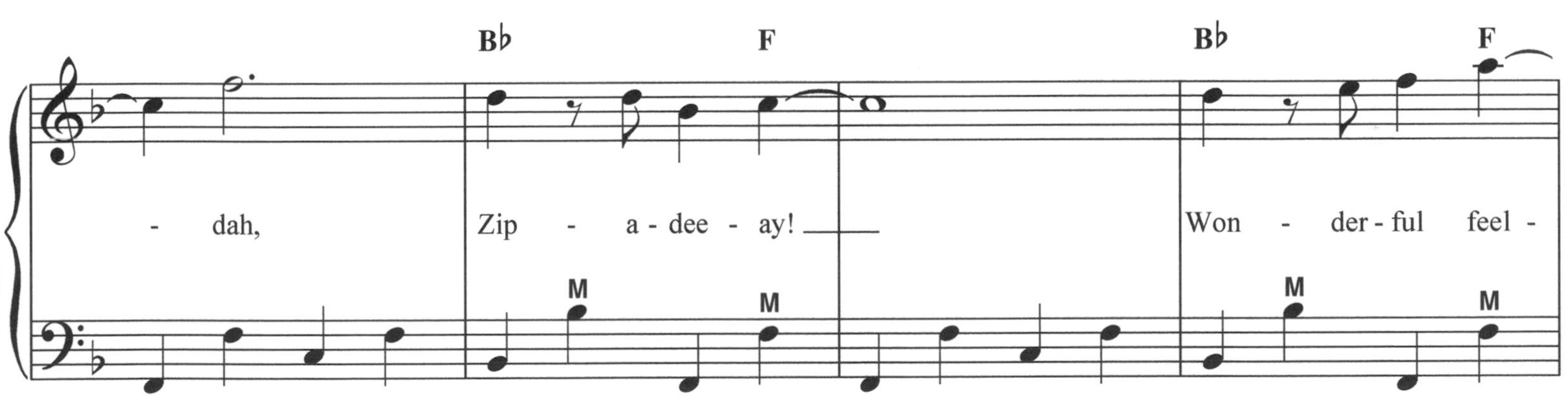
B♭
F
B♭
F
- dah, Zip - a - dee - ay! Won - der - ful feel -
M
M
M
M

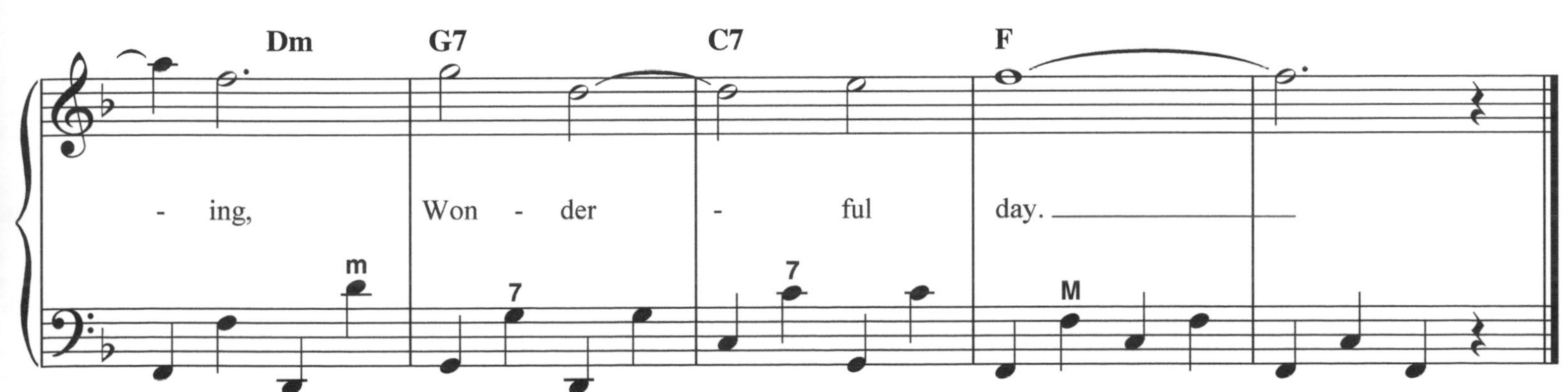
Dm
G7
C7
F
- ing, Won - der - ful day.
m
7
7
M

HAL•LEONARD

ACCORDION PLAY-ALONG

The Accordion Play-Along series features custom accordion arrangements with CD tracks recorded by a live band (accordion, bass and drums). There are two audio tracks for each song – a full performance for listening, plus a separate backing track which lets you be the soloist! The CD is playable on any CD player, and is also enhanced so Mac and PC users can adjust the recording to any tempo without changing the pitch!

1. POLKA FAVORITES

arr. Gary Meisner

Beer Barrel Polka (Roll Out the Barrel) • Hoop-Dee-Doo • Hop-scotch Polka • Just Another Polka • Just Because • Pennsylvania Polka • Tic-Tock Polka • Too Fat Polka (She's Too Fat for Me).

00701705 Book/CD Pack....................................... $19.99

2. ALL-TIME HITS

arr. Gary Meisner

Edelweiss • Fly Me to the Moon (In Other Words) • I Left My Heart in San Francisco • It's a Small World • Moon River • More (Ti Guarderò Nel Cuore) • Poinciana (Song of the Tree) • When I'm Sixty-Four.

00701706 Book/CD Pack....................................... $19.99

3. CLASSIC SONGS

arr. Gary Meisner

Carnival of Venice • Ciribiribin • Come Back to Sorrento • Fascination (Valse Tzigane) • Funiculi, Funicula • I Love You Truly • In the Good Old Summertime • Melody of Love • Peg O' My Heart • When Irish Eyes Are Smiling.

00701707 Book/CD Pack....................................... $14.99

4. CHRISTMAS SONGS

arr. Gary Meisner

Frosty the Snow Man • Have Yourself a Merry Little Christmas • Here Comes Santa Claus (Right down Santa Claus Lane) • The Most Wonderful Time of the Year • Rudolph the Red-Nosed Reindeer • Santa Claus Is Comin' to Town • Silver Bells • Winter Wonderland.

00101770 Book/CD Pack....................................... $14.99

5. ITALIAN SONGS

arr. Gary Meisner

La Sorella • La Spagnola • Mattinata • 'O Sole Mio • Oh Marie • Santa Lucia • Tarantella • Vieni Sul Mar.

00101771 Book/CD Pack....................................... $14.99

Visit Hal Leonard online at **www.halleonard.com**

Prices, contents, and availability subject to change without notice.

A COLLECTION OF ALL-TIME FAVORITES
FOR ACCORDION

ACCORDION FAVORITES
arr. Gary Meisner

16 all-time favorites, arranged for accordion, including: Can't Smile Without You • Could I Have This Dance • Endless Love • Memory • Sunrise, Sunset • I.O.U. • and more.

00359012.......................................$12.99

ALL-TIME FAVORITES FOR ACCORDION
arr. Gary Meisner

20 must-know standards arranged for accordions. Includes: Ain't Misbehavin' • Autumn Leaves • Crazy • Hello, Dolly! • Hey, Good Lookin' • Moon River • Speak Softly, Love • Unchained Melody • The Way We Were • Zip-A-Dee-Doo-Dah • and more.

00311088.......................................$12.99

THE BEATLES FOR ACCORDION

17 hits from the Lads from Liverpool have been arranged for accordion. Includes: All You Need Is Love • Eleanor Rigby • The Fool on the Hill • Here Comes the Sun • Hey Jude • In My Life • Let It Be • Ob-La-Di, Ob-La-Da • Penny Lane • When I'm Sixty-Four • Yesterday • and more.

00268724 ....$14.99

BROADWAY FAVORITES
arr. Ken Kotwitz

A collection of 17 wonderful show songs, including: Don't Cry for Me Argentina • Getting to Know You • If I Were a Rich Man • Oklahoma • People Will Say We're in Love • We Kiss in a Shadow.

00490157.......................................$10.99

DISNEY SONGS FOR ACCORDION – 3RD EDITION

13 Disney favorites especially arranged for accordion, including: Be Our Guest • Beauty and the Beast • Can You Feel the Love Tonight • Chim Chim Cher-ee • It's a Small World • Let It Go • Under the Sea • A Whole New World • You'll Be in My Heart • Zip-A-Dee-Doo-Dah • and more!

00152508 ....$12.99

FIRST 50 SONGS YOU SHOULD PLAY ON THE ACCORDION
arr. Gary Meisner

If you're new to the accordion, you are probably eager to learn some songs. This book provides 50 simplified arrangements of must-know popular standards, folk songs and show tunes, including: All of Me • Beer Barrel Polka • Carnival of Venice • Edelweiss • Hava Nagila (Let's Be Happy) • Hernando's Hideaway • Jambalaya (On the Bayou) • Lady of Spain • Moon River • 'O Sole Mio • Sentimental Journey • Somewhere, My Love • That's Amore (That's Love) • Under Paris Skies • and more. Includes lyrics when applicable.

00250269 ....$16.99

FRENCH SONGS FOR ACCORDION
arr. Gary Meisner

A très magnifique collection of 17 French standards arranged for the accordion. Includes: Autumn Leaves • Beyond the Sea • C'est Magnifique • I Love Paris • La Marseillaise • Let It Be Me (Je T'appartiens) • Under Paris Skies • Watch What Happens • and more.

00311498.......................................$10.99

HYMNS FOR ACCORDION
arr. Gary Meisner

24 treasured sacred favorites arranged for accordion, including: Amazing Grace • Beautiful Savior • Come, Thou Fount of Every Blessing • Crown Him with Many Crowns • Holy, Holy, Holy • It Is Well with My Soul • Just a Closer Walk with Thee • A Mighty Fortress Is Our God • Nearer, My God, to Thee • The Old Rugged Cross • Rock of Ages • What a Friend We Have in Jesus • and more.

00277160 ....$9.99

ITALIAN SONGS FOR ACCORDION
arr. Gary Meisner

17 favorite Italian standards arranged for accordion, including: Carnival of Venice • Ciribiribin • Come Back to Sorrento • Funiculi, Funicula • La donna è mobile • La Spagnola • 'O Sole Mio • Santa Lucia • Tarantella • and more.

00311089.......................................$12.99

LATIN FAVORITES FOR ACCORDION
arr. Gary Meisner

20 Latin favorites, including: Bésame Mucho (Kiss Me Much) • The Girl from Ipanema • How Insensitive (Insensatez) • Perfidia • Spanish Eyes • So Nice (Summer Samba) • and more.

00310932.......................................$14.99

THE FRANK MAROCCO ACCORDION SONGBOOK

This songbook includes arrangements and recordings of 15 standards and original songs from legendary jazz accordionist Frank Marocco, including: All the Things You Are • Autumn Leaves • Beyond the Sea • Moon River • Moonlight in Vermont • Stormy Weather (Keeps Rainin' All the Time) • and more!

00233441 Book/Online Audio..............$19.99

POP STANDARDS FOR ACCORDION
Arrangements of 20 Classic Songs

20 classic pop standards arranged for accordion are included in this collection: Annie's Song • Chances Are • For Once in My Life • Help Me Make It Through the Night • My Cherie Amour • Ramblin' Rose • (Sittin' On) The Dock of the Bay • That's Amore (That's Love) • Unchained Melody • and more.

00254822 ....$14.99

POLKA FAVORITES
arr. Kenny Kotwitz

An exciting new collection of 16 songs, including: Beer Barrel Polka • Liechtensteiner Polka • My Melody of Love • Paloma Blanca • Pennsylvania Polka • Too Fat Polka • and more.

00311573.......................................$12.99

STAR WARS FOR ACCORDION

A dozen songs from the Star Wars franchise: The Imperial March (Darth Vader's Theme) • Luke and Leia • March of the Resistance • Princess Leia's Theme • Rey's Theme • Star Wars (Main Theme) • and more.

00157380 ....$14.99

TANGOS FOR ACCORDION
arr. Gary Meisner

Every accordionist needs to know some tangos! Here are 15 favorites: Amapola (Pretty Little Poppy) • Aquellos Ojos Verdes (Green Eyes) • Hernando's Hideaway • Jalousie (Jealousy) • Kiss of Fire • La Cumparsita (The Masked One) • Quizás, Quizás, Quizás (Perhaps, Perhaps, Perhaps) • The Rain in Spain • Tango of Roses • Whatever Lola Wants (Lola Gets) • and more!

00122252 ....$12.99

3-CHORD SONGS FOR ACCORDION
arr. Gary Meisner

Here are nearly 30 songs that are easy to play but still sound great! Includes: Amazing Grace • Can Can • Danny Boy • For He's a Jolly Good Fellow • He's Got the Whole World in His Hands • Just a Closer Walk with Thee • La Paloma Blanca (The White Dove) • My Country, 'Tis of Thee • Ode to Joy • Oh! Susanna • Yankee Doodle • The Yellow Rose of Texas • and more.

00312104 ....$12.99

LAWRENCE WELK'S POLKA FOLIO

More than 50 famous polkas, schottisches and waltzes arranged for piano and accordion, including: Blue Eyes • Budweiser Polka • Clarinet Polka • Cuckoo Polka • The Dove Polka • Draw One Polka • Gypsy Polka • Helena Polka • International Waltzes • Let's Have Another One • Schnitzelbank • Shuffle Schottische • Squeeze Box Polka • Waldteuful Waltzes • and more.

00123218.......................................$14.99

Prices, contents & availability subject to change without notice.

HAL•LEONARD®

Visit Hal Leonard Online at
www.halleonard.com